Full Employment and Price Stability in a Global Economy

Full Employment and Price Stability in a Global Economy

Edited by

Paul Davidson

Holly Chair of Excellence in Political Economy, University of Tennessee, Knoxville, USA

and

Jan Kregel

Professor of Political Economy, University of Bologna, Italy

Edward Elgar

Cheltenham, UK • Northampton, MA, USA

Published by
Edward Elgar Publishing Limited
Glensanda House
Montpellier Parade
Cheltenham
Glos GL50 1UA
UK

Edward Elgar Publishing, Inc.
136 West Street
Suite 202
Northampton
Massachusetts 01060
USA

A catalogue record for this book is available from the British Library

Library of Congress Cataloguing in Publication Data
Full employment and price stability in a global economy / edited by
    Paul Davidson, Jan A. Kregel.
        "A selection of ... approximately 60 papers that were presented
    and discussed at the Fifth Post Keynesian Conference in Knoxville,
    Tennessee, sponsored by the Center for Full Employment and Price
    Stability, the *Journal of Post Keynesian Economics*, and the
    University of Tennessee".
    Includes index.
        1. Employment stabilization—Congresses. 2. Full employment
    policies—Congresses. 3. Employment (Economic theory)—Congresses.
    4. Price regulation—Congresses. 5. Economic stabilization—
    Congresses. 6. Competition, International—Congresses.
    7. Keynesian economics—Congresses. I. Davidson, Paul.
    II. Kregel, J. A. III. International Post Keynesian Workshop (5th :
    1998 : Knoxville, Tenn.)
    HD5713.2.F85   1999
    339.5—dc21   98–55206
                                                                            CIP

ISBN 1 85898 989 2

Printed and bound in Great Britain by Biddles Ltd, Guildford and King's Lynn

Contents

Figures

Tables

List of contributors

Paul Davidson, Holly Chair of Excellence in Political Economy, University of Tennessee, USA.

Jan Kregel, Professor of Political Economy, University of Bologna, Italy and Senior Scholar, Jerome Levy Economics Institute New York, USA.

Professor Lord Skidelsky, University of Warwick and Social Market Foundation, UK.

John S.L. McCombie, Fellow in Economics, Downing College, Cambridge University, UK.

Philip Arestis, Professor of Economics, University of East London, UK.

Malcolm Sawyer, Professor of Economics, University of Leeds, UK.

Hubert Hieke, formerly Visiting Assistant Professor of Economics, Arkansas State University, USA; now Research Fellow at the University of Mannheim, Germany.

Andrea Terzi, Associate Professor of Economics, Franklin College, Switzerland.

Fernando Carvalho, Professor of Economics, Federal University of Rio de Janeiro, Brazil.

Gary Dymski, Associate Professor of Economics, University of California-Riverside, USA.

Dorene Isenberg, Associate Professor of Economics, Drew University, New Jersey, USA.

Warren Mosler, Director of Economic Analysis, Adams, Viner and Mosler, Florida, USA.

Mathew Forstater, Visiting Scholar, Jerome Levy Economics Institute, New York, USA.

Nina Shapiro, Associate Professor of Economics, St. Peter's College, New Jersey, USA.

David Dequech, Ph.D. student, Cambridge University, UK.

Julio López, Professor of Economics, Universidad Nacional Autonoma de Mexico, Mexico.

Guadalupe Mántey, Professor of Economics, Universidad Nacional Autonoma de Mexico, Mexico.

Eric Nasica, Associate Professor of Economics, University of Nice, LATAPSES, France.

Preface

As we approach the millennium, the economic performance of many countries has deteriorated significantly not only from the post World War Golden Age of Economic Development (1948–73), but also from the go-go years of the 1980s. The 1990s started with a global recession from which only the US and the UK were able to recover and significantly reduce their unemployment rates without incurring inflation. The global economy was hit first by the Mexican currency crisis and a few years later by the Asian currency crisis which laid low those Asian developing countries that had been the model of open market economic growth. The Russian currency crisis adds an additional threatening element. Today the objective of full employment and price stability still appears to be an illusory goal for many of the economies of the emerging global market system. In a speech on 4 September 1998, Federal Reserve Chairman Alan Greenspan wondered whether the United States could remain an 'island of prosperity in a global economy threatened by recession and depression'.

This volume represents a selection of the best of approximately 60 papers that were presented and discussed at the Fifth Post Keynesian Conference in Knoxville, Tennessee sponsored by the Center for Full Employment and Price Stability, the *Journal of Post Keynesian Economics* and the University of Tennessee.

In the initial article, Lord Robert Skidelsky provides the historical background of the development of Keynes's plan for reforming the international payments system after the Second World War. Keynes's initial impetus was to provide an alternative to Germany's proposal developed by Finance Minister Walter Funk for a New Economic Order for settling payments among the nations of Europe after the war. Since the German plan has an amazing resemblance to the Euro scheme initiated on 1 January 1999, comparison of the Keynes and Funk plan is not only of historical interest but has implications for the global economy of the 21st century. The chapters by McCombie and Arestis and Sawyer discuss the advantages and disadvantages of the Euro and its implications for Europe's ability to achieve full employment without inflation. This is followed by an article by Hieke who discusses the problems of external balance and employment.

Chapters by Davidson and Terzi discuss the effect of speculation and volatile financial markets on the ability of modern money-using market-oriented economies to achieve full employment without inflation.

Following these there are two chapters that deal with banking aspects of the financial system. Carvalho discusses the implications of a bank's liquidity requirements on the modern economy. Dymski and Isenberg discuss the role of financial institutions in financing housing. Since housing quality is probably the durable that most symbolizes living standards, the role of finance in developing good housing facilities is an important social problem.

Mosler and Forstater introduce a novel way of analysing the role of money in promoting full employment and price stability. Their analysis leads to the policy proposal that these twin objectives can be readily achieved if governments establish an employer of last resort (ELR) policy. In the following article, Kregel expands the Mosler–Forstater analysis to show how it can be applicable to creating full employment and price stability in the New European monetary system.

The next two chapters turn the readers' attention to market structure and the question of employment. Shapiro demonstrates that competition *per se* is not necessarily the miracle cure for producing a full employment economy. In a similar vein, Dequech looks at the classical contention that wage and price flexibility is the solution to unemployment and finds it wanting. López and Mantey introduce a case study of the employment policies of Mexico – an open newly industrializing country. Their analysis suggests that there is a lot to be learned by not repeating the errors of the Mexican case.

Finally, Nasica analyses the role of institutions in stabilizing economies that might be otherwise unstable.

Besides bringing together economists from some 20 nations of the world for six intensive days of discussion and analysis, these Post Keynesian workshops serve another function. They produce an *esprit de corps* among the participants which encourages further professional interactions that improve the research productivity of all participants when they return to their home base.

As in the previous Post Keynesian workshops, the successful organization and supervision of the proceedings, as well as the editorial supervision of this book, are the responsibility of Louise Davidson, Editorial Office Manager of the *Journal of Post Keynesian Economics*. We would like to offer our thanks to her and all the participants of the workshop for making it yet another successful set of meetings.

Paul Davidson
Jan Kregel

1. Keynes's 'New Order': the genesis of the Clearing Union

Robert Skidelsky

I

Neither Keynes, nor anyone else in Britain, would have spent much time thinking about postwar economic arrangements in 1941 had it not been for the Lend-Lease Agreement, awaiting British signature. In Article VII, Britain was required to pledge itself to work, with the United States, to end all 'discriminatory arrangements' after the war. In July 1941, the United States had made clear to Keynes in Washington that it would not allow Britain to continue with its Ottawa Preference arrangements and wartime Sterling Area arrangements after the war. Washington was determined to yoke Britain to its free-trade agenda, and in Lend-Lease had a lever to do so. So the issue in the autumn of 1941 was how Britain could 'honestly' sign up for Article VII. The 'underlying problem' as Keynes saw it arose from America's unbalanced creditor position. Any workable postwar plan, liberal or otherwise, 'must involve a reduction of their exports relatively to their imports'.[1] The non-liberal solution, foreshadowed in the 1930s and crystallized in the first year of war, was bilateral barter. Britain – or possibly the Sterling Area – would buy from the United States only goods equivalent in value to what America was willing to receive. But what was the liberal solution? Virtually no one in Britain advocated a return to the gold standard and unfettered trade. Keynes's persuasion and events had jointly done their work. In the British view, the system which collapsed in the early 1930s had produced a persistent drain of gold to the United States, imposing deflation, impoverishment, and unemployment on most of Europe and the rest of the world. On the other hand, the non-system which had taken its place – a mishmash of competitive devaluations, trade restrictions, and exchange controls – had serious costs of its own. In the American view, affirmed most stridently by US Secretary of State, Cordell Hull, these protective devices had diminished aggregate wealth creation, soured international relations, and led directly to war. British economists were not blind to the force of such arguments. But overshadowing, and often overcoming, their liberal instincts was an acute apprehension about Britain's balance of payments problem after the war. These seemed to require the indefinite continuation of the wartime controls which Article VII apparently ruled out.

On 5 September, over a weekend at Tilton, his Sussex country house, Keynes started drafting a paper on 'post-war currency. It was meant to be his input into a Treasury planning exercise undertaken to determine how, or whether, Britain could sign up to the 'consideration' demanded by the US in Article VII in return for Lend-Lease. The question was: how could Britain's pre-war and wartime economic system be adapted to American requirements after the war? To understand how Keynes set about answering this question, we need to understand what those arrangements were, and why they had developed.

II

By historical tradition, Britain was internationalist, the United States protectionist and isolationist. Britain had virtually created the 'world economy' in the 19th century; it was its lynchpin as well as its main beneficiary. The United States, by contrast, was a largely self-sufficient periphery, with a founding myth of freedom from foreign entanglements. The shocks of the First World War and interwar years had not extinguished these historical reflexes. In the 1930s, Britain still retained a vestigial sense of responsibility for the health of the international economy: the only 'world economic conference' of the 1930s took place in London, in 1933. By contrast, the USA under Roosevelt practised a policy of monetary nationalism and political isolationism. But reorientation of policy was inevitable. The First World War had shown that the Atlantic was not broad enough to insulate the United States from European quarrels. The 1930s had shown that the United States' economy could no longer be isolated from external shocks. Britain had always been highly vulnerable to external shocks, political as well as economic. The First World War had finally destroyed the illusion of a Pax Britannica and the interwar years showed it could no longer conduct the international economic orchestra. In the 1930s Britain became more nationalist, the United States more internationalist.

The explanation lay not just in the changing facts of power, but in the way the two countries experienced the interwar years. For the United States, the 1920s were a 'good' decade, the 1930s a bad one. Britain, by contrast, had slumped in the 1920s and recovered strongly in the 1930s. The Great Depression thus figured differently in the two countries' mythologies. In the United States it was seen as an interruption of prosperity, however savage its effects; in Britain, where it was superimposed on an unemployment problem going back to 1921, it confirmed a certain pessimism about the country's industrial future. America had reacted to its plight with a burst of governmental activism – the New Deal. Britain had withdrawn into a defensive perimeter – its Empire.

In the mythology of the Great Depression, the gold standard played a very different role in the two countries. The United States had prospered under the gold standard, and slumped when it collapsed. Britain had slumped under the gold standard, and recovered when it collapsed. Reaction against the gold standard in the United States was temporary: it could hardly be otherwise when the US held over 50 per cent of the world's monetary gold. In Britain it was permanent. Responses to the trade regime are more complicated. Britain had upheld the free trade cause in the 1920s and suffered for it – or so it was thought. In the 1930s it became Protectionist. Historically, the United States had protected its manufactures behind high tariffs and exported its agricultural surpluses. Now that the infants were grown up into competitive giants, it was interested in general trade expansion. In the 1930s, US policy turned decisively towards free trade. Monetary and trade issues were heavily intertwined. The historic trade regime favoured by the United States made it very difficult for Europeans to export their manufactures to America, while lowering receipts for their farmers. This was the basis of the 'unbalanced' creditor position of the United States which undermined the gold standard. It led the British to believe that 'balanced trade' must be the precondition for restoring fixed exchange rates. In contrast to this, by the mid-1930s a consensus was emerging in the US Administration in favour of fixed exchange rates as a precondition for trade liberalization.

The 1930s was thus a decade of transition – but transition to what was unclear. The ostensible trend was towards the economics of blocs and regions. This reflected the breakdown of international cooperation during and after the Great Depression. But the hope of a revived internationalism was never quite extinguished in Britain, and was stirring in the United States.

Bedeviling Anglo-American economic relations in the 1930s was the fact that each country tended to attribute its misfortunes to the other. Basically, the Americans blamed the British for the collapse of the gold standard and the ensuing monetary disorders; the British blamed the Americans. The British view was that the United States had failed in its duty as a creditor: whether by tariff reductions, increased foreign lending, or domestic monetary expansion it should have found a way of dishoarding its vast and accumulating gold stock. In British eyes, sterling had been forced off gold in 1931 – as Keynes quipped, sterling did not leave gold, gold left sterling. The American view was that Britain had failed in its duty as a debtor. It should have deflated its economy and de-regulated its labour market in the 1920s; in 1931 it should have balanced the budget and gone on borrowing, not depreciated its currency. This was also the view in France, another gold hoarder.

The recriminations continued after the gold standard's collapse. The Americans accused the British Treasury of using its Exchange Equalization Fund to keep sterling 'undervalued' against the dollar. To avenge the injury to US exporting interests, Roosevelt forced down the value of the dollar, restoring the dollar–sterling rate by January 1934 to what it had been before September 1931, and wiping out Britain's temporary competitive advantage.[2] Even after the USA had fixed the gold–dollar price at $35 to an ounce of gold, it refused to guarantee to sell gold on demand at that price, unless Britain accepted a $5.00 pound.[3] The British interpreted this sequence of monetary events very differently. In their eyes, the Exchange Equalization Fund's purpose was to neutralize speculative gold inflows, not keep sterling undervalued. Roosevelt's policy of depreciating the dollar was interpreted as a deliberate 'beggar my neighbour' policy, since the United States still had ample gold reserves. His veto on a realignment of the two currencies strengthened the British government's resolve 'to manage sterling so as to suit our own economy... .[4]

These monetary events highlighted the fact that there was no agreed set of adjustment rules – 'rules of the game' as Keynes called them. The British were determined not to rejoin an international monetary standard unless it imposed clear duties on surplus countries. The Americans would not stabilize the international value of the dollar unless countries like Britain accepted a clear obligation to 'put their house in order', and not rely on currency depreciation and similar expedients to maintain competitiveness.

What were these expedients? The first was the sterling area, a particular bête-noire of Henry Morgenthau, US Secretary of the Treasury since 1933, who regarded it as a British-organized plot against American exports. It took shape in 1931 when twenty or so countries, based on but not limited to the British Empire, joined sterling in a downward float against the dollar. In fact, there was nothing nefarious about it, countries linking their currencies to sterling to protect their position in the British market. Typically, sterling area countries kept their currencies stable in terms of sterling, used sterling to settle their accounts with each other, and held their reserves ('sterling balances') in London. Until 1939 sterling was freely convertible into other currencies. Britain was able to use the sterling area's dollar earnings to help balance its accounts with the United States. However, the build-up of sterling balances in London – at £760 million in 1938 they exceeded Britain's gold and dollar reserves for the first time – suggests that Britain was finding it increasingly difficult to pay its way.

A more explicit discriminatory policy was the Ottawa Preference System, set up in 1932, and condemned by US Secretary of State Cordell Hull as 'the greatest injury, in a commercial way' to the United States in a long career.[5] The inspiration behind it, which went back to Joseph Chamberlain's tariff reform campaign of 1903, was to convert an empire of sentiment into a commercial and political union, on the basis of reciprocal tariff preferences for each other's products. Neville Chamberlain, the British Chancellor of the Exchequer, to whom it fell to implement his father's grand design, found little warmth in the imperial bargaining at Ottawa. The theory was that Britain would use its quasimonopsonist buying power in foodstuffs and raw materials to secure preferential tariffs for its manufactured exports in Empire countries in return for concessions to their products in the British market. The basic flaw in this strategy, which Ottawa exposed, lay in the notion of a 'natural' division between British manufactures and Dominion primary products. In practice, Canada, Australia, South Africa and India were all interested in developing their manufactures, while Britain, for many different reasons, wanted to protect its agriculture. It was also hard to reconcile the imperial vision with Britain's trade relations with third countries, many of which were members of the sterling area; an additional quirk was that Canada was part of the preference system, but not the sterling area. The Ottawa preference system turned out to be a device for tariff increases all round. The Dominions increased their tariffs on British manufactures but by a lesser amount than on foreign ones. Privileged entry for empire primary products into the British market was coupled with a complicated duty and quota system to protect British agriculture and preserve third party entry.

The important point in this context is that neither the monetary nor trading arrangements Britain adopted in the 1930s to replace the gold standard/free trade system solved its balance of payments problem. Before the First World War Britain's deficit on trading account was balanced by its earnings from financial services and from foreign investment and shipping, leaving it with a large surplus to lend abroad. In the 1930s its trade deficit widened and it started piling up short-term debt without ever recovering full employment. Its 'discriminatory' arrangements antagonized the United States without doing the job they were meant to. In the United States absorption with domestic recovery – also by no means complete – gave way to interest in the external conditions of prosperity.

From the mid-1930s, British and American economic policies started to edge towards each other, helped by the darkening international situation. The *rapprochement* was triggered off by France's decision to devalue the franc in 1936, threatening another round of competitive currency depreciation. A Tripartite Monetary Agreement was signed on 25 September 1936, by which the USA and Britain accepted the need for a franc devaluation, and the three countries agreed to promote stable exchange rates between themselves. They restored the gold convertibility of their currencies at a (temporarily) fixed rate: the gold standard on a 24-hour basis, as one wag put it. These monetary arrangements soon embraced the core Western democracies. Separately, the Bank for International Settlements in Geneva offered its member central banks facilities for granting each other reciprocal credits for commercial transactions. In July 1937, the United States negotiated a series of stabilization agreements with Latin American countries. Harry Dexter White at the US Treasury was responsible for administering them. All this marked the end of the era of competitive exchange depreciation, though it fell far short of a full-blooded return to the gold standard.[6]

These modest moves towards currency stabilization enabled some equally modest steps towards unblocking the channels of trade. The lead was taken by Cordell Hull, who had secured the passage of a Trade Agreements Act in 1934, empowering the President to negotiate reciprocal tariff reductions. Hull believed passionately that political conflicts were the result of trade barriers, and that their removal was therefore a necessary and sufficient condition for a harmonious world. The attraction of this doctrine for American opinion in general, and for exporting and banking interests in particular, was obvious – it extended America's economic reach, while preserving political isolationism. While railing against the Ottawa preference system, Hull recognized that it was Britain's response to the Hawley–Smoot tariff put up by America in 1930. The British, accepting the need for closer relations with the United States, and somewhat disenchanted with the imperial preference system, were in a mood to respond to an American initiative. The result was the Anglo-American Trade Agreement of 1938, which brought 'a marked benefit to American agriculture'.[7]

None of this had got very far by the time war broke out. One might say that the monetary and commercial relations between Britain and the United States had reached something of an impasse. In Charles Kindleberger's language, the United States would not, and Britain could not, take the lead in reconstructing a functioning world economy – this despite the growing realization by both that the state of their economic relations put a limit on their ability to recover from the Depression.

While the democracies were edging back towards a liberal economic system, Germany had developed an illiberal variant of its own. As Germany's Economics Minister from 1934 to 1937 Hjalmar Schacht pioneered an ingenious system for freeing his country from the external constraint on recovery and rearmament. Its essence was a comprehensive scheme of import licensing coupled with bilateral clearing agreements with Germany's main trading partners in Southeast Europe and Latin America. As opposed to multilateral clearing, in which the only relevant 'clearing' is of a country's balance with the rest of the world, bilateral agreements were designed to balance the payments of each pair of countries, thus obviating the need for gold movements, or indeed any foreign exchange transactions. In its simplest form, the two trading partners opened accounts for each other in their central banks, into which were paid the local currency proceeds of their sales to each other. The balances in both accounts could only be cleared (i.e. eliminated) by the exchange of goods. It was a modern form of barter trade: goods exchanged against goods, not money. By 1938 Germany had made clearing agreements with 27 countries, covering half of its foreign trade. Technically, it remained on the gold standard, but it was a gold standard maintained by exchange controls. Paul Einzig dubbed it the 'Gold Insolvency Standard' since 'any currency can be maintained stable by preventing transfers which tend to cause its depreciation'.[8] In fact, Germany was able to accumulate mark balances (credits to itself) in the bilateral clearings much as Britain was able to run up sterling balances.

Although the Schachtian system was widely regarded as illiberal and (probably wrongly) as exploitative of Germany's Danubian neighbours, it undoubtedly 'solved' Germany's balance of payments problem in a way the sterling area/imperial preference system did not do for Britain, by allowing German economic recovery to proceed to full employment.[9]

The German system started to be favourably re-evaluated only when Britain adopted the same methods to fight the war. On the outbreak of war, the sterling–dollar rate was fixed at $4.02 to the £, and imports were made subject to license. By the summer of 1940, sterling had been made inconvertible into 'hard currencies', and bilateral clearing agreements had been negotiated with non-sterling neutrals in Europe and Latin America. Under these agreements, the countries concerned were paid 'area pounds sterling' for their exports to Britain which they were free to spend anywhere in the sterling area, but not outside. In effect, all exits of foreign exchange from the sterling area were sealed off except for vital military purchases from the United States, for which Britain paid in gold and dollars. The success of the British 'control' – as the Treasury called it – in mobilizing the nation for war convinced many in 'official circles' that Schachtian methods should be made a permanent part of Britain's peacetime system.

III

The leader of this view was Hubert Henderson, Keynes's erstwhile ally, then opponent, now, like Keynes, at the Treasury. In the autumn of 1941 Henderson produced a number of memoranda setting forth the history of, and prospects for, Britain's balance of payments. His paper 'The Nineteen Thirties', dated 22 August 1941, was the first input into the Treasury's own memorandum 'Monetary and Trade Policy after the War' which started life in September; it antedated Keynes's 'Proposals for an International Currency Union' by two and a half weeks. Henderson rejected the 'Chatham House' view that the troubles of the 1930s could be blamed on economic nationalism. Economic nationalism, in its various forms, was a forced response to the speculative 'runs' which had destroyed the gold standard, the 'slump of agricultural prices' which Henderson saw as 'the main cause of the general depression', and the unbalanced creditor position of the United States. On the first point Henderson wrote: 'Under conditions of large-scale capital movements ... a country's domestic policy is placed at the mercy of the vagaries of international speculators. That is the reality ... behind the fine phrases about a freely working international system. This condition of things is ... an intolerable thraldom, to which no self-respecting community is ever likely to subject itself with its eyes open'. The country which had most successfully broken this thraldom was Germany. Under Dr Schacht it had evolved 'a really efficient system of exchange control, and the use of this system for the negotiation of payments agreements with other countries'. Schacht's 'remarkable success' showed that 'a country possessing a large manufacturing capacity need not be debarred from obtaining the supplies it wants from abroad merely because it is short of the accepted forms of international purchasing power'.

The second lesson which Henderson drew from the 1930s was that agricultural glut had replaced traditional agricultural shortage. Falling agricultural prices had been the main factor in the collapse of the gold standard. Attempts to stabilize agricultural prices had taken the form of Protectionism, the Imperial Preference System, and commodity regulation schemes. They would remain a permanent part of the economic landscape until primary producers had diversified into manufacturing behind tariffs. Henderson believed that such a process was bound to hit the exports of manufactured goods from countries like Britain. This was an important source of the export pessimism which runs like a leitmotif through his wartime pronouncements.

A third lesson from the past was that market forces would not be allowed to adjust balance of payments disequilibria. Creditor countries like the United States had shown they would not reduce tariffs; debtor countries like Germany and Britain could not accept a system which forced deflation and unemployment on them. Thus it was 'reckless in the extreme', Henderson thought, to expect reductions in the US tariff and an expansion of American foreign lending to bring about the even greater 'creditor adjustment' which would be required after the present war. All countries would in future manage their foreign trade and exchange-rate policy in the interests of domestic policy.

The conclusion Henderson drew from all this was that countries which had rejected *laissez-faire* in their domestic policies would not place themselves once more in the 'straightjacket' of an 'automatic' international system.

> For my part [Henderson concluded] I do not believe that the new wine of industrial planning can be put in the old bottles of the gold standard, Free Trade, the most favoured-nation clause and the open door. I am convinced that a satisfactory international system can only be built along lines which provide adequate scope for national policies of planning and control, and that in such a system quantitative regulation, exchange control and bilateral agreements have a legitimate part to play. That ... is one of the morals that emerge from the story of the nineteen thirties.[10]

Henderson was a nationalist, not imperialist. He argued that Britain would face 'two disequilibria' in its balance of payments after the war: with the United States and with the sterling area. The implication of this was that Britain might have to balance its accounts bilaterally with sterling area countries as well as with the United States.[11]

Henderson's views were a representative, though not uncontested, British reaction to the experiences of the the interwar years. All those who commented on his 'Nineteen Thirties' paper agreed that Britain would need to retain its trading and exchange control systems after the war. The issue was whether it could 'honestly' pledge itself to work, with the United States, to dismantle these systems in due course, or whether they were, as S.G. Waley minuted, 'good in themselves' and never to be given up.[12] Dennis Robertson (Treasury), Sir Arnold Overton (Board of Trade), Sir Frederick Leith Ross (Treasury, seconded to Office of Economic Warfare), James Meade (Offices of the War Cabinet) and Roy Harrod (Prime Minister's Office) took the 'liberal' side, with Robertson favouring flexible, rather than managed, exchange rates.

A deliciously acidulous exchange between Henderson and Robertson gives a flavour of the early debate. Robertson alleged that Henderson's argument amounted to trying to get Britain a larger share of a poorer world's wealth 'by making cunning bargains à la Schacht'. What was needed was for creditor and debtor nations 'to do their economic duty in that state of life unto which it has pleased God (assisted by Adolf Hitler) to call them'. Americans should 'buy funny things and travel about and work shorter hours and open the gates again for Poles and Dagoes to work in the castle grounds'; the British should accept their relative poverty and share it round through 'family allowances' and so on, instead of 'maintaining a value for our monetary unit which doesn't reflect our diminished power of export, and then trying to make up for that by driving clever bargains with people who will probably out-Schacht us in the end'.[13] Henderson accused Robertson of suffering from the 'Geneva complex'. This consisted in blaming all the world's troubles (including the war) on the economic nationalism of Britain and the United States, and 'an almost morbid desire that no "herd" of which he forms a part should be guilty of any injustice to another "herd".' In fact, the aggressive psychology of the dictators was driven far more by contempt for 'Geneva idealism' than by trade restrictions. Rather than accept mercantilist policies by Britain, Robertson would prefer 'any degree of reduction in our standard of living', his guilt as a 'bourgeois and bachelor' leading him to bear his share of the necessary sacrifice.[14] Henderson, as we can see, was quite as ready to apply *ad hominem* arguments to Robertson, as he had been to Keynes.[15]

Where did Keynes stand? Harrod recalls running into him about this time in a Treasury corridor. He was leaning against a door-post. 'You must give up the bilateralist approach,' I said, 'and come down on the American side'. 'No', he said, 'I must pursue both lines of thought ... both'. His expression was enigmatic. He seemed to be transfixed with a curious immobility that was unlike him. Some deep inscrutable thoughts were proceeding. Even his great brain was baffled by this problem'.[16]

Harrod is right to say that Keynes's inclinations were internationalist. But they were heavily qualified by an instinctive mistrust of the United States which went back all the way to the failure of the Americans to support his 'Grand Scheme for the Rehabilitation of Europe' in 1919.[17] Keynes's visceral feeling was that Britain was the only country in the world fit to 'conduct the international orchestra'. If it was no longer able to do so, it must preserve its monetary independence. He first asserted this doctrine in his *Tract on Monetary Reform* (1923), as against the consensus view that Britain should return to the gold standard as soon as possible. The United States could not be trusted to 'manage' an international monetary system in the general interest. The best solution, therefore, was to divide the world into sterling and dollar currency blocs.[18] In 1924 he developed arguments for restricting foreign lending.[19] In the *Economic Consequences of Mr. Churchill* (1925) Keynes first stated his view that the price of debtor adjustment was mass unemployment. 'Deflation does not reduce wages automatically. It reduces them by causing unemployment'.[20] In the *Treatise on Money* (1930) he stated the case for interest rate autonomy: the central object of national monetary policy should be to maintain a rate of interest consistent with full employment. This was incompatible with a '*laissez-faire* attitude to foreign lending'.[21] In his 'National Self-Sufficiency' articles of 1933 he broadened the case for national monetary sovereignty to include the possibility of making social experiments. 'We each have our own fancy. Not believing we are saved already, we would each like to have a try at working out our own salvation ... and to be free as we can make ourselves from the interferences of the outside world'.[22] In a letter to a German correspondent, W. Luck, on 13 October 1936, Keynes restated the doctrine of the *Tract* in the light of his later theoretical and practical reflections:

1. In general I remain in favour of independent national systems with fluctuating exchange rates.
2. Unless, however, a long period is considered, there need be no reason why the exchange rate should in practice be constantly fluctuating.
3. Since there are certain advantages in stability ... I am entirely in favour of practical measures towards de facto stability so long as there are no fundamental grounds for a different policy.
4. I would even go so far ... as to give some additional assurance as to the magnitude of the fluctuations which would normally be allowed ... Provided there was no actual pledge, I think that in most ordinary circumstances a margin of 10 per cent should prove sufficient.
5. I would emphasise that the practicability of stability would depend (i) upon measures to control capital movements, and (ii) the existence of a tendency for broad wage movements to be similar in the different countries concerned.[23]

Keynes's bias against permanently fixed rates of exchange and unlimited capital mobility was therefore long-standing. It reflected Britain's much weaker pull on the world's gold supplies and the failure of the United States to do its 'duty' as the world's leading creditor nation. The theory of the matter had also become clear to him. America's tendency to stockpile gold at Fort Knox was a practical illustration of liquidity preference. Sterilizing gold inflows was the major source of high world interest rates and deflation.

On the other hand, Keynes also toyed with the idea of an 'ideal' system which might overcome this problem. The most complete sketch of such a system is to be found in his *Treatise on Money*. The essential condition was to ensure that countries never had to deflate because of a shortage of gold. The 'ideal arrangement' would be to set up a supranational bank with the power to create a fiduciary reserve asset (supernational bank money or SBM) which would count equally with gold as legal reserves of the member central banks. It would be able to lend SBM to the central banks of countries in temporary balance of payments difficulties in proportion to their deposits of gold and securities, and would vary the total quantity of SBM so as to stabilize its value in terms of a basket of commodities.[24] The main feature of this scheme – to secure a *compulsory* initial redistribution of reserves from surplus to deficit countries and to provide automatic overdrafts for countries in temporary difficulties – was to be repeated in his Clearing Union proposal.

In the 1930s, Keynes took no interest in Hjalmar Schacht's system of bilateral clearing agreements. Why then was the Schachtian system so much on his mind in the summer of 1941? The reason is twofold: Britain, as we have seen, had itself adopted 'Schachtlan' methods to fight the war, and in the autumn of 1940 Keynes had got personally involved in a propaganda exercise designed to counter Germany's postwar plans.

In the summer of 1940 Hitler was master of Western and Central Europe. In a rare effort to make Germany's conquests more palatable to its victims, satellites, and European neutrals, his Economics Minister Walther Funk announced a 'New Order' at a press conference in Berlin on 25 July 1940. It had two elements. Germany and Italy would use their combined productive power to reconstruct Europe after the war; and payments within Europe would be cleared multilaterally, instead of bilaterally as in Germany's prewar system. Germany would set up a payments union managed by a central clearing office in Berlin. Within the Union there would be fixed exchange rates and planned trade, with credits and debits being offset by the Clearing Office. Trade with outside countries would be regulated by bilateral agreements made by the Union: European imports from the United States would exactly balance European exports to the United States. In any case, gold would no longer function as a means of payment and America's gold stock would become redundant.[25] The plan was the work of able technocrats in the Reichsbank and Economics Ministry. It offered all the continental countries of non-Soviet Europe the benefits of multilateral clearing: it was in fact the German answer to the 'fortified' sterling area. It was also the first blueprint for the economic union of Europe.[26]

The 'New Order' dossier arrived on Keynes's desk on 19 November 1940, with a note from Harold Nicolson at the Ministry of Information suggesting that he do a broadcast for American and Dominion audiences to discredit it. The dossier did not in fact contain a coherent account of the Funk Plan, consisting of snippets from German newspapers and broadcasts, stitched together by the Ministry of Economic Warfare. However, Keynes had got a better idea of the German scheme from Claude Guillebaud's favourable comment on 'Hitler's New Economic Order for Europe', submitted to the *Economic Journal* (which Keynes still edited) and published in December 1940, and this influenced his reply to Nicolson. He wrote back to Nicolson that a broadcast on the lines implied by the Ministry of Economic Warfare's comments was hopeless: it was no use trying to outflank Funk by offering Europe the blessings of universal free trade and the gold standard. In fact, the Funk plan was 'excellent and just what we ourselves ought to be thinking of doing. If it is to be attacked, the way to do it would be to cast doubt and suspicion on its bona fides'.[27]

Keynes did not broadcast on the Funk Plan but he produced some propagandist points for use by the Foreign Office: Britain and the countries of the sterling area could offer neutrals – and an eventually liberated Europe – far more of what they needed for reconstruction and trade than could Germany and its allies; Germany would exploit its position, as it had before the war, to get 'something for nothing', whereas Britain's debts would be repaid; Funk's talk of a rational division of labour was merely a cloak for concentrating industry in Germany and pastoralizing the rest of Europe; because of the lack of food and raw materials in its space, Germany would be bound to start new wars to carry its imperialist exploitation overseas.[28] More reflective was a letter he wrote to Sigismund Waley:

> If Hitler gets his new Europe going properly, with barter replacing gold, and with all the nations playing the cultural and ethnographical roles allotted to them, while the Vatican provides the slave states with a philosophy of life, then England can be made to look like an intolerably disruptive pirate nuisance in the eyes of Europe. We would become the real aliens, the Protestant dissenters, the Berbers of the North. In Hitler's favour is the fact that he has the will and ambition to govern Europe, and that Rome, Berlin and Munich are the natural places to do it from. But as long as the blockade is effective he is compelled to loot, and while he has to loot the conquered territories, his propaganda must fail.[29]

Much more important than his propagandist exercises was Keynes's acceptance of the fundamental postulates of Funk's permanent system:

> I have assumed [he wrote on 1 December 1940] that we shall continue our existing exchange controls after the war, and that we do not propose to return to *laissez-faire*

currency arrangements on pre-war lines by which goods were freely bought and sold internationally in terms of gold or its equivalent. Since we ourselves have very little gold left and will owe great quantities of sterling to overseas creditors, this seems only commonsense ... The virtue of free trade depends on international trade being carried on by means of what is, in effect, barter. After the last war *laissez-faire* in foreign exchange led to chaos. Tariffs offer no escape from this. But in Germany Schacht and Funk were led by force of necessity to evolve something better. In practice they have used their new system to the detriment of their neighbours. But the underlying idea is sound and good. In the last six months the Treasury and the Bank of England have been building up for this country an exchange system which has borrowed from the German experience all that was good in it. If we are to meet our obligations and avoid chaos in international trade after the war, we shall have to retain this system. But this same system will serve to protect the impoverished European countries and is an essential safeguard against a repetition of what happened last time.[30]

In a letter he wrote to Ashton-Gwatkin of the Foreign Office on 25 April 1941, Keynes expanded on these initial observations, as follows.

(i)   Capital exports would be restricted to the case where the capital exporting country had a favourable trade balance with the capital importing country.

> Whatever one might wish, something of the sort seems to be inevitable, since we shall no longer have a cushion of gold or other liquid assets, by means of which the immediate effects of unbalanced capital movements can be handled.

(ii) Large elements of multilateral clearing would exist within the Sterling Area, but payments agreements would be required to handle relations between the area and the outside world.

> Unquestionably [this] would involve a discrimination against the United States if she persisted in maintaining an unbalanced creditor position. Again, whether we like it or not, this will be forced on us. We shall have no means after the war out of which we can pay for purchases in the United States except the equivalent of what they buy from us.

(iii) The exchange rate between sterling and the dollar should be fixed by agreement, but the rate at which it was fixed would no longer be so important.

> For, with a proper system of payments agreements which would prevent an unbalanced situation from developing, there would be no longer much object in depreciating the exchange. The method of depreciation is a bad method which one is driven to adopt failing something better. The currency system I have in view would be that something better. If USA inflates more than we do, we might even *appreciate* sterling.

(iv) The postwar sterling area could be extended to countries like Holland and Belgium. But even within the closed area it would still be necessary to guard against an 'unbalanced position' of a member country.

> There would have to be some arrangement by which an unbalanced position up to an agreed figure would have to be cared for by credit arrangements. But, if the maximum were reached, then the unbalanced debtor would have to resrict its purchases until it was in balance again.

(v)   The essence of the system was 'trading goods against goods'. If Argentina bought maize from Britain, it would have to spend its sterling in Britain or in the Sterling Area. Britain's role as the world's largest importer would give it a huge bargaining power to negotiate payments agreements with outside countries.

(vi) 'The difficulty is to know quite how far it is safe to go in the direction of a complete freedom of transactions within the sterling area'. If Britain found itself with an adverse balance of payments as a result of countries like Argentina using their export earnings to Britain to buy too many goods from other sterling area countries then 'we should have to insist that the Argentine seller of maize must spend his sterling in the United Kingdom'.

(vii)

> The necessity for some such plan as the above arises essentially from the unbalanced creditor position of the United States. It is a necessary condition of a return to free exchanges that the United States should find some permanent remedy for this unbalanced position. Sooner or later one can only suppose that she will have to do so. But it would be very optimistic to believe that she will find the solution in the immediate post-war period, even if she tries to mitigate her task by making large presents for the reconstruction of Europe.[31]

Keynes's letter to Ashton-Gwatkin was a first, very uncertain, bash at his own Clearing Union plan, which he would draft that autumn. It is what his Clearing Union might have looked like *without the United States* in it. The crucial point was the priority given to commercial planning. If trade between the Sterling Area and the United States was to be on a barter (bilateral clearing) basis, monetary issues like the sterling–dollar exchange rate and creditor versus debtor adjustment became secondary. Also noticeable are Keynes's doubts about whether Britain's balance of payments would be able to support multilateral clearing within the sterling area.

It would be a mistake to believe that Keynes was *advocating* a 'Schachtian' world for Europe after the war, only one managed by Britain, not Germany. It is also important to be clear about the context in which these ideas were put forward. Until America entered the war at the end of 1941, Keynes could not assume that America would play any part in constructing a new international economic order, one which would provide a 'permanent remedy' for its 'unbalanced position'. The Atlantic Charter was some months ahead, Russia was not yet involved in hostilities. If Britain 'won the war' in these circumstances, it would be left responsible for the 'economic reorganization of Europe' – or more realistically, it would be left *à deux* with a presumably post-Nazi Germany. An economic settlement would therefore of necessity have to build on the 'Schachtian' arrangements of the 1930s, as developed during the war itself, hence, too, the importance Keynes attached to the continuing 'economic leadership [of Germany] in central Europe'.[32]

At the same time, Keynes did not think of Schachtian devices merely as a *pis aller*. Even an 'ideal system' which included the United States, would not be a return to the gold standard. In his reading of interwar history, currency manipulation and tariffs alike were weapons in the 'blind struggle' of countries to escape from the shackles of the gold standard, with a tendency to produce war.[33] The Schachtian system (in its 'good' sense) avoided this by ensuring that 'goods exchanged for goods' not gold. The doctrine that exchange controls were better than currency depreciation became a permanent part of Keynes's thinking. It also became Treasury and Bank of England orthodoxy.

IV

'I believe that the only fundamental issue' Kahn wrote to Keynes on 19 August 1941 'is what degree of American co-operation would be necessary to justify a return to what might be called a liberal economic system and whether there is sufficient hope of persuading the Americans ... to make the necessary concessions'.[34] Keynes's perplexity is captured in his reply. He was not 'seriously worried by the rather unexpected strength of the laissez-faire school' which he had found in Washington. 'For ... we shall start in practice *de facto* with a[n exchange] control and ... what actually will be evolved from that is extremely unlikely to be *laissez-faire*'. The really interesting question was the 'technical problem' of adapting the *de facto* system to peacetime condition.[35] This is the problem he tried to solve in his plan for a Clearing Union, drafted at Tilton in the first weekend of September 1941. It was done, he told Kahn, in an effort 'to make my ideas concrete' and 'to press others who have different ideas to do the same'. Keynes's method, as always, was to lead from the front and force others to make clear the nature of their disagreement.

The fruit of his weekend's drafting was two papers, 'Post War Currency Policy', and 'Proposals for an International Currency Union'. The first of them, divided into four parts, 'The Secular International Problem', 'Our Contemporary British Problem', 'The Analysis of the Problem', and 'The Alternatives Facing Us', provided the intellectual background for the 'Proposals'. To avoid a confused exposition, we will start with the first and third sections, before summarizing the second and fourth. The two questions Keynes set out to answer were: what was wrong with the gold standard? And what were the special problems Britain would face after the war?

On the first question, the key passage reads: 'To suppose that there is a smooth adjustment which preserves equilibrium if only we trust to methods of *laissez-faire* is a doctrinaire delusion which disregards the lessons of historical experience without having behind it the support of sound theory'.[36] Keynes claimed, provocatively, that in the previous five hundred years there had been only two periods, each of about fifty years, when the use of commodity money in international trade had 'worked' – the silver inflation period of the 16th century and the gold standard of the late 19th century, when 'the system of international investment pivoting on London transferred the onus of adjustment from the debtor to the creditor position'. So, far from currency *laissez-faire* having promoted the international division of labour, it had forced countries into Protectionism to escape currency disorders.

Keynes continued his historical lesson by dismissing the 'false' alternatives to the gold standard which had proliferated between the wars. They included the use of fluctuating exchange rates; credit and loan arrangements based on a 'false analogy' with 19th century conditions when loans were self-liquidating 'because they themselves created new sources of payment'; competitive deflations and exchange depreciations; tariffs, preferences, and subsidies. In the 1930s Schacht had 'stumbled in desperation on something new which had in it the germs of a good technical idea', namely, to cut the knot by discarding the use of international currency and substituting it for barter between countries. The fact that it was used in the service of evil should not blind us to its possible technical advantages in the service of good. Keynes then quoted from Henderson's 'Nineteen Thirties' paper: 'If Germany had wished for butter instead of guns and aeroplanes, there is no reason to doubt that Dr. Schacht's expedients would have enabled her to obtain the butter instead of the metal from overseas'.[37]

What of the theory? Keynes traced the failure of the gold standard to the fact that it threw the strain of adjusting a balance of payments disequilibrium on the countries least able to support it – those in trouble rather than those doing well. Adjustment, he wrote, was '*compulsory* for the debtor and *voluntary* for the creditor'. The country gaining gold had the option of hoarding its gold inflow rather than adding it to its money supply, the country losing gold had no choice but to reduce its money supply. Nor could it rely on the capital market, since a surplus country was under no compulsion to lend. The result was to give the system a deflationary bias, which produced a competitive struggle for wages and markets without, in fact, restoring satisfactory equilibrium. A further defect of the system was that it failed to discriminate between the flow of 'refugee, speculative and investment' capital. The system of unlimited capital mobility only worked because, in the 19th century, the flow of money corresponded to the development of new resources, unlike in the interwar years, when speculative flows dominated investment flows. 'The flow of refugee and speculative funds, superimposed on [the favourable trade balance of the United States] brought the whole system to ruin' between the wars. There was no guarantee against a repetition of massive hot money flows after the war, when the position of wealthowners would be threatened everywhere, and the 'whereabouts of "the better 'ole" will shift with the speed of a magic carpet'.[38]

Britain would start the peace in a 'state of extreme disequilibrium'. A large part of its visible and invisible exports would be lost in the war, there would be an abnormally high demand for imports for postwar reconstruction, and sterling balances were accumulating in London. Britain would need to increase its exports by between 50 and 100 per cent. It might even find it necessary to match imports and exports bilaterally with countries like Argentina – which would mean a shrinking of multilateral clearing within the sterling area. Keynes's mistrust for the United States emerges in a lengthy digression to the effect that the United States had not adjusted its creditor position after the last war and was even then attempting to force its wheat exports, by international convention, on impoverished East European countries. To give up Schachtian measures, in the absence of an American commitment to better alternatives, would be 'madness'. Anyone who agreed to such a surrender 'would be as great a traitor to this country as if he were to sign away the British navy before he had a firm assurance of an alternative means of protection'.[39]

What alternatives did Britain face? The United States would probably offer 'liberal relief to Europe during the reconstruction period, some reduction of tariffs and restriction of agricultural exports, and a general stimulus to demand via the New Deal'. The first was a temporary measure, the second would probably not be on an adequate scale, the third would offer 'great, and perhaps adequate relief' but could not be relied on.[40] If all that was on offer was 'currency disorders ... mitigated and temporarily postponed by some liberal Red Cross work by the United States', Britain would have no alternative but to refine and improve 'the Schachtian device'.[41] It would end the war with 'a well developed' payments and clearing system which might evolve into a permanent peacetime system, mitigating the objectionable features of bilateralism. It could stabilize and balance its trade at a high volume by continuing to buy foodstuffs and raw materials in bulk from countries willing to take its exports. A serviceable Schachtlan regime might be worked out. But Keynes would prefer first to approach the United States with an 'ideal' scheme, which would 'preserve the advantages of an international means of payment universally acceptable, while avoiding those features of the old system which did the damage'. While it might not be so helpful as *ad hoc* relief measures for the transitional period, it would be better in the long run. It would enable Britain to sign up honestly to the 'blessed word [non] -discrimination. If not this, we can ask, what then? Now that you are fully seized of the essential elements of the problem, what alternative solution do you offer us?'[42]

By this route Keynes came to his 'Proposals for an International Currency Union'. Its object 'must be to require the chief initiative [in adjustment] from the creditor countries, whilst maintaining enough discipline in the debtor countries to prevent them from exploiting the new ease allowed them in living profligately beyond their means'.[43] Its starting point was the wartime system of exchange controls operated by all countries. On this base Keynes erected a global system of multilateral clearing.

Member central banks would hold 'clearing accounts' in a new institution, the International Clearing Bank (ICB). All residual international transactions were to be settled through these accounts. Member central banks would buy and sell their own currencies among themselves against debits and credits to their accounts at the Clearing Bank.[44] These balances would be held in 'bank money' (he later called this 'bancor'). Each national currency would have a fixed, but adjustable relation to a unit of ICB's bank-money, which itself was expressed in terms of a unit of gold. This was like the gold standard. Unlike the gold standard, central banks could sell gold for bank-money at the ICB's price, but could not buy it with bank-money. So bancor, not gold, was the ultimate reserve asset of the system.

The object of the ICB was to maintain balance of payments equilibrium between each member country and the rest of the world. Persisting overdrafts and credits in the clearing accounts would reflect deficits and surpluses in countries' balance of payments. Keynes sought to bring a simultaneous pressure on surplus countries to reduce their surpluses and deficit countries to reduce their deficits, and this aim was reflected in the rules governing the quantity and distribution of the ICB's reserve assets. The initial bias in favour of deficit countries was assured by equipping each member bank with an automatic overdraft facility (called the 'index quota') equal to half the average value of its country's total trade for the five previous years, but the distributional rules were designed to bring a symmetric pressure to bear on member banks to discharge all their credits and debts (that is, balance their countries' external accounts) over the course of a year. Thus, though at any one time a member bank could overdraw its account up to the maximum of its quota, corrective mechanisms were supposed to come into play to prevent overdrafts reaching their quota limit except for very short periods. A bank whose annual average overdraft was more than a quarter of its index-quota would be designated a 'deficiency bank' and allowed to depreciate its currency by not more than 5 per cent at the end of that year; if its overdraft over the year was more than half its quota it would be designated a 'supervised bank', and might be *required* to reduce the value of its currency by up to 5 per cent, to hand over any free gold, and prohibit capital exports. Interest would be charged on overdrafts, rising in line with the debt-quota ratio. A persistently profligate member could be expelled from the Union. There were similar provisions to liquidate persisting surpluses – any member bank in persistent credit would be allowed or required to revalue its currency (in steps of 5 per cent), be required to unblock any foreign-owned investments, and be required to pay interest of 5 or 10 per cent a year on credits running above a quarter and half of its quota, respectively. A credit balance exceeding the full amount of its quota at the end of the year would be confiscated.[45]

'The heart of the matter' as Professor Moggridge writes 'was to encourage balance of payments adjustment'.[46] But Keynes also suggested that the ICB open clearing accounts for a supranational policing body 'charged with preserving the peace and maintaining international order'; a reconstruction and relief organization; and commodity control schemes. These bodies would be given overdraft facilities up to an agreed maximum (presumably on the same quota system as applied to the member central banks). The reconstruction and relief agency would acquire additional financial facilities from the Reserve Fund into which would be paid the interest payments on, and proceeds of confiscated, surplus balances. Keynes wrote:

> By this means all risk is avoided of any country being required to assume burdensome commitment for relief and reconstruction, since the resources will be provided in the first instance by those countries having credit balances on their Clearing Accounts for which they have no immediate use and are voluntarily leaving idle, and in the long run by those countries which have a chronic international surplus for they have no beneficial employment.

The ICB would be managed by a Board of eight governors and a chairman. Britain, the Commonwealth, the USA and the USSR would have one each, there would be two from Europe, one from Latin America, and one other. The fact that Britain and its Empire could outvote the United States, which would be providing the ICB with most of its money, was a felicitous touch.[47]

Keynes had made no attempt to explain or advocate his proposals. As a result they had been widely misunderstood within the Whitehall departments to which they were circulated, and sometimes attacked on the basis of the misunderstanding. He tried to remedy this omission in the second draft of his plan, circulated on 18 November 1941. This will help us get a better idea of the logic and purposes of his scheme. The following are the important points:

(1) The Currency Union was a generalization of the 'essential principle of banking ... within any closed system ... this ... is the necessary equality of credits and debts, of assets and liabilities. If no credits [i.e. liabilities] can be removed outside the banking system but only transferred within it, the Bank itself can never be in difficulty'. Keynes might have added that it

was a generalization of a British-type of banking system, in which overdrafts did not give rise to corresponding 'real' liabilities: credits and debts were purely fiduciary. This was to be an important difference from Harry Dexter White's Stabilization Fund which only made collateralized loans. Unlike a national bank, the International Bank would need to be governed by rules, not discretion, especially in regard to maximum permitted overdrafts and provisions to ensure clearing, so that the movement of individual balances in either direction was checked in good time.

(2)   The plan aimed to substitute an expansionary for a contractionary pressure on world trade. This might be done by the Federal Reserve Board redistributing gold, or providing the Bank of England with temporary overdrafts. However, this would be subject to 'extraneous, political reasons', putting some countries into obligation to others, and in any case, Britain was unlikely to be a major recipient of US bounty. So it would be better to persuade the United States to enter 'into a general and collective responsibility ... that a country finding itself in a creditor position *against the rest of the world as a* whole should enter into an obligation to dispose of this credit balance ... This would give us, and all others, the great assistance of multilateral clearing...'

(3)   'If we lack the productive capacity to maintain our standard of life, then a reduction in this standard is not avoidable. If our price levels are hopelessly wrong, a change in the rate of exchange is inevitable. But if we possess the productive capacity and the difficulty is the lack of markets as a result of restrictive policies throughout the world, then the remedy lies in expanding opportunities for export by removal of restrictive pressures, not in contracting imports'.

(4)   'The purpose of the overdraft facilities is mainly to give time for the necessary adjustments to be effected, and to secure prior agreement that they *will* be made'.

(5)   Adjustment should be symmetric between creditors and debtors. But 'I do not contemplate that the sanction ... by which creditor balances in excess of a stipulated amount were confiscated, would ever come into force in practice. The main point is that the creditor should not be allowed to remain passive. For if he is, an intolerable task is laid on the debtor country'.

(6)   An advantage of the plan was that it provided 'an automatic register of the size and the whereabouts of the aggregate debtor and creditor countries respectively. The danger signal is shown to all concerned...'

(7)   The rules governing changes in exchange rates were designed to make the creditors contribute to the change by appreciating their currencies, while avoiding changes from being neutralized by 'unjustified competitive depreciations elsewhere'.

(8) Keynes admitted that the most potent criticism of his plan was the inadequacy of discipline against debtor countries. But at the moment there was no discipline at all; the force of a collective sanction should not be underestimated; and 'a small expenditure of faith and a readiness to allow actual experience to decide are not too much to ask, when so much else is at stake'.

(9) The new system should make it possible to proscribe protective expedients like high tariffs or preferences, export subsidies, import quotas or prohibitions, barter agreements, and so on, 'except when they are required'.

(10) Central controls of capital movements would be permanent. This would involve all members of the Union in setting up or maintaining the *machinery* of exchange control for all transactions, though a general open licence would be given for current trade. This did not imply an end of international investment. But it was important to distinguish between 'genuine new investment for developing the world's resources' and 'floating funds', and between temporary credits from surplus to deficit countries and flights of capital from deficit to surplus countries. 'There is no country which can, in future, safely allow the flight of funds for political reasons or to evade domestic taxation or in anticipation of the owner turning refugee. Equally, there is no country that can safely receive funds which cannot safely be used for fixed investment and might turn it into a deficiency country against its will and contrary to the real facts'. So all remittances would be canalized through central banks and the resulting balances cleared through the ICB; the proceeds from the sale of foreign-owned assets, actual or prospective, could not be repatriated except under licence; the interest and sinking funds of foreign loans could be freely repatriated; except for small working balances, floating and liquid funds would only be lent and borrowed between central banks.[48]

The first draft of Keynes's Currency Union has a very Schachtian feel to it. Technically, it was an essay in global Schachtianism: 'a *generalised* payments agreement'.[49] Multilateralism was to be let out on licence, made possible by the inclusion of the United States. It reflected Keynes's view that a 'liberal' international system had to incorporate Schachtian elements in perpetuity. But his Clearing Union also had a much shorter-term objective. Britain and the European countries would start postwar life as 'deficiency' areas, which would require massive US support if they were to avoid both import controls against American goods and a catastrophic reduction in their living standards. So Keynes attempted to strike a deal by which American support would be made unconditional as a *quid pro quo* for free entry of American exports as demanded by Article VII. The Clearing Union was an attempt to handle both short-term and long-term problems in a single framework. Or, to put it another way, it was an attempt to multilateralize hegemonic functions (including keeping the peace) which Britain had previously performed, but which it did not want the United States to perform.

His plan reflected a British critique of interwar US policy which was bound to militate against its acceptance by the United States. He implied, without quite saying so, that Britain had 'done its duty' as a creditor in the 19th century, but the US had failed to do so between the wars, and therefore it must now be forced to.[50] In fact, Keynes had sketched in the historical background in an amazingly cursory, and occasionally confused way, as though he was too tired – as he may well have been after his summer labours in Washington – to argue his case properly.

But the problem went deeper. The Clearing Union Plan was a straightforward application to policy of Keynes's 'liquidity preference' theory. In his vision of economic life, the speculative demand for money balances was normally positive. This is what gave the gold standard a deflationary bias. It is in terms of this schematism that the interwar years are seen as an (admittedly extreme) example of the 'normal' case, unlike the 19th century when 'special factors' produced a spirit of business optimism sufficient to offset 'normal' deflationary tendencies.[51] The purpose of the Clearing Union (as of Keynesian policy generally) was to make quasi-permanent the expansionary forces which had occurred only intermittently and haphazardly in the past. But a Clearing Union with this philosophy was likely to be endorsed only by those who accepted the Keynesian analysis, or by those, like the British and Europeans, who had special reasons for wanting a share of American surpluses.

Even those who accepted that liquidity-preference could be a problem, and had been a problem between the wars, were divided on how to apportion the blame for it. The more general American view was that its causes lay in the profligacy of the debtor rather than the avarice of the creditor countries: for reasons connected with their internal policies debtor countries had not been safe places in which to invest money. Keynes admitted the force of the criticism that the sanctions on debtors were inadequate in his scheme. Its corrective requirements did not extend to their domestic policies. But like in the parable of the Prodigal Son he hoped that generosity by the creditor countries would secure better behaviour by debtors. However, this moral hypothesis was undermined by the unconditional character of the creditor guarantee that he sought. Politically, this was something the Americans would never accept. The current East Asian financial crisis raises the same kind of issue. Who is to blame: the East Asian countries for pursuing unsound domestic policies, or the international 'speculators' who invested in them and then pulled the plug? Beyond this: are 'currency disorders ... mitigated or temporarily postponed by ... Red Cross work by the United States' a satisfactory basis for a world monetary system?

Keynes's Clearing Union was designed to avoid exchange-rate wars. An interesting puzzle is why he did not advocate clean floating. The technical answer is that he did not believe the Marshall–Lerner condition – that the sum of the price elasticities of demand for exports and imports must sum to more than one for a devaluation to improve the terms of trade – was generally valid. As he explained to Henry Clay:

> A small country in particular may have to accept substantially worse terms for its exports in terms of its imports if it tries to force the former by means of exchange depreciation. If therefore we take account of the terms of trade effect there is an optimum level of exchange such that any movement either way would cause a deterioration of the country's merchandise balance.[52]

The 'terms of trade' argument against currency depreciation had re-emerged in the debates over German reparations in the 1920s in which, of course, Keynes was heavily involved. Empirical studies in the 1930s suggested that elasticity pessimism was justified. This may explain the low priority Keynes gave to exchange rate adjustment in his Clearing Union. Today it is more usually assumed that the Marshall–Lerner condition will be satisfied after a lag.[53]

V

This chapter has tried to explain the historical and intellectual sources of Keynes's Clearing Union plan. To appreciate its profound differences from the Harry Dexter White plan for an International Monetary Fund we would need to juxtapose the two schemes. But this much can be said.

The Clearing Union idea is rather obviously borrowed from the Germans. In fact, both sides copied each other so much that one can talk about a 'European' perspective on postwar economic problems, understandably since the 'unbalanced' US creditor position was a common European problem. The steps taken by Britain in 1940 to pool gold and foreign exchange reserves and prevent them draining out of the sterling area were modelled on the 'Schachtian device'. The Funk Plan's attempt to multilateralize clearing within Continental Europe was influenced by the 'fortified' sterling area. Keynes's Clearing Union was the Funk Plan globalized, with the addition of an overdraft facility. The barbarism of Hitler's political project has overshadowed and obscured the substratum of common economic logic.

The Clearing Union plan, then, had three sources. Technically, it was based on Schacht's barter model. Economically, it reflected Keynes's view that the sterling area/imperial preference system would not solve Britain's postwar balance of payments problem. Politically, it was premised on the need to appease the United States. The fact that Keynes had, as he told Harrod, pursued 'both lines of thought', simultaneously, soon put his plan into a pole position.

He used Schactian arguments and devices to reach liberal conclusions. So his plan provided a potential point of agreement between the Schachtians and liberals in Whitehall.

APPENDIX. THE SCHACHTIAN SYSTEM

Under a bilateral clearing agreement, a German importer from, say, Hungary, instead of paying marks to the Hungarian exporter for exchange into pengos, would pay the marks into a Hungarian clearing account with the Reichsbank. German exporters to Hungary were paid marks from this fund. The opposite process took place in Budapest. No local currency was traded in the foreign exchange market. A foreign exchange market in so-called 'Aski' marks was allowed to develop for trade with countries not covered by clearing agreements. An exporter to Germany could obtain a credit in Aski marks which he could sell at a discount to the importer of goods from Germany, who could thus pay the German price. The Schachtian system was an alternative to a mark devaluation, which was rejected both on anti-inflationary grounds, and because devaluation would have increased the nominal value of Germany's external debt (including reparations) denominated in gold marks.

It was widely believed at the time that Germany exploited its position as the chief market and leading supplier for countries in the Danubian basin, by 'buying cheap and selling dear'. In fact, Germany often bought above, and sold below, the world market price, in order to tie clearing account countries into the German economic system. As a result it was able to get essential imports of food and raw materials on long-term contracts, while delaying the export of its own manufactures needed for rearmament purposes. This delay was reflected in the accumulation of mark balances in its partners' Reichsbank accounts, which represented credits to Germany by its small trading partners. But this was advantageous to them. Clearing account countries had to print additional local currency to pay their exporters, which, in the prevailing conditions, raised employment rather than prices.[54] The domestic counterpart of the Schachtian system was the issue of credits or Mefo-Bills to German industry, which in four years restored full employment.

The Schachtian system represented *in toto* a way of escape from both the inflation and balance of payments constraints on pursuing a full employment policy. 'Without this control it is scarcely conceivable that Germany could have maintained so high a rate of external expansion on the basis of so small a volume of imports, while, if imports had not been restricted, recovery would have been checked by the resulting adverse balance of payments'.[55] The state paid money to businessmen to hire more workers and buy essential imports up to the level of full capacity, cutting off inflationary pressure through wage and price controls and balance of payments pressure by restricting imports or paying IOUs for imported goods. As such it was certainly the most extreme version of Keynesian policy ever practised in peacetime, though probably devoid of any direct stimulus from Keynes himself.

It is interesting that Keynes never paid the slightest attention to this type of application of his ideas. His printed preface to the German edition of the *General Theory* (CW, VII, xxvi) makes no reference to, or shows knowledge of, the 'Schachtian' system; as far as can be established he made no reference to it between 1933 and 1940, either in public or private. It is highly unlikely that he knew nothing about it. It is likely that he did not want to give the Nazi regime the slightest excuse to use his name as an *imprimatur*. The more intriguing possibility is that he did not in fact approve of 'Keynesian' policy carried to these lengths in peacetime. This is hinted at in a passage from the preface to the German edition of the *General Theory*, omitted from the *Collected Writings* version referred to above, when Keynes explicitly writes that his 'theory of output as a whole', while 'applicable' to German conditions, was 'worked out having the conditions of Anglo-Saxon countries in mind – where a great deal of laissez-faire still prevails'.[56]

NOTES

1. CW. XXIII. p.208 (CW ≡ Collected Writings).
2. To what extent Roosevelt's bizarre gold-buying policy of 1933 was conceived as a retaliation against sterling's depreciation is disputed. He certainly justified it in these terms. (See B. Rowland, p.202 in B. Rowland (ed.) *Balance of Power or Hegemony: The Interwar Monetary System*, 1976.) However, some see it mainly as an attempt to raise US domestic prices (J.K. Galbraith, *Money: Whence it Came, Where it Went*, pp. 210–11, 1975.). Probably the simplest explanation is that Roosevelt and his advisers had only a vague idea of what they were doing.
3. Ian M. Drummond, *The Floating Pound and the Sterling Area* 1931–1939, 1981, p.257.
4. S.G. Waley, 1936, q. ibid. p.205.
5. Arthur Schlesinger. Jr., *The Coming of the New Deal*, 1959, p.253.
6. For a summary, see J.K.Horsefield, *The International Monetary Fund 1945–1965*, vol. 1, 1969, pp.6–7.
7. Cordell Hull Memoirs. i. 1948, p.530.
8. Paul Einzig, *Hitler's 'New Order' in Europe*, 1941, p.66.
9. For a fuller discussion of the Schachtian system, see Appendix.
10. H.D. Henderson, 'The Nineteen Thirties', 22 August 1941, T 247/121.
11. Ibid. Henderson. 'The Balance of Payments Problem', 25 September 1941.
12. S.G. Waley. 8 November 1941. T 247/116. This Treasury file contains the reactions to Henderson.
13. D.H. Robertson note, 22 August 1941, T 247/121.
14. Ibid. Henderson to Sir Richard Hopkins, 30 October 1941.
15. In 1930 he had accused Keynes of being unable to accept a 'conservative conclusion' as 'inconsistent with your self-respect' (see R. Skidelsky, *John Maynard Keynes*, ii, 1992, p. 366). This was a thinly veiled allusion to Keynes's membership of the Bloomsbury Group, whose contributions to its literary pages he had so disliked when he edited the *Nation*.

16. Roy Harrod, *Life of John Maynard Keynes*, 1951, p.526. See E.F. Penrose, *the Peace*, 1953, p.17 for a similar comment.
17. R. Skidelsky, *John Maynard Keynes*, i, 1983, p. 370; D.E. Moggridge, *Maynard Keynes, An Economist's Biography*, 1992, p. 309.
18. CW IV, pp.139–40.
19. Skidelsky. ii. pp.183–7.
20. CW IX, p.219.
21. CW VI, p.299.
22. CW XXI, pp.239–40.
23. CW XI, p.501.
24. CW VI, pp.354–61.
25. A. van Dormael, *Bretton Woods, Birth of a Monetary System*, 1978, pp.5–7: see also Harold James, 'Post-War German Currency Plans' in Christoph Buchheim, Michael Hutter and Harold James *Zerrissene Zwlschenkriegszeit. Wirtschaftshistorische Beitrage*, 1994, pp. 205–18.
26. The existence of this important fascist root of European Union has been ignored, largely for political reasons, but partly because it was regarded as fraudulent. Certainly Hitler had no interest in it. His mind was already set on extending the war to Russia. This does not mean that the technocrats who devised the Funk Plan thought it fraudulent. They were probably expecting the postwar era to start very soon, and were making economic preparations for it. (For further details, see Paul Einzig, '*Hitler's 'New Order' in Europe*', 1941, pp.25–6; John Laughland, *The Tainted Source: The Undemocratic Origins of the European Idea*, 1997, ch.2.)
27. CW XXV, p.2.
28. JMK and E. Playfair. 'Que Quiere Decir el Area', November 1940, JMK 'Proposals to Counter the German 'New Order' ', 1 December, 1940. CW XXV, pp.3–16.
29. JMK to S.Waley. 11 November, 1940. T 247/85.
30. Ibid. pp.8–9.
31. Ibid. pp.16–19.
32. Ibid. p.9.
33. JMK. *The General Theory of Employment, Interest and Money*, CW VII, pp.348–9. Hubert Henderson agreed: 'Of the various expedients which different Governments employed in the 1930s none produced more unfortunate results than deliberate exchange depreciation. It was the least helpful to countries'. q. Dormael, *op. cit.* p.129.
34. Keynes Papers. L/K/135.
35. JMK to RFK, 21 August 1941, MY-W, p.20.
36. Ibid. pp.21–2.
37. Ibid. pp.22–3.
38. Ibid. pp.27–31.
39. Ibid. p.27.
40. Ibid. pp.31–2.
41. Ibid. p.24.
42. Ibid. pp.32–3.
43. Ibid. p.30.
44. As in the following example. An American exporter sells goods to an English importer. He expects payment in dollars. The English importer applies to the Bank of England for dollars. The ICB debits the British clearing account and credits the US account the cost of the transaction. The Bank of England receives the dollar equivalent of the credit from the American central bank, which it pays to the British importer who then pays the American exporter.
45. Ibid. pp.33–7. These provisions can be illustrated by figures. The Bank of England's initial quota (overdraft facility) would have been $3.1 bn, or 770m at an exchange rate of $4.03 to the £. It would have been allowed a maximum overdraft of £192.5m over the year (a quarter of its quota) without any corrective measures being called for. If its overdraft averaged over D85m a year it would have been declared a 'supervised' bank, required to devalue its currency by 5 per cent, stop exporting capital, and hand over gold. It would also face rising interest charges on its debt. Conversely, if its credit balance averaged over D85m a year, it would have been

required to revalue its currency, release frozen foreign-owned balances (e.g. sterling balances) and pay interest of 10 per cent on any amount over 1385m. Any excess over the full quota of 1770m would have been confiscated.

46. Moggridge. *op. cit.* p.674.
47. CW XXV, pp.38–41.
48. Ibid. pp.44–54.
49. Ibid. p.52.
50. Ibid. pp.30–149.
51. For Keynes's 'special factors' theory of the 19th century see CW VIL, p.307.
52. JMK to H. Clay, 2 December 1940. T 247/116. See also CW YXV, pp.28–9.
53. For example, Wendy Carlin and David Soskice, *Macroeconomics and the Wage Bargain*, 1991, pp.292–3.
54. See L. Neal, 'The Economics and Finance of Bilateral Clearing Agreements: Germany 1934–1938', *Ec. Hist. Rev.*, 32, 1979, pp. 391–404.
55. Claude Guillebaud, *The Economic Recovery of Germany 1933–1938*, 1939, p. 72.
56. See B. Schefold, 'The General Theory for a Totalitarian State? A Note on Keynes's Preface to the German Edition of 1936', reprinted from the *Cambridge Journal of Economics*, **4**(2), June 1980, pp.175–6, in John Cunningham Wood, *John Maynard Keynes: Critical Assessments*, vol. 2, 1983, pp.416–7.

2. Economic integration, the EMU and European regional growth

John S.L. McCombie[1]

INTRODUCTION

The introduction of a common currency for Europe has now come to fruition, although without the initial participation of Denmark, Greece, Sweden and the UK.[2] The drive towards full monetary union was so strong that in one or two cases the convergence criteria were effectively fudged.[3]

The purpose of this chapter is to review the likely effects of the single market and the proposed common currency on the growth of the European regions. The term 'region' is defined very broadly. This is because with the introduction of a common currency a large majority of the European nations will become, in effect, European regions on a par with the larger regions of the US. While there has long been a concern over the dangers to social cohesion that economic integration may bring (Emerson *et al.*, 1992; Dignan, 1996) and which led to the introduction of European aid for the depressed European regions from the mid-1970s, there are still wide regional disparities in terms of per capita income and unemployment. At present, almost one in four of the European Union (EU) regions has a per capita level of income that is below three-quarters of the EU average. These form a poverty belt, which includes many of the peripheral regions such as those in Greece, Portugal (with the exception of Lisbon), rural Spain, southern Italy and the former East Germany. There are also regions in the UK and Austria included in the belt. This has raised the question as to whether the single economic market (SEM), together with the introduction of a common currency, is likely to ameliorate or exacerbate the position, especially in the absence of substantial European-wide fiscal transfers.

The most optimistic view is that economic and monetary union will lead to a faster growth of Europe with a gradual convergence in regional per capita incomes. Underlying this is the orthodox neoclassical view that market forces are equilibrating and will lead automatically to convergence in the various indicators of regional disparities. It is, however, possible that the outcome will be a faster overall growth of Europe, but with regional disparities increasing and even possibly some regions performing worse than if there had been no integration in the first place. Finally, it is conceivable that the overall growth of Europe may be actually reduced and some countries would find that, divested of their macroeconomic policy instruments, their growth rates would be lower than if they were not part of the EU. This could be, for example, if an independent European central bank, in pursuing policies putatively designed to reduce inflation, actually reduced the growth of demand and hence the overall rate of growth. This, of course, denies the existence of the classical dichotomy in which money has no effect on real variables and on which much of the supposed advantages of the common currency are predicated.[4]

This chapter argues that while the SEM may raise the long-term growth of Europe (although this is problematic), the unfettered workings of the market are likely to lead to forces making for greater regional disparities. The introduction of the common currency greatly reduces national discretionary macroeconomic policy, including exchange rate adjustments. It also is likely, under present proposals, to weaken the effectiveness of the automatic fiscal stabilizers (Eichengreen, 1997). These are all likely to exacerbate regional problems, because of the absence of sufficient fiscal transfers at the EU level.[5] This could lead to greater polarization in Europe, which could ultimately threaten its social cohesion.[6]

THE SINGLE ECONOMIC MARKET AND THE EUROPEAN REGIONS

Although it is a somewhat artificial distinction, it is useful to consider separately the effects of the progressive economic integration of the European regional markets and the likely impact of a common currency. Generally, the consensus of opinion (certainly the view of the European Commission) is that increased integration will provide substantial economic benefits for Europe as a whole. The conventional neoclassical theory, stemming from Ricardo's principle of comparative advantage, suggests that increased integration, defined as greater freedom for the movement of both goods and factors of production, leads to improved allocative efficiency by allowing for greater specialisation. Regions (or countries) benefit from specialising in the production of goods that use intensively their abundant factors of production. The fact that regions differ in their productivity or their wage levels is, of course, no cause for concern, as the law of comparative advantage suggests no region will be made worse off by integration. This is not to say, however, that there may not be a significant redistribution of income accruing to the different factors of production. This occurs because the returns to the scarce factor of production decline as the factor becomes relatively more abundant with integration. In addition, it is argued that the increased movement of factors of production causes the progressive eradication of both the interregional and intraregional misallocation of factors of production (McCombie, 1988a). Factors will move to where their marginal productivity is highest, leading to an overall increase in output. Of course, the Heckscher–Ohlin theorem shows that free movement of goods can be a substitute for factor mobility in bringing about the equalisation of factor prices. However, as is well known, these results rely on a number of restrictive assumptions; namely perfect competition and the associated full employment of resources, together with identical well-behaved production functions exhibiting constant returns to scale.

The early predictions of the theories, at least in the simple models, do not stand up well to empirical testing. The classic study was Borts and Stein's (1964) work on US regional growth, which found the model did not perform well (see the discussion in McCombie, 1988a). Furthermore, there is little support for the Heckscher–Ohlin theory at the US regional level, apart from some weak evidence in favour of the theory when changes in industrial concentration, are considered (Moroney and Walker, 1966).

Another argument is that with greater integration comes greater competition and hence improved productive efficiency, especially in the presence of oligopolistic industries. It is conceded that in the short run there may be underutilisation of resources due to the structural change. (See, for example, Neary, 1978) on the problem of short-run capital specificity.) Nevertheless, it is argued that such costs are not a reason against integration. They are likened by Krugman (1989), for example, to investment costs needed to adopt new technology or 'to the losses suffered by the buggy manufacturers with the coming of the automobile'. Of course, a necessary assumption of this is that the unemployment of resources is short term and the impact of integration does not adversely affect the rate of growth of any country (or region). These assumptions will be disputed below.

Kaldor (1972, 1981) has long challenged a central assumption of this approach, arguing that increasing returns to scale are the mainspring of economic growth and their existence overturns the main conclusions of the above neoclassical analysis. Kaldor (1981), taking Ricardo's famous example of the case of the opening of trade between Portugal and England, shows that in the circumstances when there are increasing returns in manufacturing and diminishing returns in agriculture, the opening of trade between the two countries, far from being beneficial for both, could result in one country (Portugal, in the example) being 'a much poorer country than before'. There is a certain irony in the fact that the importance of increasing returns has only recently come to be emphasised in orthodox economic theory, first in the 'new' or 'strategic' trade theory and secondly in the 'new growth theory'.

Krugman (1989) has examined the implications for European integration within the conventional neoclassical approach. He considers that the existence of increasing returns is demonstrated by the importance of intra-industry trade, which allows increased specialisation in production to realise the benefits of economies of scale. He cites the liberalising of trade between the US and Canada as a case in point. This allowed Canada to specialise in a narrower range of automobile products which it was able to produce on a scale and efficiency comparable to the US. While the disadvantages of integration with increasing returns have been appreciated in the literature, according to Krugman they turn out to be relatively minor. They include the possibility of increased barriers to entry in some industries and greater monopoly profits. If a country (region) can gain a more than proportionate share of such industries, this will be at another country's expense. This provides a rationale for strategic trade policies, which may be traced back to Friedrich List, whereby it is optimal for a country to subsidise exports to gain market share and reap the benefits of increasing returns to scale. This may be globally suboptimal if countries all choose to subsidise the same industry. However, this is unlikely to be a serious issue in the EU as such measures are forbidden. Other possible disadvantages to European integration include the possibility of reciprocal dumping whereby oligopolistic firms spatially price discriminate. Firms keep prices high in their own country and sell at much lower margins in their competitors' countries. This could in principle lead to the same good being shipped in opposite directions with a waste of transport costs.

Nevertheless, it was Kaldor (1970) who was one of the first to appreciate that increased integration, while it may increase aggregate growth, could actually lead to increased disparities between the various constituent regions.[7] However, while it could be argued that increasing returns are likely to lead to significant benefits for the newly integrated market as a whole, this may be to the absolute disadvantage of one, or more, of the regions concerned. Growth occurs in a circular and cumulative manner in the presence of increasing returns to scale and regions may be caught in vicious, as well as virtuous, circles of growth (Myrdal, 1957).

Kaldor's is essentially a demand-orientated approach. A faster growth leads to increased competitiveness (of either the price or the non-price variety) which leads to a faster growth of exports. This in turn, through the Harrod foreign trade multiplier, feeds back into faster growth. Of course, regional growth is not explosive; we do not observe production in some regions completely collapsing, but the main driving force is for divergence. This, of course, may be limited, or even completely offset, by such factors as regional policy, the increasing shortage of land, greater congestion costs, and labour shortages in the prosperous regions.

Since the existence of increasing returns to scale is the *sine qua non* of this approach, I shall next consider the empirical evidence and then the consequences for regional growth.

THE EVIDENCE FOR INCREASING RETURNS TO SCALE

The controversy over whether constant returns or increasing returns to scale exist has reigned ever since Adam Smith's (1776) *Wealth of Nations*. For some commentators, it is almost axiomatic that the whole of capitalist development is inextricably bound up with the progressive exploitation of increasing returns. (See Kaldor, 1977, for an exposition of this view.) The rationale can be traced back to Smith's dictum of the division of labour being limited by the extent of the market, so graphically demonstrated by his famous example of the pin factory. Associated with this is the *reductio ad absurdum* argument that if there were constant returns at every level of production, given the existence of transport costs, everyone would end up producing individually everything they consumed. This is because, as there would be no benefit from size, such a structure of production would minimize transport costs.[8] Regional economists have long pointed to the existence of increasing returns and agglomeration economies as the reason for the existence of cities and the spatial concentration of production. There is a certain irony that much of this literature on the returns to scale and the importance of space has only been recently rediscovered by mainstream economists (Krugman, 1991). There is little doubt that one of the reasons of the prevalence of the assumption of constant returns in neoclassical economics has been the mathematical difficulties that the abandonment of the postulate of perfect competition poses. It is not coincidental that the development of the theoretical modelling of the new trade theory and the new growth theory, with their emphasis on increasing returns to scale, had to wait until the belated development of the imperfectly competitive models.

Kaldor (1972) traces the origins of the neglect of increasing returns precisely to the middle of the fourth chapter of Volume I of the *Wealth of Nations*, where Smith gets 'bogged down in the question of how values and prices for products are determined. One can trace then a more or less constant development of price theory from the subsequent chapters of Smith through Ricardo, Walras, Marshall right up to Debreu and the most sophisticated of present day Americans. The basic assumption of this theory is constant costs, or constant returns to scale'. Although Kaldor (1972) considers increasing returns at the empirical level to be self-evident, ever since the debate over Clapham's (1922) 'empty economic boxes', the econometric evidence has proved contradictory. The original work of Cobb and Douglas, from their seminal paper in 1928 to the plethora of their cross-industry studies in the 1930s and 1940s, not only found constant returns to scale but that the output elasticities did not significantly differ from their factor shares, a result which they claimed showed that markets were competitive and factors were paid their marginal products. (However, most of these results were spurious. See McCombie, 1998a).

Work by Hildebrand and Liu (1965) and Moroney (1972), using the logarithm of the levels of the output and the inputs for US regional data at the 2-digit SIC, found some evidence of increasing returns to scale, but these were generally small. Griliches and Ringstad (1971), using firm data for the Norwegian regions, also found similar results.

The whole question of the existence of increasing returns to scale has been recently re-opened by Hall's (1990) work. Using time-series value added data, he regressed the growth of output on the growth of the factor inputs weighted by their shares in total costs, rather than in total revenue. (Consequently, his procedure did not rely upon the assumption of perfect competition.) He found evidence of substantial increasing returns to scale. But criticisms were not long in coming. Caballero and Lyons (1989, 1992) argued that the model was misspecified, because externalities had a potentially important role to play, and Hall made no allowance for them. They extended the Hall model by including the growth of total manufacturing in the specification of the individual industry production functions to capture the influence of externalities. They found the coefficient on this variable was statistically significant and positive. The estimates of the industry returns to scale, *per se*, were much smaller than those found by Hall and close to constant returns to scale. The controversy did not end here. Marchetti (1994), Basu and Fernand (1995) and Basu (1996) all argue that gross output is preferable to the use of value added.[9] When gross output is used, it is found that the externality effect is insignificant and generally it is not possible to rule out constant returns to scale. The main problem with these time-series studies is that no adjustment is made for changes in capacity utilisation. Consequently, the estimates of 'increasing returns' may be merely capturing the short-run Okun effect. The growth of materials demonstrates few (if any) changes in its utilisation over the cycle (i.e. the recorded growth rate of materials accurately reflects its usage). It can be shown that this will reduce the weight given to the Okun effect and the estimates using gross output suggest constant returns to scale. (See McCombie, 1998b, for an argument as to why the estimates must for *a priori* reasons give constant returns to scale.)

Of more relevance for our argument here are the estimates of the Verdoorn Law (Kaldor, 1966). This is the relationship between the growth of productivity (p) and manufacturing, or industry, output (q) and takes the form $p = \alpha + \beta q$, where a statistically significant Verdoorn coefficient (β) indicates increasing returns to scale. The Verdoorn relationship is deceptively simple and issues that have been explored in the literature include the effect of the omission of the capital stock; simultaneous equation bias; misspecification due to the diffusion of innovations; measurement errors: and second order identification problems. (See McCombie and Thirlwall, 1994, Chapter 2 for a detailed discussion of these issues.) Notwithstanding this, the Verdoorn law suggests the presence of substantial increasing returns to scale. McCombie and de Ridder (1984) estimated the law using US state data over the last decade of the Golden Age (1963–73) and found that the estimates of returns to scale were in the range of 1.33 to 1.65. (McCombie, 1985, found similar results using US state statistics at the 2-digit SIC level.) These results have been confirmed by more recent studies. Leon-Ledsma (1998), using cross-regional data over the period 1962–91 for Spain, finds a Verdoorn coefficient of about one-half and returns to scale of between 1.37 and 2.24, depending upon the exact specification of the model. Bernat (1996) using US state data for 1977–90 found a significant Verdoorn coefficient, although slightly lower than the traditional value of one half. Fingleton and McCombie (1998) found a value of one half for the EU regions using data for the NUTS 2 regions. What is interesting is that the last two studies explicitly took into account the spatial nature of the data by estimating models that had a spatial error process. In both studies, there is evidence that the economic performance of one region is significantly affected by that in the surrounding ones and there are significant spatial technological spillovers.[10] Harris and Lau (1998) estimated the Verdoorn law using time-series data for the UK standard regions within an error correction model. They likewise found evidence of substantial returns to scale. Consequently, there is a great deal of evidence of substantial increasing returns to scale at the regional level.

However, before turning to the explicitly spatial implications of increasing returns to scale for regional growth, it is useful to first discuss Baldwin's (1989) estimates of the possible effects of the SEM for Europe as a whole.

EUROPEAN ECONOMIC GROWTH AND INCREASING RETURNS TO SCALE

Baldwin (1989) was one of the first to attempt to quantify the overall likely benefits of the SEM. His estimates were based on the use of the aggregate production function and neoclassical new growth theory. He took as his starting point the Cecchine Report's estimates of possible static welfare gains of between 2.5% and 6.5% of European GDP obtained by raising the level of output for any given level of factor inputs. Baldwin noted that this increase in output would also increase the rate of saving. Hence, under neoclassical assumptions, the rate of investment would also rise. This would lead to further medium-run dynamic gains. Under constant returns to scale, he estimates that the medium-run effect is about 40% of the static effect.

One of the standard results of the Solow model is that the steady state rate of growth is independent of the share of GDP that is invested. Hence, so long as there are diminishing returns to the produced factor of production, while there will be a temporary increase in productivity growth, the European economy will once again reach the same steady state growth rate as before. [11] However, the new growth theory has shown that that this result no longer holds if the output elasticity of capital, broadly defined, is greater than, or equals, one and so diminishing returns to capital do not set in.

There is a problem, however, that if the output elasticity is greater than one, there will be infinite output in a finite time. As this is implausible, to say the least, Baldwin restricts his consideration to the case where the coefficient is just below unity, which is the mean value that estimation of national production functions, without a time trend, gives him. [12] Baldwin considers that the effects of the SEM might raise the growth rate by between 0.3 and 0.9 percentage points. When it is appreciated that the one-off creation of the single market could raise the trend rate of growth of Europe by up to one-third, it can be seen just how powerful are the effects of increasing returns and perhaps how implausible are these estimates. [13] Of course, as Baldwin admits, these are very much 'back of the envelope' calculations, but they do suggest that the dynamic gains accruing by raising the growth rate are likely to be much more important than the static gains stressed by the Cecchine report.

The role of increasing returns to scale (broadly defined) plays a key role in the cumulative causation model. Kaldor (1970) postulated a two-sector model where growth was initially determined by the growth of agricultural demand and then later, with the decline of the importance of this sector, by the growth of exports working through the Harrod foreign trade multiplier. In the formalisation by Dixon and Thirlwall (1975), the growth of manufacturing productivity is determined by the growth of manufacturing output, via the Verdoorn Law. The growth of the demand for output is a function of the growth of relative prices and the income elasticity of demand for exports. (The latter represents factors affecting non-price competitiveness, including differences in the structure of production, which are likely to be especially important in the regional case.) Prices are determined by a constant mark-up on unit labour costs. The supply side is not explicitly modelled since it is assumed that there is either unemployed labour in the region and/or sufficient migration which will provide an elastic supply of labour. It is, nevertheless, a simple matter to incorporate a labour constraint by making the growth of regional wages a function of the elasticity of the labour supply. As the labour supply becomes less elastic in a fast-growing region, this will have the effect of offsetting the increasing improvement in relative prices through the Verdoorn effect. Consequently, the growth of demand will falter, restricting output growth and putting a brake on the cumulative causation process. The rate of growth of the capital stock is as much a consequence of output growth as a cause of it, as a faster growth of output *pari passu* creates the resources necessary for capital accumulation. Consequently, a faster growth of output, by increasing the rate of growth of productivity, will improve the degree of price competitiveness, provided that all the gains are not absorbed in higher real wages. In the Dixon and Thirlwall model, the small-region assumption is made in that the faster growth of the region under consideration will not affect the growth of the rest of the world. Whether or not the region's growth rate converges to an equilibrium value or is explosive depends upon the size of the price elasticities, the Verdoorn coefficient, and the income elasticity of demand for the region's exports. Dixon and Thirlwall (1975) consider these to be of a magnitude such that it is likely that growth will eventually be at an equilibrium rate. However, if this is faster than that of the rest of the world, there will be widening productivity differentials. This is also true if the growth rates are the same, but the initial levels of productivity differ. Even if the small region assumption is relaxed, Dixon and Thirlwall (1978) consider that in a two-region model, the growth of the two regions will converge to equilibrium rates.

The new growth theory derives similar results to that of the Kaldorian model, although the underlying assumptions differ. (A region can sell all that it produces and there is no explicit role in the model for the growth of demand.) Bertola's (1993) model gives a good example of the implications of this approach for European integration. The first case he examines is where there are two regions, each with a Cobb–Douglas production function, $Q_i = A_i K_i^{\alpha} L_i^{\beta} (i = 1,2)$, where Q, K, L, and A denote output, capital, labour and the level of technical efficiency. To endogenise growth, the level of technical efficiency is assumed to be a function of the region's capital stock, namely, $A_i = \eta K_i^{\mu}$, and $\alpha + \mu = 1$. If region 1 has a higher rate of return than region 2 and capital is mobile, then region 2's capital will move there. This would benefit the owners of capital, but not labour in region 2, which would consequently become unemployed. If both factors are mobile, they would both move to region 1, leaving region 2 deserted. This would be optimal, in the narrow sense of maximising the level and rate of growth, although the owners of any fixed factor in region 2, say land, would be made worse off.

The second case that Bertola examines is where an externality is introduced into the production function whereby output in region 1 is also a function of region 2's capital stock, through the latter's effect on region 1's and vice versa. He examines a number of different situations. Where there is endogenous growth and interregional labour mobility, under certain circumstances it can be shown that the migration of workers in response to wage differentials can lead to the situation where there is no production in either region! This is simply a curiosum, a result of the unrealistic assumption that no production can take place in one region in the absence of production in the second region. Labour myopically responding to the wage differential period-by-period will eventually all move from, say, region 2 to region 1. As a result the capital stock in region 2 tends to zero, and so also will production in region 1, because of its multiplicative dependence on K_2. The use of different specifications do not lead to such a dramatic and implausible outcome, but the outcome of labour mobility is still suboptimal. The conclusions of the model are that integration is likely to lead to the spatial concentration of production and in the presence of spatial externalities this could be suboptimal, unless there is a taxation regime to internalise the externalities. However, there is, as Wyplosz (1993) points out, a problem with these types of endogenous growth models in that growth is a function of the size of the population, which is clearly contradicted by empirical evidence.

Other neoclassical models also come up with similar dramatic results. Fani (1984) postulates a two-region economy with increasing returns to scale in the non-tradable sector and demonstrates how there will be a permanent growth rate difference between the two regions, leading to increasing regional disparities, given even the smallest initial difference in the regional capital stocks.

These models are unrealistic in that it is unlikely that productivity growth rates will diverge permanently, or that production will become concentrated solely in one region. What it does suggest, however, is that there are powerful forces making for growth disparities which may eventually be offset by other forces (such as shortages in land or increasing congestion costs).

The models discussed above have been at a high level of aggregation using the aggregate production function or, in the case of the Verdoorn law, a variant of the technical progress function. Nevertheless, similar insights have been produced by the 'new economic geography' derived primarily from the influential work of Krugman (1991), to which we now briefly turn.[14] Krugman's work considers the conditions under which regional concentration of production occurs. In a simple two-region model Krugman shows that the spatial concentration is likely to be greater, the greater is the degree of returns to scale, the lower the transport costs and the larger the more footloose manufacturing sector (since some industries such as agriculture and services are likely to be location specific). Firms have a choice whether to locate plants in both regions where they incur two sets of fixed costs (which is the cause of the increasing returns to scale in this explanation) and minimise transport costs or to locate solely in one region. Here they reap greater benefits of increasing returns but have greater expenditure on transport costs. Also, it is assumed that part of the firm's output is used as an intermediate input in other firms' production processes. This gives an added reason for firms to locate where there are other firms. A firm will locate where the demand is and this will depend upon where other firms have located. There is thus a process of cumulative causation at work which will lead to the persistence of location patterns long after the initial reasons for their establishment, which may be due to no more than chance factors, have disappeared. Krugman points to the rise and persistence of the US manufacturing belt as a case in point. This process has much in common with Arthur's (1989) notion of path dependency and lock-in. Suppose that initially firms locate randomly, but the probability of a firm locating in a region is a function of the share of firms that have located there already (in other words we are dealing with non-linear probabilities). Eventually a particular region will come to be the major centre of concentration, and other firms who have located elsewhere will go out of business as they cannot fully benefit from the external economies of scale. Where the agglomeration occurs may be just due to a historical accident.[15] (For a survey of the new economic geography, see Ottaviano and Puga, 1997.)

Europe and the US make a useful comparison. The US contains four major regions (the Northeast, the Midwest, the South and the West) which are comparable in size to the largest four European countries (Germany, France, the UK and Italy). Given the long period of the integration of the US space economy, the cost of transporting goods (including impediments that need to be overcome such as information costs, tariffs, exchange rate fluctuations) is much lower than in Europe, and so we should expect a much greater specialisation of industry in the US. This is precisely what Krugman (1991) finds. The implication is that with economic integration, there may be greater concentration of industry in Europe with the core areas gaining at the expense of the periphery – a further example of cumulative causation.

IS EUROPE AN OPTIMUM CURRENCY AREA?

The creation of a common currency has far-reaching implications beyond those inherent in the accomplishment of economic integration. A huge volume of literature has developed on the subject, most of it taking as its starting point Mundell's (1961) theory of the optimum currency area. Generally, the emphasis on this approach has been on the extent to which regions, or nations, within a common currency area can weather short-run shocks. However, it is also necessary to extend this analysis to consider the effect of a common currency on long-run growth. Given that individual countries will no longer have the macroeconomic instruments of exchange rate variation and independent monetary and fiscal policies, the key question is whether the introduction of a single currency will lead to other effective adjustment mechanisms. A common way of assessing this has been to compare the experience of the US regions with that of the European countries.

If shocks to the EU countries were significantly more asymmetric than shocks to the US regions, this could pose serious problems if (or rather when) a single currency is adopted. This would not necessarily be conclusive evidence because the introduction of a single currency may well alter the adjustment mechanisms in Europe (by, for example, increasing the degree of labour mobility)[16] but such comparisons can be nevertheless instructive.

For Europe to satisfy the conditions for an optimum currency area, one or more of the following conditions must be satisfied. First, shocks to the European economy should be symmetric, in that they affect all countries and regions simultaneously and to the same extent. If this were the case, then macroeconomic policy measures taken by a central European bank could be sufficient. It may be, however, that if the central bank is more concerned with, say, the control of inflation than unemployment, the contracyclical action it takes may not be optimal for all countries. For example, a country with a more Keynesian-minded government and an independent macroeconomic policy may have introduced more radical reflationary policies than would occur under a single currency. Nevertheless, let us pass by this question.

Secondly, and this is important if shocks are asymmetric, the optimum currency literature suggests that there should be a sufficiently high degree of labour and/or capital mobility between the regions. An alternative if this is not the case is that there should be a sufficiently high degree of real wage flexibility. We shall have reason to question these conclusions below, but first it is necessary to examine the question as to whether or not the European regions are subject to asymmetric or symmetric shocks.

If shocks are more symmetric in the US than in Europe, it has been argued that this would result in less relative price variability between the US regions than between the European countries. It has been argued that the increasing economic integration of Europe will make the regions of Europe more homogeneous and so any shocks will become progressively more symmetric. However, we have seen above that the new economic geography suggests that the opposite is more likely to be true. Greater integration will lead to more specialisation and a greater dependence on trade and exports for a region's vitality, and this is likely to lead to greater asymmetric shocks. (At the national level, the composition of exports does not vary greatly between the advanced countries, but this is not the case at the regional level.) This instability will reflect the greater exposure of the regions to the impact of changes in technology and tastes. Thus, the effectiveness of other adjustment mechanisms becomes of greater importance.

Krugman (1993) points to the emergence of serious problems in the US regions, which are not readily solvable within the common currency area of the US. One example he gives is that of New England (and in particular the state of Massachusetts). In the early 1980s, Massachusetts underwent an economic revival based on the production of mini-computers, advanced medicine and precision military hardware. But in the late 1980s the bottom fell out of those markets and within four years the unemployment rate increased fourfold. If it were a country, Massachusetts would have devalued or employed Keynesian demand management expansionary policies. In fact, in so far as the latter was concerned, a fiscal crisis actually forced the state to adopt a deflationary policy.

The rise in unemployment led to emigration, and Krugman considers that there is little likelihood that New England will turn itself around.

There have been a number of studies that have examined the question of the degree of asymmetric shocks. Since changes in relative regional product prices reflect changes in supply and demand conditions, they can be used as a measure of the degree to which shocks are asymmetric. The argument is that the greater the asymmetric shocks, the greater the degree of variation in spatial relative prices. Eichengreen (1990a) cites Poloz (1990) who found somewhat surprisingly that real exchange rate changes between Canadian provinces were more variable than between France, Italy, the UK and Germany. However, Eichengreen discounts that evidence because of the much greater degree of specialisation of the Canadian provinces compared with the European countries, which would lead one to expect the observed greater price variability. Instead, Eichengreen prefers to use a comparison of variability of the consumer price index of the US states with the real exchange rates of 12 European countries. He finds that the real exchange rates have typically varied more than those of the US states have by a factor of 3 or 4. de Grauwe and Vanhaverbeke (1993) also compared the variability of the real exchange rate of 50 European regions with that of five European countries (Germany, France, Spain, the UK and the Netherlands) over the period 1977–85. Using unit labour costs to measure prices, they found that regional price variations were less than were those at the national level.

What do these studies tell us? Because the variation in relative prices is less at the regional level than at the country level, the individual countries may be nearer to an optimal currency area than Europe as a whole. This is because the shocks are less asymmetric at the regional level.

However, there is a caveat to this argument. Large asymmetric shocks may bring little change in relative prices at the US regional level because of national wage-bargaining and price-setting policies, whereas relatively small asymmetric shocks may induce large fluctuations in the real exchange rate at the European national level. Thus the degree of variability of regional prices *vis-à-vis* exchange rate fluctuations may not be a good indicator of whether the US regions or the EU nations are subject to a greater degree of asymmetry in their shocks.

A second measure Eichengreen (1990a) used was the degree of correlation between the movement of share prices on Canadian regional stock exchanges compared with those of Paris and Dusseldorf.[17] The rationale is that share prices will reflect the degree of profitability of the companies. Given that profitability declines in a downturn of the economy, we would expect shares to likewise fall. Thus, if the dispersion of regional shocks was smaller in Canada than Europe, we should expect the changes in share prices to be more highly correlated in Toronto and Montreal than in Paris and Dusseldorf. This Eichengreen finds to be the case. Even in the 1980s, when there was the greatest correlation of share prices on the various European exchanges, share prices were still five times as variable as on the Canadian exchanges.

Bayoumi and Eichengreen (1993) try to disentangle the effects of supply and demand shocks using a simple neoclassical synthesis AD/AS model. In this approach, unlike the post-Keynesian one, an increase in demand has merely a temporary effect on output and leads to only an increase in the price level in the long run. (This is because of the neoclassical assumption that the long-run aggregate supply curve is independent of demand conditions.) An outward shift in the aggregate supply curve, however, will lead to a permanent increase in output and a fall in the price level. This enables the authors to try to separate the two effects. They find that supply shocks have been larger in magnitude and less correlated across the regions in Europe than in the US and that the adjustment to shocks is faster in the US. This provides further evidence that Europe would have greater difficulty in operating as a common currency area, compared with the US. Bayoumi and Eichengreen (1993) also find that there is a core of European countries (Germany and its immediate neighbours) which experience smaller and more highly correlated shocks than those outside this core. This leads them to suggest that a two-speed, rather than a one-speed, approach to the EMU is more appropriate, since the latter could well lead to an increase in the core/periphery disparities in Europe.

LABOUR MOBILITY BETWEEN THE EUROPEAN REGIONS

Since the evidence suggests that the shocks to the European countries are largely asymmetric, the next important adjustment mechanism we need to consider is whether the degree of labour mobility is able to compensate for this. What evidence there is suggests that mobility in the US is much greater than intra and international mobility within Europe. (For a survey of the various issues, see Begg, 1996.) This is not surprising given the greater cultural, political, and linguistic differences between the European countries compared with the US regions. Also, the fact that there has been historically much greater migration to the US means that society there is potentially more spatially mobile than in Europe. Nevertheless, the EMU will see the reduction in the administrative barriers to migration, as professional qualifications issued by a member state will be recognised by the other EU countries. (The right to employment of an individual of one EU state in the other countries is already established.)

It is possible, of course, that the relative lack of migration in Europe is due to the fact that adjustment occurs through other mechanisms. However, there is strong evidence that this is not the case. Boltho (1989) found that the variation in spatial per capita income levels was greater in Europe than in the US. Moreover, the persistence of unemployment over time is very much greater for

Europe, especially for the UK and Italy which have the highest correlation between regional unemployment rates for 1975 and 1987. There is no significant correlation for the US (OECD, 1989) (see also Evans and McCormick, 1994). The evidence suggests that this lack of persistence in regional unemployment rates in the US is due to the fact that labour migration reacts to reduce regional unemployment rates rather rapidly. However, this does not mean that European regional labour markets are moribund. Jackman (1998) points out that the UK regions have experienced noticeable differences in employment growth rates (from 1974 to 1997, employment grew in the South East and East Anglia by 25%, whereas at the other extreme employment fell by 15% in the North and Northeast). However, regional unemployment disparities, while large, have not worsened over this period. This suggests that the regional labour supply and employment have grown at roughly the same rate. There has been significant structural change in the UK over this period with the decline of heavy industry and engineering in the North and the West Midlands and the growth of, especially, services in the South East. As Jackman (1998) observes, 'the remarkable thing is that, as jobs have been going South, workers have been following them'. Nevertheless these flows are proportionally smaller than those compared with the US. This also seems to be true in the rest of Europe. In the short run, a fall in demand is met by rising unemployment and a fall in participation rates, but in the longer term, emigration is an important safety valve.

Eichengreen (1990b) confirms this picture by comparing various indicators of the dispersion of regional unemployment in the EU and US from 1960 to 1988. He finds that the dispersion is significantly greater in the US than in Europe and considers that this is primarily due to the faster labour market adjustment. Using an error correction model he finds that the speed of adjustment of unemployment to the long-run regional rate, which differs between regions, is about 25% faster in the US than Europe. Moreover regional unemployment differentials are smaller in the US than Europe. To account for this in terms of differences in the size of the shocks 'one would have to argue that the shocks in Europe were not only larger but more persistent, which does not seem particularly plausible' (Eichengreen, 1990b). He concludes that 'even if the EC manages to replicate the degree of integration enjoyed in the US, significant regional imbalances will continue to arise' (Eichengreen, 1990b). This is because of the lack of fiscal federalism in the EU on a scale comparable to that found in the US and the negligible migration between the EU member states. (See also Eichengreen, 1993.)

REGIONAL WAGE FLEXIBILITY

The standard neoclassical argument is that the persistence of regional unemployment rates in the European regions is attributable to real wage rigidity, which is seen as the result of market imperfections. The fact that in Europe regional unemployment rates within countries are much greater than between countries is put down to national pay bargaining effectively reducing the regional dispersion in real wages. For example, in the UK, the 1988 White Paper on Employment explicitly cited the failure of real wages to fall in those areas where unemployment was high as a cause of the persistence of these high rates. The existence of multi-employer industry-wide pay bargaining, it was held, established wage differentials that were insufficient to encourage especially skilled labour to move into areas where there was low unemployment. This led to legislation in the UK throughout the 1980s to deregulate the British labour market. Public sector employers were also put under pressure to move away from national to regional pay bargaining.

Walsh and Brown (1991), however, show that multi-employer agreements in the UK, which originated in the late 19th century, had steadily declined from the 1950s onwards, although there had been an acceleration of this rate in the 1980s. They found a paradox. During the 1970s and 1980s there had been a reduction in interregional pay differentials (if the South East is excluded) at a time when there has been a strong trend towards decentralisation in pay bargaining arrangements. The reason is that small firms benefit from economies of scale by having a joint bargaining structure with other firms and so have maintained links with other firms in this respect. The position with the larger firms is more complicated with major changes to their organisational structures taking place over the last couple of decades. While there has been a move to link pay to performance in profit centres, there has been a reluctance to respond to local labour market conditions by introducing parallel pay structures. Thus, while there has been an *ad hoc* response to labour shortages in the South East of Britain by increasing wages, it has not led to explicit regional pay bargaining. Indeed, Walsh and Brown invoke the efficiency wage argument as to why this is a rational response on the part of firms.

It is generally assumed that European labour markets exhibit less wage flexibility than do those in the US (Eichengreen, 1993). Nevertheless, even though US labour markets are flexible, several studies have concluded that money wages are relatively inflexible (Layard *et al.*, 1991; Bean, 1994). The evidence also suggests that periods of high wage flexibility in Europe coincide with periods of rapid and unsustainable inflation – a condition which the EMU is designed to eliminate (Jackman, 1998). With a common currency and greater transparency concerning wage rates across countries, there is also the possibility that relative real wages may become progressively more difficult to alter at the national as well as the regional level.

However, we need to next examine the question as to whether, even if we do have high wage flexibility and labour (and capital) mobility, this will necessarily automatically reduce regional disparities within a common currency.

WOULD LABOUR AND CAPITAL MOBILITY AND FLEXIBLE REGIONAL WAGES NECESSARILY BE SPATIALLY EQUILIBRATING?

Underlying the above empirical studies has been the assumption that increased factor mobility could be a substitute for exchange rate flexibility. We have seen that there is empirical evidence that when demand falls in a particular region, the response of labour is to migrate, especially in the US and to a lesser extent in Europe (Eichengreen, 1990b). The conclusion is that the evidence suggests that in Europe, migration is not responsive enough to counter asymmetric shocks in the short run (Begg, 1996). In a longer-term context, it is possible that the migration of factors of production could exacerbate conditions in an already depressed region. There is a great deal of evidence that migration is age and skill selective. It is the younger more skilled workers that leave. Thus, a migrant actually transfers embodied human capital with him or her. In the long run, the decline in the skills base may well decrease the attractiveness of the region to new employers. Although not directly related to migration, some indirect evidence is provided by Bradley and Taylor (1996) who studied the relationship in the UK between local education performance and regional competitiveness. They concluded, 'the available evidence suggests a cumulative process which results in economic divergence. The cumulative causation process identified ... indicates that localities with a poor economic performance also tend to be saddled with a poor educational performance.'

Thus while emigration from the depressed regions may have long-run detrimental effects, it is by no means clear that immigration into the prosperous regions is without its problems. With many of the prosperous regions experiencing overcrowding and congestion, the increase of migration into these areas may lead to significant negative externalities.

Moreover, we have already seen that in the presence of increasing returns to scale, both labour and capital migration could lead to increased concentration of production and a greater polarisation effect. Although, as noted above, these may, it is true, be offset to some extent by rising congestion and land prices, leading to spread effects.

A further problem is that even with a common currency with perfect capital mobility, balance-of-payments problems do not disappear. McCombie and Thirlwall (1994) have examined this in a two-region model. There is not space to go into this model in detail. However, some of the implications may be examined. Let us assume that there is negative shock in demand for the periphery's exports. The rate of growth of output falls and this will set up negative multiplier effects, leading to (or increasing) unemployment in, particularly, the non-traded sector. Part of the fall in demand will be compensated for by automatic fiscal transfers from the central government. (Estimates suggest that in the US with its large degree of fiscal federalism, this may be as much as 33 cents for every dollar decline in income.) The periphery may attempt to maintain its level of expenditure by borrowing from the rest of the economy to cover its balance-of-trade deficit. However, to maintain the previous rate of growth would require an ever-increasing flow of capital. Eventually, the necessary regional collateral will become exhausted and the progressive decline in the region's assets will have a depressing effect on its growth of spending. Eventually, income will have to adjust and the growth of the periphery will decline until the basic balance (i.e. the current account plus long-term capital flows, including government fiscal transfers) is brought back into equilibrium (McCombie, 1988b).

Capital mobility may bring further long-term problems. Suppose there is a decline in regional profitability for some reason. With perfect capital mobility, this may lead to a substantial reduction in the region's investment and an outflow of capital. The neoclassical model, with its assumption of malleable capital, assumes that the consequent fall in the capital–labour ratio will lead to an improvement in the rate of return. But to the extent to which new technology is embodied in investment, this may not occur leading to a further deterioration in the periphery's position as its proportion of outmoded capital stock increases. Consequently, less than perfect capital mobility may mean that investment still persists in a poorly performing country (region) giving it a breathing space to recover, which would not otherwise exist with perfect capital mobility. With increasing returns to scale, we have seen that capital mobility may lead to greater regional disparities.

Krugman (1993) advances a somewhat different explanation where a depressed region simply sheds both people and capital. 'The implication is that relative output and employment of regions should look more like a random walk than a process that returns to some norm' (Krugman, 1993). This, he argues, is different from the deterministic cumulative causation mechanism. It is just that the adverse random shocks to the region cumulate over time, which suffers a decline in output and employment and lack of investment in new industries.

If there is lack of labour mobility, then a fall in demand is likely to lead to an increase in unemployment. Would wage flexibility solve the problem? The neoclassical assumptions underlying the demand for labour assume that, given a well-behaved production function, the volume of employment will be determined at the level where the marginal revenue product of labour equals the wage. As the latter falls, by the necessity of these assumptions, output and employment must increase. In the Keynesian case, the outcome is ambiguous. A fall in real wages will simultaneously represent a further decline in demand for output, through the dual decision hypothesis. The net effect on employment depends upon whether the increased demand from the rest of the world, resulting from the corresponding fall in prices of the region's exports, outweighs the fall in regional demand resulting from the wage cuts (McCombie, 1998b). If it does not, cutting the regional wage may actually exacerbate the situation. Wage flexibility may be a necessary condition for increasing employment, but it certainly is not sufficient.

CONVERGENCE OR DIVERGENCE IN REGIONAL PRODUCTIVITY GROWTH? AN ASSESSMENT OF THE EMPIRICAL EVIDENCE

It is somewhat ironical that at a time when major advances were being made in endogenous growth theory, empirical testing seemed to provide strong support for the orthodox Solow one-sector neoclassical growth model, albeit sometimes augmented by proxies for human capital (Barro, 1991; Mankiw *et al.*, 1992). The standard Solow approach assumes a well-behaved aggregate production function, perfectly competitive markets and an exogenous rate of technical change that is assumed to be spatially invariant. As is well known, in the steady state the growth of productivity is equal to the rate of technical progress and so productivity growth should be identical in all regions. However, this merely applies to the steady state. Suppose for some reason that a region is below its equilibrium capital–labour ratio (why this should be the case is never made clear). Then it can be shown that its growth of this ratio will be faster than the steady state rate and, consequently, productivity growth will be commensurably faster. In a seminal paper Barro and Sala-i-Martin (1991) showed that by linearising the transitional dynamics, the speed of convergence could be obtained from the regression of productivity growth on the initial level of productivity.[18] This method has been widely applied using cross-regional, as well as international data, and provides a measure of what has become known as unconditional β convergence. While a higher share of investment in GDP will not affect the steady state rate of growth, it will affect the equilibrium level of productivity at any point in time. Thus, conditional β convergence occurs when the investment–output ratio and other variables that may affect the steady state level of productivity are explicitly included in the regression equation.

A complementary measure of the reduction in disparities is σ convergence, which is said to exist if the standard deviation of the logarithm of per capita income levels declines over time. β convergence is a necessary but not sufficient condition for σ convergence to occur. This is because shocks may well lead to a (temporary) increase in the standard deviation, even though there is overall convergence to the equilibrium growth rate. There has now been considerable work on estimating the rate of convergence using regional data (see, for example, Barro and Sala-i-Martin, 1991, 1995; Dewhurst and Mutis-Gaitan, 1995; Armstrong, 1995; and Mas *et al.*, 1995).

What is interesting is that most of these studies find a rate of convergence of around 2% per annum across many of the different regional data sets, which is slower than the neoclassical model would predict. Moreover, it must be remembered that while the coefficient is often significant, the *t*-value is usually quite low and the fit of the regression is often poor. Also, Galli (1997) finds very little evidence for persistent convergence in 11 European countries at the industry level. He arrives at the 'general conclusion that convergence is not an inevitable process, but rather a cyclical phenomenon alternating with divergence'.

An attempt to assess the impact of the SEM within this framework is the European Commission (1996) report using a study by Cambridge Econometrics for the period 1975–87 and 1987–93. The study compared the growth of the European countries in the periods before and after 1987 (i.e. when the SEM first effectively came into operation) and with the US and Japan. The study also used the Barro and Sala-i-Martin type regressions for the EU nations and the EU regions. It is difficult to draw any firm conclusions because of the shortness of the time period and the fragility of the estimated coefficients (i.e. the estimates of a particular coefficient are sensitive to inclusion or exclusion of other variables). This is not unusual in these types of regressions (Levine and Renelt, 1992). The results suggest that convergence in Europe was weaker or non-existent in the late 1980s, compared with some tendency to convergence earlier, but it is difficult to be categorical.

The question arises as to the extent to which these types of regressions constitute a test of the Solovian neoclassical growth model. There are a number of problems, not least because the relationship is compatible with a number of other hypotheses or underlying assumptions. I set out a few of the more important reservations or qualifications below.

Does the aggregate production function exist? There are considerable doubts as to whether this is the case. The Cambridge Capital Theory Controversies showed that there is not necessarily a unique inverse relationship between the rate of profit and the capital–labour ratio, which is a necessary assumption for the predictions of the neoclassical growth model (Harcourt, 1972). There are also insurmountable aggregation problems which also cast doubt on the very existence of a well-behaved aggregate production function (Fisher, 1992). One cannot point to the good fits that are often obtained to the estimation of production functions in support of the argument that they are reasonable approximations (after all, no model can capture the totality of the reality) because of the underlying accounting identity (McCombie, 1998a, b).

The importance of sectoral growth. The rapid growth of some of the countries of continental Europe was due to the large intersectoral transfer of labour from low productivity agricultural to the high productivity manufacturing sector and more recently from manufacturing to the service sector (see Cornwall, 1977, for a convincing critique of the neoclassical model along these lines). The sectoral composition of growth is important for the understanding of growth and is at variance with the equilibrium assumptions underlying the single sector neoclassical model (Cornwall and Cornwall, 1994). In particular, the Keynesian regional growth model stresses the importance of the growth of demand for a region's output, and hence the key role of the structure of output. As we have seen, these factors are captured by differences of the income elasticity of demand for the region's exports.

The closed economy assumption. Although the regression analysis is applied to pooled regional data, the underlying theory is usually based on a closed economy. For example, one of the standard predictions of the model is that the lagging region with the lower capital–labour ratio will have a higher rate of return. In these circumstances, with perfect capital mobility there should be instantaneous convergence. (Why should there be *any* investment in the region with the lower rate of return? A related question, which we have noted above, that is not satisfactorily answered by the neoclassical model is why did these differences in the capital–labour ratios occur in the first place?) Of course, it is possible to construct open economy models within this framework and introduce various factors that prevent instantaneous adjustment, but they nevertheless remain unsatisfactory, especially in the period where there has been virtually free capital mobility in Europe. In many of the international Barro-type regression models, the degree of openness of an economy has been included by the use of the share of trade in output, which has not always found to be statistically significant. However, Thirlwall and Sanna (1996) have shown that theoretically it is the growth, and not the share, of exports that should be included and this invariably is highly statistically significant and robust. It is not possible to understand the reasons why growth rates differ without considering the international or interregional economy, trade interlinkages and the balance-of-payments constraint (McCombie and Thirlwall, 1994; Thirlwall, 1980, 1997; and Thirlwall and Sanna, 1996).

The importance of the diffusion of technology. One assumption that may well be inappropriate is that all regions share the same level of technology. Differences in the levels of productivity may wholly or partly reflect differences in the level of technology and the significant coefficient on the initial level of productivity may be capturing the diffusion of technology from the more to the less advanced regions. Fagerberg and Verspagen (1996), in particular, stress this point. They examined the growth of 70 regions for six EU countries over the postwar period. They began with the standard neoclassical convergence model and found that the convergence process seems to have come to an end in the early 1980s. They augment the standard model with variables designed to capture differences in technological capabilities; namely R&D employees and EU supported investment (EUI) projects. Generally, these variables increased the explanatory power of the model and exhibited the expected sign. Surprisingly, the inclusion of investment–output ratio did not prove to be statistically significant. The results provide strong support for the hypothesis that R&D expenditure increases growth. They further split the sample into three: (i) the high unemployment peripheral regions, (ii) the intermediate unemployment regions (including many of the large urban centres) and (iii) the low unemployment regions. The estimates suggest three different growth clubs. The R&D and EUI had little impact where it is most needed, namely, in the high unemployment regions. The real winners were the low unemployment regions. Not only do they have lower unemployment; they also have higher GDP per capita and faster growth than the other regions. Here are found the well known 'growth poles'. What is disconcerting is that the policies seem to have little impact on the poorest regions where the need is greatest.[19]

Regional policy. In a democracy, it would be surprising if the political process allowed the regional growth rates of GDP per capita to diverge to any great extent. Regional policy, the spatial distribution of government procurement expenditures and the provision of social overhead capital may all have a significant effect in reducing regional disparities. Button and Pentecost (1995) examine the extent of convergence in regional unemployment rates in Great Britain and Germany. They found little consistent pattern of convergence and even where there was in Germany, it coincided with a period of active regional policy. In the UK, changes in regional unemployment rates seem to be largely determined by (cyclical) changes in demand and there does not seem to be any long-term convergence to the national rate (see also Baddeley *et al.*, 1998 a,b).

There have been some attempts to test other models of growth that differ from the simple (if not simplistic) neoclassical approach. An important first step in this direction is the study of Cheshire and Carbonaro (1995). They argue that the more appropriate economic spatial unit is the Functional Urban Region (FUR), which is similar to the US Standard Metropolitan Statistical Area (SMSA), but has the advantage that it is based on employment criteria and journey to work patterns. They use the largest 122 FURs in their study. The basic formulation begins with the standard neoclassical convergence model; namely the growth of GDP per capita is expressed as a function of the initial level of per capita GDP.

Also included is the growth of per capita income in the remainder of the nation in which the FUR is located. This acts as a control for national effects (e.g. different education and training policies and national cyclical fluctuations). Other dummies were introduced to control for fixed effects not captured by the national growth rates. The impact of the SEM was captured (admittedly imperfectly) by the change in economic potential. This is a measure of the degree of economic interaction a region or FUR has with the surrounding areas. Thus, unlike the standard neoclassical model, spatial variables were explicitly included in the regression. Other regressors included variables intended to capture other factors affecting the growth of GDP per capita such as R&D expenditures.

What is of particular interest from the results is that the logarithm of the per capita income variable proved to be fragile. When it was the sole regressor, it was negative and statistically significant, suggesting convergence. However, with the progressive introduction of other variables, the coefficient switches sign to suggest divergence, although it is statistically insignificant. In the preferred model it is negative again, but statistically insignificant. From this Cheshire and Carbonaro (1995) conclude that 'the most plausible interpretation is that there are some forces producing convergence and others producing divergence and the actual outcome over time is determined by the net effect of those forces ... It does not seem helpful to measure convergence in the way that has been done to date'. This sums up the state of play in the convergence literature at the moment.

CONCLUSIONS

This chapter has examined the evidence and the theoretical arguments as to whether the emergence of a single economic market and a common currency is likely to improve or worsen existing regional disparities. The neoclassical approach of the 'old' growth theory suggests that the workings of the free market should lead to convergence, although this may be temporarily offset by shocks. However, once we allow for increasing returns for which there is substantial empirical evidence, there are strong forces that will lead to greater disparities, although these may be constrained to some extent by congestion, land and labour shortages in the prosperous regions and by the effect of regional policy. The introduction of a common currency will remove the possibility of the European nations from pursuing independent macroeconomic policies. There is a real danger that in the likely absence of an effective EU regional policy, there will be a growing polarisation in Europe between the prosperous core and the disadvantaged periphery.

NOTES

1. The author is Fellow in Economics, Downing College, Cambridge.
2. Denmark, Sweden and the UK have opted out of the first wave, and Greece does not meet the entry criteria.
3. An example is the French government's decision to count France Telecom's reserves as part of general revenues.
4. For critical views of the Maastricht Treaty and the current proposals for a common currency, see Arestis and Sawyer (1998) and Rothschild (1998).
5. It should be emphasised that while Tony Thirlwall and I (see, for example McCombie and Thirlwall, 1994) have long argued that non-price competition is much more important in trade between the advanced countries than price competition, this does not mean that there is no role for exchange rate adjustments in the short run. We have argued that, by and large, exchange rate changes are ineffective in allowing a country to increase its balance-of-payments equilibrium rate of growth. However, they may be necessary for correcting deficits around the equilibrium growth rate, especially in the face of substantial differences in national inflation rates.
6. While significant interregional transfers which occur within a country that partially offset regional differences in per capita income pass almost without comment, the same cannot be said when such transfers cross national boundaries.
7. Although mention should also be made of Myrdal (1957) and Hirschman (1958).
8. This argument, however, is perhaps not so convincing as might be initially thought. Suppose that there are indivisibilities in production, and because of a fixed factor of production, marginal and average costs fall with the increase in output. When full capacity is reached, it is necessary to employ another fixed factor. With the increase in the volume of output and the progressive employment of more fixed factors, Samuelson's 'asymptotic homogeneity theorem' shows that the conditions of production will approximate to constant returns to scale, despite the indivisibilities. Moreover, do we necessarily expect the productivity of Switzerland to be much smaller than that of the UK because of the smaller size of the former's GDP? This has led to the emphasis on the importance of dynamic increasing returns to scale such as learning by doing, induced innovation, etc.
9. This is because, in the words of Marchetti (1994), value added is 'an economic concept without any physical counterpart' and there are problems in the construction of value added data that can lead to it being spuriously correlated with a number of other variables. On the other hand, gross output is sensitive to changes in the classification of production between industries. If a firm subcontracts work previously done in-house to a firm in another industry grouping, this may lead to a change in productivity in both industries purely because of the change in classification. (This would occur if the productivity of the transferred activity differed from that of either, or both, of the two industries.) Consequently, it is not clear which of the two measures is to be preferred.
10. This is perhaps not all that surprising given that the spatial areas are determined, *faute de mieux*, by administrative or political rather than economic considerations.
11. Note that this result holds in a closed economy even if there are increasing returns to scale, provided that capital is subject to diminishing returns.
12. There is a problem here that is akin to the Harrod knife-edge problem. If the coefficient even slightly exceeds unity, unbounded growth occurs leading to implausible magnitudes in a short time. Solow (1994, p. 50) demonstrates that with an output elasticity of capital of 1.05, under plausible assumptions, 'a country like Germany or France will achieve infinite output in about 200 years, or even a shorter time from "now"'. If the coefficient is slightly less than unity (even though there may be overall returns to scale) we are back in the Solow world, albeit with a long transition period. It is only when the coefficient is exactly unity that we have the result that increasing the investment–output ratio will raise the steady state rate of growth. It would be a remarkable coincidence if the coefficient just happened to take this value, and as Solow points out, there is no convincing explanation that would make this value endogenous and provide a mechanism by which it converges to unity.

13. There has been no noticeable acceleration in Europe's growth rate in the last few years. In fact, the necessity of meeting the Maastricht criteria has actually depressed growth in a number of European countries.
14. While the results will come as no surprise to regional economists, Krugman's work has alerted the rest of the economics profession to the importance of space and the consequences of its neglect in, for example, international trade theory. As Krugman (1991, p.9) notes: 'Pervasive increasing returns and imperfect competition; multiple equilibrium everywhere; an often decisive role for history, accident and perhaps sheer self-fulfilling prophecy: These are the kind of ideas that are now becoming popular'.
15. An example Krugman gives is the development of the carpet industry in Dalton, which originated there from the making of a tufted bedspread by Catherine Evans. Of course, there are many examples where there was a more economic reason for the initial development of an industry, like proximity to coal in the case of the steel industry.
16. As Wyploz (1997) argues rhetorically 'would the United States have passed the currency area tests a century ago? And had it failed, all things considered, was it a mistake for the country to adopt a single currency?'
17. The Canadian stock exchanges were used in preference to US regional stock exchanges because many of the same companies are quoted on the latter exchanges, whereas in the Canadian case there are non-overlapping listings.
18. GDP per capita is often used instead of the more correct measure, namely productivity, because of data limitations.
19. There is one difficulty with the specification of their model. Does the initial level of per capita income reflect differences in technology (and levels of efficiency) or differences in the initial capital–labour ratio? Since Fagerberg and Verspagen do not assume that every region has the same level of technology (unlike the pure neoclassical model), they cannot rule out the former and there is no way to disentangle the effects in their model. This problem is also encountered by Fingleton and McCombie (1998).

REFERENCES

Arestis, P. and Sawyer, M. (1998), 'The Single European Currency: Prospects and an Alternative Proposal', *Zagreb International Review of Economics and Business*, **1**, pp. 27–44.
Armstrong, H.W. (1995), 'An Appraisal of the Evidence from Cross-sectional Analysis of the Regional Growth Process within the European Union', in Armstrong and Vickerman (1995).
Armstrong, H.W. and Vickerman, R. (1995), *Convergence and Divergence Among European Regions*, London: Pion.
Arthur, B. (1989), 'Competing Technologies, Increasing Returns and Lock-in by Historical Events', *Economic Journal*, **99**, pp. 116–31.
Baddeley, M., Martin, R. and Tyler, P. (1998a) 'Transitory Shock or Structural Shift? The Impact of the Early 1980s Recession on British Regional Unemployment', *Applied Economics*, **30**, pp. 19–30.
Baddeley, M., Martin, R.L. and Tyler, P (1998b), 'European Regional Unemployment Disparities: Convergence or Divergence', *European Urban and Regional Studies*, **5**, pp. 195–215.
Baldwin, R. (1989), 'The Growth Effects of 1992', *Economic Policy*, **9**, pp. 248–81.
Barro, R. (1991), 'Economic Growth in a Cross Section of Countries', *Quarterly Journal of Economics*, **CVI**, pp. 407–55.
Barro, R.J. and Sala-i-Martin, X. (1991), 'Convergence', *Journal of Political Economy*, **100**, pp. 223–51.

Barro, R.J. and Sala-i-Martin, X. (1995), *Economic Growth*, New York: McGraw Hill.

Basu, S. (1996), 'Procyclical Productivity: Increasing Returns or Cyclical Utilisation?' *Quarterly Journal of Economics*, **100**, pp. 719–51.

Basu, S. and Fernand, J.G. (1995), 'Are Apparent Spillovers a Figment of Specification Error?', *Journal of Monetary Economics*, **36**, pp. 165–88.

Bayoumi, T. and Eichengreen, B. (1993), 'Shocking Aspects of European Integration', in F. Torres and F. Giavazzi (eds), *Adjustment and Growth in the EMU*, Cambridge: Cambridge University Press.

Bean, C. (1994), 'European Unempolyment: A Survey', *Journal of Economic Literature*, **32**, pp. 573–619.

Begg, I. (1996), 'Factor Mobility and Regional Disparities in the European Union', *Oxford Review of Economic Policy*, **11**, pp. 96–112.

Bernat, G.A. (1996), 'Does Manufacturing Matter? A Spatial Econometric View of Kaldor's Laws', *Journal of Regional Science*, **36**, pp. 463–77.

Bertola , G . (1993), 'Models of Economic Integration and Localised Growth', in F. Torres and F. Giavazzi (eds), *Adjustment and Growth in the EMU*, Cambridge: Cambridge University Press.

Boltho, A. (1989), 'European and United States Regional Differentials: A Note', *Oxford Review of Economic Policy*, **5**, pp. 105–15.

Borts G.H. and Stein, J.L. (1964), *Economic Growth in a Free Market*, New York: Columbia University Press.

Bradley, S. and Taylor, J. (1996), 'Human Capital Formation and Local Economic Performance', *Regional Studies*, **30**, pp. 1–14.

Button, K. and Pentecost, E. (1995), 'Regional Economic Convergence in Great Britain and Germany' in Armstrong and Vickerman (1995).

Caballero, R.J. and Lyons, R.K. (1989), 'The Role of External Economies in US Manufacturing', National Bureau of Economic Research, Working Paper no. 33.

Caballero, R.J. and Lyons, R.K. (1992) 'External Effects in US Procyclical Productivity', *Journal of Monetary Economics*, **29**, pp. 209–26.

Cheshire, P. and Carbonaro, G. (1995), 'Convergence and Divergence in Regional Growth Rates: An Empty Black Box', in Armstrong and Vickerman (1995).

Clapham, J.H. (1922), 'Of Empty Economic Boxes', *Economic Journal*, **32**, pp. 305–14.

Cobb, C.W. and Douglas, P.H. (1928), 'A Theory of Production' *American Economic Review (Supp.)*, **18**, pp. 139–65.

Cornwall, J. (1977), *Modern Capitalism: Its Growth and Transformation*, London: Martin Robertson.

Cornwall, J. and Cornwall, W. (1994), Growth Theory and Economic Structure, *Economica*, **61**, pp. 237–51.

de Grauwe, P. and Vanhaverbeke, W. (1993), 'Is Europe an Optimum Currency Area?: Evidence from Regional Data', in P.R. Masson and M.P. Taylor, *Policy Issues on the Operation of Currency Unions*, Cambridge: Cambridge University Press.

Dewhurst, J.H.L. and Mutis-Gaitan, H. (1995), 'Varying Speeds of Regional GDP per Capita Convergence in the European Union, 1981–91', in Armstrong and Vickerman (1995).

Dignan, A. (1996), 'Regional Disparities and Regional Policy in the European Union', *Oxford Review of Economic Policy*, **11**, pp. 64–95.

Dixon R.J. and Thirlwall, A.P. (1975), 'A Model of Regional Growth Rate Differences on Kaldorian Lines', *Oxford Economic Papers*, **27**, pp. 201–14.

Dixon, R.J. and Thirlwall, A.P. (1978), 'Growth Rate Stability in the Kaldorian Regional Model', *Scottish Journal of Political Economy*, **25**, pp. 97–9.

Dunford, M. (1993), 'Regional Disparities in the EC. Evidence from the REGIO Data Bank', *Regional Studies*, **27**, pp. 727–43.

Eichengreen, B. (1990a), 'Is Europe an Optimum Currency Area?', Centre for Economic Policy Research, Discussion Paper no. 478.

Eichengreen, B. (1990b), 'One Money for Europe? Lessons from the US Currency Union', *Economic Policy*, **10**, pp. 119–86.

Eichengreen, B. (1993), 'Labour Markets and European Monetary Unification', in Masson, P.R. and Taylor, M.P., *Policy Issues on the Operation of Currency Unions*, Cambridge: Cambridge University Press.

Eichengreen, B. (1997), 'Saving Europe's Automatic Stabilisers', *National Institute Economic Review*, **159**, pp. 92–8.

Emerson, M., Aujean, M. and Catinat, M. (1992), *The Economics of 1992*, Oxford: Oxford University Press.

European Commission (1996), 'Economic Evaluation of the Internal Market', *European Economy, no. 4.*

Evans, P. and McCormick, B. (1994), 'The New Pattern of Regional Unemployment: Causes and Policy Significance', *Economic Journal*, **104**, pp. 633–47.

Fani, R. (1984), 'Increasing Returns, Non-traded Inputs and Regional Development', *Economic Journal*, **94**, pp. 308–23.

Fagerberg, J. and Verspagen, B. (1996), 'Heading for Divergence? Regional Growth in Europe Reconsidered', *Journal of Common Market Studies*, **34**, pp. 431–48.

Fingleton, B. and McCombie, J.S.L. (1998), 'Increasing Returns and Economic Growth: Some Evidence for Manufacturing from the European Union Regions', *Oxford Economic Papers*, **50**, pp. 89–105.

Fisher, F.M. (1992), *Aggregate Aggregation Production Functions and Related Topics* (Monz, J. ed.) London: Harvester Wheatsheaf.

Galli, R. (1997), 'Is There Long Run Convergence in Europe?' *International Review of Applied Economics*, **11**, pp. 333–68.

Griliches, Z. and Ringstad, V. (1971), *Economies of Scale and the Form of the Production Function*, Amsterdam: North Holland.

Hall, R.E. (1990), 'Invariance Properties of Solow's Productivity Residual', in P. Diamond (ed.), *Growth/Productivity/Employment*, Cambridge, MA: MIT Press.

Harcourt, G.C. (1972), *Some Cambridge Controversies in the Theory of Capital*, Cambridge: Cambridge University Press.

Harris, R.I.D. and Lau, I. (1998), 'Verdoorn's Law and Increasing Returns to Scale in the UK Regions,1968–91: Some New Estimates Based on the Cointegration Approach', *Oxford Economic Papers*, **50**, pp. 201–19.

Hildebrand, G. and Liu, T.C. (1965), *Manufacturing Production Functions in the United States, 1957*, Ithica, New York: Cornell University Press.

Hirschman, A. (1958), *The Strategy of Economic Development*, New Haven: Yale University Press.

Jackman, R. (1998), 'EU Labour Markets and Monetary Union', *Economic Outlook*, **22**, pp. 12–17.

Kaldor, N. (1966), *The Causes of the Slow Economic Growth of the UK. An Inaugural Lecture*, Cambridge: Cambridge University Press.

Kaldor, N. (1970), 'The Case for Regional Policy', *Scottish Journal of Political Economy*, **17**, pp. 337–48.

Kaldor, N. (1972), 'The Irrelevance of Equilibrium Economics', *Economic Journal*, **82**, pp. 1237–55.

Kaldor, N. (1977), 'Capitalism and Industrial Development: Some Lessons from Britain's Experience', *Cambridge Journal of Economics*, **1**, pp. 193–204.

Kaldor, N. (1981), 'The Role of Increasing Returns, Technical Progress, and Cumulative Causation in International Trade', *Economie Appliquee*, **34**, pp. 593–617.

Krugman, P. (1989), 'Economic Integration in Europe: Some Conceptual Issues', in A. Jacquemin and A. Sapir (eds), *The European Internal Market – Trade and Competition*, Oxford: Oxford University Press.

Krugman, P. (1991), *Geography and Trade*, Leuven: Leuven University Press.

Krugman, P. (1993), 'The Lessons of Massachusetts for EMU', in F. Torres and F. Giavazzi (eds), *Adjustment and Growth in the EMU*, Cambridge: Cambridge University Press.

Layard, R., Nickell, S. and Jackman, R. (1991), *Unemployment, Macroeconomic Performance and the Labour Market*, Oxford: Oxford University Press.

Leon-Ledsma, M.A. (1998), 'Economic Growth and Verdoorn's Law in the Spanish Regions, 1962–1991', paper presented to the 5th *Journal of Post Keynesian Economics* Workshop, Knoxville, Tennessee, US, 21 June – 1 July, 1998.

Levine, R. and Renelt, D. (1992), 'A Sensitivity Analysis of Cross-Country Growth Regressions', *American Economic Review*, **82**, pp. 942–63.

McCombie, J.S.L. (1985), 'Increasing Returns and the Manufacturing Industries. Some Empirical Issues', *The Manchester School*, **53**, pp. 55–75.

McCombie, J.S.L. (1988a), 'A Synoptic View of Regional Growth and Unemployment I – The Neoclassical Theory', *Urban Studies*, **25**, 267–81.

McCombie, J.S.L. (1988b), 'A Synoptic View of Regional Growth and Unemployment II – The Post-Keynesian Theory', *Urban Studies*, **25**, pp. 399–417.

McCombie, J.S.L. (1998a), '"Are There Laws of Production?" An Assessment of the Early Criticisms of the Cobb-Douglas Production Function', *Review of Political Economy*, **10**, 141–73.

McCombie, J.S.L. (1998b), 'Solow's "Technical Change and the Aggregate Production Function" Revisited', University of Cambridge (mimeo.)

McCombie, J.S.L. and de Ridder, J.R. (1984), 'The Verdoorn Law Controversy: Some New Empirical Evidence Using US State Data', *Oxford Economic Papers*, **36**, pp. 268–84.

McCombie, J.S.L. and Thirlwall, A.P. (1994), *Economic Growth and the Balance-of-Payments Constraint*, Basingstoke: Macmillan.

Mankiw, G.N., Romer, D. and Weil, D.N. (1992), 'A Contribution to the Empirics of Economic Growth', *Quarterly Journal of Economics*, **107**, pp. 407–37.

Marchetti, D.J. (1994), 'Procyclical Productivity, Externalities and Labor Hoarding: A Re-examination of Evidence from U.S. Manufacturing', EUI Working Paper ECO no. 94/13, Florence: European University Institute.

Mas, M., Perez, F., Uriel, E. and Maudos, J. (1995), 'Growth and Convergence in the Spanish Provinces', in Armstrong and Vickerman (1995).

Moroney, J.R. and Walker, J.M. (1966), 'A Regional Test of the Heckscher-Ohlin Hypothesis', *Journal of Political Economy*, **74**, pp. 573–86.

Moroney, J.R. (1972), *The Structure of Production in American Manufacturing*, Chapel Hill: North Carolina Press.

Mundell, R.A. (1961), 'A Theory of Optimum Currency Areas,' *American Economic Review*, **50**, pp. 657–65.

Myrdal, G. (1957), *Economic Theory and Underdeveloped Regions*, London: Duckworth.

Neary, J.P. (1978), 'Short-Run Capital Specificity and the Pure Theory of International Trade', *Economic Journal*, **88**, pp. 488–510.

OECD, (1989), *Employment Outlook*, Paris.

Ottaviano, G.I.P. and Puga, D. (1997), 'Agglomeration in the Global Economy: A Survey of the "New Economic Geography"', Centre for Economic Performance, London: LSE.

Poloz, S. (1990), 'Real Exchange Rate Adjustment Between Regions in a Common Currency Area', Bank of Canada (mimeo).

Rothschild, K.W. (1998), 'Some Considerations on the Economics and Politics of the EU and the Maastricht Treaty', in P. Arestis (ed.) *Method, Theory and Policy in Keynes, Essays in Honour of Paul Davidson*, Vol. 3, Aldershot: Edward Elgar.

Solow, R.M. (1956) ,'A Contribution to the Theory of Economic Growth', *Quarterly Journal of Economics*, **70**, pp. 65–94.

Solow, R.M. (1994), 'Perspectives on Growth Theory', *Journal of Economic Perspectives*, **8**, pp. 45–54.

Thirlwall, A.P. (1980), 'Regional Problems are Balance-of-Payments Problems', *Regional Studies*, **14**, pp. 419–25.

Thirlwall, A.P. and Sanna, G.(1996), 'The Macrodeterminants of Growth and "New" Growth Theory: An Evaluation and Further Evidence', in P. Arestis (ed.), *Employment, Economic Growth and the Tyranny of the Market: Essays in Honour of Paul Davidson*, Vol. 2, Aldershot: Edward Elgar.

Thirlwall, A.P. (1997), 'Factor Mobility, Trade and "Regional" Economic Differences: What Should We Tell Our Grandchildren?' University of Kent at Canterbury, (mimeo).

Walsh, J. and Brown, W. (1991), 'Regional Earnings and Pay Flexibility', in A. Bowen and K. Mayhew (eds) *Reducing Regional Inequalities*, London: Kogan Page.

Wyplosz, C. (1993), 'Discussion' [of Bertola], in F. Torres and F. Giavazzi (eds), *Adjustment and Growth in the EMU*, Cambridge: Cambridge University Press.

Wyplosz, C. (1997), 'EMU: Why and How It Might Happen', *Journal of Economic Perspectives*, **11**, pp. 3–22.

3. Prospects for the single European currency and some proposals for a new Maastricht

Philip Arestis and Malcolm Sawyer

1. INTRODUCTION

This chapter pursues a number of themes related to the proposals for an Economic and Monetary Union (EMU) in the European Union (EU). In particular we critically review the Maastricht Treaty arrangements and convergence criteria for the single currency, review the current position and present a proposal for a new Maastricht. We begin with a brief review of the convergence criteria and of some key elements of the institutional arrangements which would underpin the EMU; the exchange rate and the budget deficit criteria and the proposals for an independent central bank are also discussed. We argue that the Maastricht criteria have some but rather limited validity in relation to the formation of the EMU. The criteria relate only to convergence over interest and inflation rates, and much broader convergence is required. The criteria also relate budget deficit to GDP and government debt to GDP ratios, and the attainment of such ratios imposes (and will continue to impose) a substantial deflationary bias onto the European currencies. The following section reports on the present position relating to the convergence criteria (which broadly shows that there must have been a considerable degree of 'fudge' for the criteria to have been met). Section 4 draws up an alternative proposal which seeks to overcome the deflationary biases in the Maastricht proposals, and finally section 5 summarises and concludes.

2. MAASTRICHT AND CONVERGENCE CRITERIA

The convergence criteria under the Maastricht Treaty for a country's membership of the single currency and, by implication, membership of the independent European System of Central Banks (ESCB) are (1) a high degree of price stability, with an inflation rate within 1.5 per cent of the three best-performing member states; (2) 'healthy' government finance, defined as a maximum ratio of 3 per cent government deficit to GDP at market prices, and a maximum ratio of 60 per cent of government debt to GDP at market prices; (3) observance of the normal ERM fluctuation margins for at least two years without any devaluation among the member state currencies; and (4) long-term interest rate levels that do not exceed two percentage points from the nominal long-term government bond rates of the three best-performing member states in terms of price stability.

The proposed ESCB comprises two important institutions: the national central banks and the European Central Bank (ECB) – and its precursor the European Monetary Institute (EMI), which will disappear once the ECB is set up. National central banks will not be abolished; they will become operating arms of the ESCB and have to be independent from the national governments. It is envisaged that such an institution would be accountable to the European Parliament through monitoring of its performance, and in that way some degree of democratic accountability would be retained. The ESCB can decide whatever definition of price stability it might choose; but there is no clear accountability in the sense of imposing any sanctions or introducing any incentives to change personnel, whenever the ESCB failed to meet the objectives it sets for itself. The key points in the ESCB mandate are the following. First, to maintain price stability, using whatever monetary policy will be necessary regardless of the costs involved in unemployment and lost output. Second, to support the general economic policies of the EU, provided that it does not interfere with the objective of price stability. Third, to act in accordance with the free market economy principles. Fourth, to set interest rates, to conduct foreign exchange operations and to manage member states foreign exchange reserves. Fifth, to ensure smooth functioning of the payment system which links banks across the EU.[1]

Thus, the institutional arrangements involve the creation of an 'independent' (of political control) Central Bank at the European level, given the sole policy objective of zero inflation, which is to be achieved via the movement of interest rates, presumably through its influence on the demand and supply of money and hence ultimately the rate of inflation. There is a complete separation between the monetary authorities (in the form of the Central Bank) and the fiscal authorities (in the form of national governments). The monetarist theory which underlies much of the advocacy of the independent central bank (see Arestis and Sawyer, 1997) accepts the classical dichotomy, so that while monetary policy can guide the rate of inflation, the levels of output and employment are set on the supply-side of the economy (at the 'natural rate' or at the NAIRU) leaving no role for fiscal policy. The *Stability and Growth Pact* clearly stipulates that the national budget deficits would be constrained by the threats of fines on any country which exceeds the 3 per cent of GDP norm. A country which fails to keep its budget deficit within the 3 per cent limit will have to pay in the first instance a penalty equivalent to the payment of a non-interest-bearing deposit. If the situation persists the penalty becomes a fine equivalent to between 0.2 and 0.5 per cent of GDP, depending on the size of the 'excess' deficit. We would assume that any fine would be levied in respect of the *ex post* budget deficit since budget deficit forecasts are subject to both error and to manipulation (although this would also apply to deficit outcomes). But if the prospect of fines impact on national government decision making, then a government would aim for deficits substantially below 3 per cent of GDP in each year, regardless of the stage of the business cycle, to avoid unforeseen events pushing the actual deficit over 3 per cent of GDP. Furthermore, the penalty clause would add to the deficit it is meant to cure, and as such it would face enormous national opposition (Goodhart, 1996, p.246).

This constraint on the budget deficit clearly limits the use of national fiscal policy for demand management purposes. If a government is running a budget deficit near to the 3 per cent of GDP margin, then a degree of approval would have to be obtained from the EU for any actions involving expenditure which would take the deficit over 3 per cent. Any budget deficit which does occur would have to be financed by borrowing, and the rationale for the limits on the national budget deficits is the externality effects of one country's budget deficit on the general level of interest rates within the European Union. This non-monetisation of deficits is an (almost) inevitable corollary of the different tiers of government responsible for fiscal matters and for monetary ones. This seems to involve something of a contradiction. Interest rates are to be used by the Central Bank to influence the money supply so that interest rates are seen as a monetary phenomenon. But here interest rates are seen as influenced by loanable funds considerations.

Exchange Rate Considerations

The criterion concerning exchange rates requires that observance of the normal ERM fluctuation margins for at least two years without any devaluation. When the Maastricht Treaty was agreed in December 1991, the normal ERM band was 2.25 per cent either side of a currency's central exchange rate against the DM (although some currencies were observing a 6 per cent margin). The ERM crisis of 1992–93, however, introduced the 15 per cent band for all currencies, with the exception of the DM and the guilder which remained in the 2.25 per cent band. The 'letter' of the Treaty suggests that the 15 per cent band is the relevant one, although it could well be argued that the 'spirit' is the 2.25 per cent band. Whatever it may be, however, it is the case that what is meant by 'normal fluctuation' margins is vague. What is crystal clear, however, is the EMI (1995) statements, that 'Under current circumstances, it is not advisable to give a precise operational content to the Treaty provisions regarding exchange rates which could be mechanically applied also to forthcoming periods' (p. x), and that 'the requirement to be a member of the ERM remains an element of the Treaty' (p. 33). But however the Treaty is interpreted, we would argue that the relevant criteria would be low variability of the exchange rate (relative to other EU currencies) akin to the 2.25 per cent band. We would argue this for two reasons. First, since the single currency is the ultimate fixed exchange rate, preparations in the broadest sense for the single currency are much enhanced by stability of exchange rates in the period leading to the introduction of the single currency. Second, it enables a judgement to be made as to whether the exchange rate is at the 'right' level. Any judgement on the appropriate rate would be clouded by variations in the exchange rate, given the lagged effects of the exchange rate and the general finding that temporary fluctuations in the exchange rate do not feed through fully into prices.

A considerable degree of prior stability of the exchange rate (against relevant currencies) is a basic requirement for entry. The entry into a single currency obviously involves accepting a rate of exchange between each of the member currencies and the ECU, and it is a decision which is almost irreversible. If the exchange rate is in some relevant sense set incorrectly then it would have enormous and long-lasting ramifications for the economy. The British experience over the return to the Gold Standard in 1925 with an overvaluation of around 10 per cent and the entry into the ERM in 1990 at an overvaluation of around 15 per cent show the dangers of an incorrectly set exchange rate. Overvaluation raises the question of what is the correct value of the currency: our benchmark is an exchange rate which is compatible with a sustainable trade position and full employment. The question arises as to whether there is a mutually consistent set of exchange rates which would be compatible with full employment in each of the member countries. For the UK, the prevailing exchange rate is clearly not consistent with full employment given the current levels of demand in other European countries, although it may be if all EU countries achieved full employment. The calculation of the appropriate level of the exchange rate is fraught with difficulties and the advantage of a substantial period of stable exchange rates is that it would help to establish whether the prevailing exchange rate is the right one. We would stress that we are arguing here for both a stable exchange rate prior to any entry into a single currency and one which has been consistent with a healthy foreign trade position and high employment levels.

Budget Deficits

The criteria for a budget deficit of 3 per cent of GDP and a government debt of 60 per cent of GDP are given as 'reference values' and their precise status is a matter of considerable debate, especially since there is no prospect of many countries meeting the debt ratio requirement and there is considerable doubt over whether some of the major countries really meet the deficit criteria. While the other criteria have a clear rationale in terms of a single currency (in the sense that, following the introduction of a single currency, there would be a fixed exchange rate and near equality of inflation rates, interest rates, etc.), that cannot be said for the budget deficit and government debt criteria. Concern over the government budget deficit should arise from the possibility that it will lead to mounting national debt, and that will be the case (for a constant primary deficit, that is excluding interest payments, relative to GDP) when the (post tax) rate of interest exceeds the rate of growth. This condition masks a basic problem namely that if it is not met then the 3 per cent overall deficit (including interest payments) can be maintained only by a growing surplus on the government budget excluding interest payments on the national debt.

The Independent European System of Central Bank

The ESCB will be confronted with a very important issue in the conduct of monetary policy, which is the appropriate choice of monetary policy instruments. Two differing, but not necessarily inconsistent, methods suggest themselves: monetary targeting and inflation targeting. In terms of monetary targeting, it is pointless to demand that the ESCB attempts to control the money stock when that is essentially endogenous and not controllable by the Central Bank (for example, Arestis, 1997, Chapter 3). The experience with monetary targetry as pursued for example by Germany, the USA and the UK is quite revealing in this context. The target was never met in the 1980–84 period in the UK; five cases of completely unsuccessful experience with monetary targetry. In the USA it was met twice out of the eight times a target was set over the period 1979–86. In Germany the outurn was within the target range (the spread of which was generally of the order of four percentage points) in 12 out of the 23 cases it was set, covering the period 1975–97, although in nine cases the upper end of target range was only marginally met. It is ironic that the German monetary authorities still insist that the future European Central Bank should use money supply targetry, a 'suitable anchor' in their view, as the main instrument of monetary policy (reported in the *Financial Times*, 19 December, 1997). Presumably this is at variance with the views of other EU central bankers who have either abandoned monetary targetry (for example the UK) and those who never attempted them (most of the rest of the EU countries). The alternative method is inflation targeting, which operates in UK, Sweden and Finland. This method requires more analysis and explanation in terms of the channels through which monetary policy affects the inflation target, and it also involves a great deal of forecasting in terms of the expected magnitudes of the activity variables. The choice between the two methods is still open, although there is no reason in principle why a monetary target cannot be complemented by an inflation target, the problems referred to above notwithstanding. However, given the enormous uncertainties surrounding the EMU, a more discretionary approach is more likely.

The danger is, of course, that price stability is attempted through the use of unemployment deliberately to achieve lower inflation rates (and that may well be ineffectual and/or costly). Central bankers, with their heavy emphasis on 'sound' money, are prone to pursuing deflationary policies without giving sufficient attention, if any, to full employment and growth targets. The justification for this focus on money and inflation has come from appeal to the classical dichotomy, and the declaration that monetary restraint has no effects on the supply-side potential of the economy. We would see another two serious problems with these proposals. The first arises from the crucial assumption that appointed central bankers are to be trusted more than elected governments. But since central bankers see themselves as the custodians of international capital, the formation of monetary policy will be geared more to the interests of international financial capital rather than to those of the EU (see Coakley and Harris, 1983). Indeed, there is the danger that an independent central bank will act mainly in its own interest. There should thus be democratic control over its activities, which would potentially avoid or contain the problems just alluded to. For example, the European Parliament could be given a significantly enhanced role in this respect. This would be a step perfectly in line with the Maastricht Treaty, which actually imposes limited requirements for accountability.[2] The second, and potentially more serious problem, is that changes in the common monetary policy are likely to have asymmetric effects across the Union in view of differences in the timing and amplitude of cycles, as well as in the institutional and behavioural characteristics of the member countries. So that 'Differences in the responsiveness of other financial markets to changes in money market interest rates and differences in the net financial positions and interest sensitivities of personal, corporate or financial sectors will mean that the burden of adjustment will not be evenly distributed' (Arrowsmith, 1995, p. 84). An additional problem emerges from the transmission mechanism of monetary policy to the rest of the economy which is significantly different across the member states. This would contribute substantially to the asymmetric effects referred to above.

Limited Maastricht Benefits

It is generally recognized that the direct benefits of a single currency are rather limited, and arise from the reduction in transactions costs involved in EU trade. 'The likely amounts are not however very large, and once the one-off costs of converting to the euro are taken into account as well, the net transactions savings do not provide a strong reason for moving to the euro' (Currie, 1997, p. 6). Estimates of the transition costs to the euro are of the order of $30 billion

(*Financial Times*, 24 November 1997). The major effects, for good or ill, of a single currency will arise from the institutional and policy framework within which the euro is embedded. We would see the current proposals for that institutional and policy framework as derived from a 'new monetarist' perspective. This is based on the classical dichotomy with a separation between the real and the monetary sides of the economy with the (equilibrium) level of unemployment (effectively the NAIRU) and output determined on the supply-side of the economy and the level of prices (and hence the rate of inflation) set by the rate of expansion of the money supply. The monetary and financial sector is viewed as essentially stable and, of course, the classical dichotomy serves to, in effect, insulate the real side of the economy from the monetary side. The stock of money cannot be directly controlled, but the Central Bank can use its discount rate (or equivalent) to influence monetary conditions, thereby affecting the rate of inflation. The general level of interest rates is seen, by the financial markets at any rate, to depend on the credibility of the monetary authorities of the country concerned. Those with anti-inflationary credentials are rewarded with lower interest rates. An independent central bank is seen as one device for securing these credentials.

Another important cost consideration is that as the EMU is launched the EU may become more prone to financial upheavals. This would come about in view of the vast movements of financial assets as a result of the liberalisation of financial markets, which will increase dramatically the amount of funds floating within the euro area seeking profitable opportunities – and there may very well be many of them in view of the expected 'tough' stance on interest rates to establish credibility. Institutions are required to safeguard EMU from potential financial and banking crises; they are completely absent at the moment.

3. CURRENT PROSPECTS

In accordance with the Maastricht Treaty, the European Commission and the European Monetary Institute reported on 25 March 1998 to the EU Council of Economic and Finance ministers (ECOFIN Council for short) the possible participants to the EMU and to the single European currency. The ECOFIN Council in its turn made definite recommendations in early May 1998 to a specially composed meeting of the Heads of State or of Government in Brussels. To qualify for EMU membership on 1 January 1999 countries had to meet the Maastricht criteria as explained above. The reports of both the European Commission (1998) and the European Monetary Institute (1998), recommended that the following eleven countries had met the necessary conditions to join the EMU, and adopt the euro, on 1 January 1999: Belgium, Germany, Spain, France, Ireland, Italy, Luxembourg, the Netherlands, Austria, Portugal and Finland.

In addition to the five Maastricht criteria discussed above, there is an additional important condition which also has to be met, that of national central bank independence. This criterion refers to the statutes of National Central Banks regarding their independence and whether price stability is the prime objective of monetary policy. Belgium, Germany, Ireland, Italy, the Netherlands, Portugal and Finland have legislation which meets the criterion of independence and price stability. Spain, France, Luxembourg and Austria have national legislation in place which if enacted at the date of the establishment of the ECB would meet this criterion. Greece is another country with relevant national legislation which is compatible with this criterion. Sweden's planned legislative changes are yet to be adopted, but the current legislation is not compatible with this criterion. The UK and Denmark have negotiated opt-out arrangements.

The two reports, EC (1998) and EMI (1998), confirm that with a few exceptions, which will not jeopardise the overall functioning of the ESCB, the statutes of almost all national central banks are compatible with the Maastricht Treaty.

Strictly speaking, France and Luxembourg are the only countries which pass all the convergence criteria. But nine more countries have been deemed as meeting all the convergence criteria when really they do not. It is apparent from Table 3.1, where the current convergence situation of all EU country members is reported, that seven of them – Belgium, Germany, Spain, Ireland, the Netherlands, Austria and Portugal – fail on the debt/GDP criterion, one on the ERM participation for at least two years (Finland), and one on both of these criteria (Italy). In terms of the countries which will not participate from the birth of the EMU, Greece is the only country that meets none of the convergence criteria. Sweden fails both the debt and the ERM participation criteria, and is excluded from the first round. The UK and Denmark both belong to the category of failing only one criterion, this being the ERM participation and the debt/GDP ratio, respectively. The UK and Denmark, of course, negotiated the right to abstain from any move to the EMU and the single currency. In Table 3.1 it is also shown that the EU Council decisions of 26 September 1994, 10 July 1995, 27 June 1996, and 30 June 1997, according to which ten countries, Belgium, Denmark, Spain, Finland, Italy, Austria, Portugal, Sweden, UK and Greece were declared as 'excessive deficit' countries, the Commission has recommended abrogation for the first nine; Greece remains an 'excessive deficit' country. These nine countries join Denmark, Ireland, Luxembourg, the Netherlands and Finland, which have already met this public finances criterion.

Member countries appear to have made substantial progress in terms of meeting the Maastricht criteria in 1997 (EC, 1998; EMI, 1998). The inflation data indicate that with the exception of Greece, all the other EU member states have inflation rates less than 2 per cent, which is below the reference value of 2.7 per cent. The government budgetary positions show that, with the exception

Table 3.1 Convergence situation of potential EMU members

	Inflation rate (consumer)			Budget deficit as % of GDP			Debt as % of GDP			Long-term interest rate Aug 1997	ERM band
	1996	1997	1998	1996	1997	1998	1996	1997	1998		
Reference value	2.5	2.6	3.1	3.0	3.0	3.0	60.0	60.0	60.0	8.0	
Germany	1.5	1.9	2.3	3.8	3.3	2.9	60.7	62.2	62.7	5.7	±15%++
France	2.0	1.1	1.3	4.1	3.2	3.2	55.4	57.7	59.2	5.6	±15%++
Italy	3.9	1.8	2.1	6.7	3.2	3.0	123.8	122.9	121.2	6.6	±15%+
UK	2.9	2.6	2.7	4.7	2.0	0.6	57.8	54.5	52.4	7.1	free floating[x]
Spain	3.5	2.0	2.2	4.4	3.0	2.6	69.8	69.0	68.2	6.2	±15%++
Netherlands	2.1	2.3	2.3	2.3	2.1	1.8	78.0	73.6	71.2	5.5	±15%++
Belgium	2.1	1.6	1.9	3.2	2.8	2.6	127.4	125.1	122.8	5.7	±15%++
Sweden	0.8	1.0	2.0	2.5	2.1	0.0	77.7	77.1	73.9	6.5	free floating[x]
Austria	1.9	1.5	1.6	3.9	2.5	2.5	70.0	68.0	67.6	5.7	±15%++
Denmark	2.2	2.5	2.6	1.4	-0.5	-0.5	69.9	66.4	63.2	6.2	±15%++
Finland	0.6	1.3	2.3	3.1	1.9	0.4	58.8	59.4	57.9	5.8	±15%+
Portugal	3.1	2.2	2.3	4.0	2.9	2.9	66.0	62.9	61.7	6.3	±15%++
Greece	8.2	5.7	4.7	7.4	4.7	4.1	111.8	108.0	104.2	9.6	free floating[x]
Ireland	1.6	1.7	2.1	0.9	0.8	0.8	72.8	67.5	65.0	6.3	±15%++
Luxembourg	1.8	2.0	2.0	0.1	0.1	0.1	5.9	5.7	5.5	5.9	±15%++
Number of countries meeting criteria											
Yes	10	14	14	5	11	13	4	4	4	14	12
No	5	1	1	10	4	2	11	11	11	1	3
All countries	15	15	15	15	15	15	15	15	15	15	15

Note: + ERM member for less than two years; ++ ERM member for at least two years; [x] not an ERM member.

Source: IMF World Economic Outlook, September 1997.

of Greece, all countries had government deficits of 3 per cent of GDP or less, and three countries achieved a budget surplus. Despite the EC's (1998) and EMI's (1998) critical attitude of the one-off measures taken by a number of countries which contributed to their 1997 figures, the reports conclude that on the whole the deficit reductions are sustainable. The government debt criterion is only met by four countries as stated above. The EC and the EMI report that substantial progress has been recorded during 1997 for those countries with a debt/GDP ratio above the 60 per cent reference value; and since for these countries, this ratio has been diminishing and approaching the reference value of 60 per cent at a satisfactory rate, the expectation is for a continuation of a sustained decline in this ratio in the years to come. Similarly, in the case of ERM participation, the 11 countries which are thought by the Commission and the EMI to have met the criteria, appear to have enjoyed exchange rate stability with their currencies trading very close to the unchanged central rates during 1996 and 1997. The Irish currency, however, deviated from the reference range of 2.25 per cent significantly. The Italian and Finnish currencies have participated in the ERM only since November 1996 and October 1996, respectively, and the Greek currency only entered the ERM on 16 March 1998. The Swedish and UK currencies did not participate in the ERM during the reference period. The interest rate criterion is met by all country members, with the exception of Greece. The average long-term interest rate in the 14 countries converged to levels of between 5.5 and 7 per cent, below the reference rate of 7.8 per cent. The overall conclusion, then, is that with the exception of the inflation rate and the interest rate, the other three criteria have not been passed as comfortably as it might appear from the claims made by the EC (1998) and the EMI (1998).[3]

There is a critical question at this stage as to whether the sustainability of outcomes, which appear to satisfy the convergence criteria, are as robust as the two reports (EC, 1998; EMI, 1998) claim them to be. One aspect of this is that there are business cycles and the extent to which the convergence criteria are met may depend on the state of the business cycles in the member countries. In particular, it would be expected that recessions would make the budget deficit condition more difficult to achieve than boom conditions. The current situation and the decision taken by the Commission and the EMI are presented against the background of an economic situation in Europe which is portrayed as sound. It is thus claimed that the economic fundamentals in Europe are healthy, with low inflation, favourable monetary conditions, high profitability of investment and sustained external demand (EC, 1998; EMI, 1998). Another aspect is that one particular criterion became the most important for the euro decision-makers, this being the deficit to GDP criterion; perhaps because it was thought so paramount by the financial markets. It is of some interest to note the degree to which measures have been taken with the specific aim of ensuring that the deficit criterion has been met. It is widely accepted that a number of 'creative' devices were adopted and implemented by a number of countries with respect to the deficit position. This appears to have been particularly the case in a number of major countries, France, Germany, Italy and Belgium.[4] It is estimated (EMI, 1998) that the impact of these temporary deficit-reducing measures accounted for between 0.1 and 1 per cent of GDP in 1997.

While it is important to acknowledge that some 'success' was achieved in 1997, and further improvements are expected in 1998 (EC, 1998; EMI, 1998), the point ought to be made that such success has been achieved at a high cost in terms of unemployment. As Table 3.2 shows, the picture is really bleak when the unemployment experience is taken on board. Rates of unemployment well above the 10 per cent mark still exist in a number of EU member countries, and with the exception of Luxembourg, all EU unemployment rates are well above 5 per cent. Countries which managed to improve on meeting the convergence criteria over the 1996–8 period have experienced high and rising unemployment rates. We may refer in particular to Austria, Finland, France, Germany, Italy and Spain. In the case of all these countries, improvement in terms of meeting the convergence criteria did take place, but at significantly high costs in terms of their unemployment rates. Furthermore, countries outside the EU do not appear to have been experiencing the same high unemployment rates, as EU members. If we take the average unemployment rates for EU countries and non-EU countries, as reported in Table 3.2, the point is made clearly. But what is more important is that as we move from 1992 to 1997 the difference in the averages of the two sets of countries widens, and after 1995 the gap remains the same. Indeed countries which are comparable to the EU countries, Canada and the USA in particular, have actually been enjoying falling unemployment rates continously since 1992. Norway is another good example of a country which has chosen to remain outside the EU and her unemployment rate has been falling steadily since 1993. We may even refer to the UK case where since 1992, when the UK left the ERM mechanism, unemployment has been falling steadily with the exception of 1993 when it increased slightly.

The lack of trust between Northern and Southern EU states has produced the *Stability and Growth Pact* which imposes increased restrictions on the freedom of EU countries to use fiscal policy. This appears to lead to a fairly conservative monetary policy (Miller, 1997). Even if countries met the criteria and joined the single currency, they would have to abide by the *Stability and Growth Pact*. This system of financial penalties for member countries which breach the budget deficit criterion, implies that deflationary policies and high unemployment rates would not disappear by the mere fact of qualifying to join the EMU. As suggested earlier, the current alleged convergence may very well be unsustainable which implies that further costs in terms of unemployment are likely to ensue in view of the *Stability and Growth Pact*. Furthermore, countries which do not meet the debt/GDP criterion will be under severe pressure to produce fiscal surpluses.

Table 3.2   *Standardized unemployment rates: seasonally adjusted and GDP*
growth rates, 1997**

EU Country	Unemployment rate (%)						Growth rate (%)
	1992	1993	1994	1995	1996	1997*	
Austria	3.6	4.2	3.8	3.9	4.4	6.6	1.7
Belgium	7.3	8.9	10.0	9.9	9.8	9.7	3.0
Denmark	9.2	10.1	8.2	7.2	6.9	6.4	3.1
Finland	13.0	17.7	17.4	16.2	15.3	15.3	6.2
France	10.4	11.7	12.3	11.7	12.4	12.6	2.4
Germany	6.6	7.9	8.4	8.2	8.9	9.5	2.0
Greece (i)	7.9	8.6	8.9	9.7	9.8	10.0	3.1
Ireland	15.4	15.6	14.3	12.3	11.8	10.8	7.3
Italy	9.0	10.3	11.4	11.9	12.0	12.2	1.9
Luxembourg	2.1	2.7	3.2	2.9	3.3	3.7	3.7
Netherlands	5.6	6.6	7.1	6.9	6.3	5.6	2.9 (+)
Portugal	4.2	5.7	7.0	7.3	7.3	6.2	3.3
Spain	18.5	22.8	24.1	22.9	22.1	20.9	3.1
Sweden	5.6	9.5	9.8	9.2	10.0	10.7	1.3
UK	10.1	10.4	9.6	8.8	8.2	7.4	3.9 (+)
Average for EU Countries	8.6	10.2	10.4	9.9	9.9	9.4	3.3
Non-EU Country							
Australia	10.7	11.0	9.8	8.6	8.6	8.7	3.3
Canada	11.3	11.2	10.4	9.5	9.7	9.5	3.7
Japan	2.2	2.5	2.9	3.1	3.4	3.4	–0.3
Norway	5.9	6.1	5.5	5.0	4.9	4.2	4.6
USA	7.5	6.9	6.1	5.6	5.4	5.2	3.9 (+)
Average for Non-EU Countries	7.5	7.5	6.9	6.4	6.4	6.2	3.1

Notes: (i) Labour Market Trends and Ministry of National Economy (Greece); * these are average figures of the first two quarters in 1997; ** the figures refer to the first two quarters of 1997 or to the first three quarters of 1997 (+).

Source: OECD Economic Outlook.

This will be necessary in order to ensure that the debt/GDP ratio is diminishing and approaching the 60 per cent reference value at a satisfactory rate. There are thus potentially very high costs in terms of both attempting to meet the Maastricht criteria and maintaining the imposed discipline once within the EMU. The clear implication is that the introduction and use of euro under these conditions would have severe deflationary effects. At the same time, possible hysteresis effects imply that the deflation for entry into the EMU will have long-lasting effects. It is also pertinent to note that Table 3.2 provides ample evidence of the argument that countries like Germany, Finland, France, Italy and Spain have deflated their economies in their attempts to meet the single currency criteria. Even more seriously, they will have to go on doing so, thus further increasing their unemployment rates. This is not helped by the apparent flexible treatment of the Maastricht Treaty, whereby the criteria have been interpreted generously, and a number of countries have joined despite their failure to meet all the criteria as argued above.[5] This is reinforced by the argument that there is political will and institutional momentum for a January 1999 start.

A potentially more serious situation may develop since the EMU includes countries which meet the Maastricht criteria only marginally and/or only through 'creative' accounting. This may very well mean that fiscal deficits and inflation rates are higher than if the membership of EMU were narrower, and especially so if the *Stability and Growth Pact* is implemented rather weakly. Under these circumstances the ECB is likely to offset this fiscal laxity by being more deflationary in its attempt to achieve price stability. Erratic movements in interest rates may ensue implying a volatile and, quite possibly, an overvalued euro thus deteriorating even more the unemployment situation.[6] Furthermore, the ECB will lack reputation when it starts, and as such it would need to establish an instant reputation as a stable and strong currency in the eyes of the markets, especially financial markets. Also, given that the ECB will lack transparency, it will have to be increasingly more conservative through the use of the rate of interest to establish credibility. These arguments suggest that higher interest rates than otherwise would almost be a certainty, and this would add to an already appalling unemployment record in the EU. There would probably be political pressures in countries with double-digit unemployment rates (see Table 3.2) and this may force them to inflate their economies. But then this would involve severe penalties for the countries concerned in view of the *Stability and Growth Pact*. In any case, financial markets may force further increases in interest rates and the ECB, which would be expected to resist political pressures from national governments, would not be averse to such temptations.

4.   A NEW MAASTRICHT

We start from a rather more Keynesian perspective. The prevalence of unemployment is an unfortunate stylised fact of most peace-time industrialised economies during most of this century. We do not propose a mono-causal explanation of unemployment but rather see an inadequacy of aggregate demand, a financial system which has deflationary tendencies and effects, lack of productive capacity to employ the available labour, balance of trade and inflationary constraints, unemployment as a disciplining device, as among the more significant causes (some of which are more important at a particular time and country than others). Forces of cumulative causation operate in market economies to generate disparities between regions and countries, so that even if full employment can be achieved in the more prosperous regions the less prosperous regions are still left with substantial unemployment. We take the view that the real and the monetary sectors in any economy are closely linked. Proposals for a new Maastricht have to address two issues: first, what convergence criteria should be satisfied before a single currency is established, and second, what institutional arrangements should accompany the single currency. We turn to these issues in turn.

There is some clear sense in the requirements that interest rates and inflation rates should be aligned in those countries joining a single currency, and we would propose to retain those convergence criteria. There is also clear sense in the criteria on stability of exchange rate over a preceding two-year period, and indeed we would interpret that criteria rather more strictly than appear to be the current intentions. But the level of the exchange rate is not independent of the level of economic activity, and hence a criterion for the convergence of the levels of economic activity is also required. It cannot be overemphasised that a currency entering the euro at an overvalued level will cause substantial adverse effects. Think of the deflation that would have to be endured to reduce prices in a country by say 10 per cent in order to offset an overvaluation of that order; or the difficulties which an economy would endure if the exchange rate was 'right' when that economy had say 20 per cent unemployment and others had 10 per cent. The convergence criteria on the level of economic activity comes in three parts. First, there should be the requirement that the average rate of unemployment (over the course of a business cycle) is broadly the same, and that the convergence of unemployment to take place around a low level (say within 2 percentage points).[7] Locking together economies with very different levels of unemployment, especially in the context of very small fiscal transfers, is a recipe for long-term disparities of unemployment. Second, that the business cycles in the countries concerned are broadly in line with each other. Clearly if one country is at the top of the cycle and another at the bottom, the appropriate fiscal and monetary policies are quite different: at a minimum a single currency necessarily imposes a common monetary policy on participating countries (and we would argue for a degree of common fiscal policy, as discussed below). Third, the risk of asymmetric policy responses to deal with unemployment, and the reform of the welfare state, should be contained if at all possible. This risk requires more than ever, close co-operation of the EU member states on economic policy, especially in the area of fiscal policy.

It may be useful to draw on the 'optimum currency area' literature for guidance on the convergence criteria. This literature suggests that there should not be big differences in underlying economic conditions. And yet, in terms of the structural rates of unemployment and the cyclical levels of economic activity within the EU, the differences are significant. The disparities in the structural rates of unemployment are striking. As Table 3.2 shows, Austria, Belgium, Denmark, Germany, Luxembourg, the Netherlands, Portugal and the UK have unemployment rates below 10 per cent, while of the remaining seven, five (France, Greece, Ireland, Italy, Sweden) have rates above 10 per cent, and two (Finland and Spain) have rates above 15 per cent. The cyclical levels of economic activity show a similar story. The continent's bigger economies remain sluggish, while the smaller ones are enjoying more buoyant conditions. In Table 3.2 the average GDP growth rate of the big economies (France, Germany, Italy, Sweden, UK) is shown to be around 2.3 per cent, while that of the smaller countries (Austria, Belgium, Denmark, Finland, Greece, Ireland, Luxembourg, Netherlands, Portugal, Spain) is around 3.8 per cent. Furthermore, it would be desirable for a single currency to be used in an economic area within which there is openness of goods markets and mobility of factors of production (labour, capital) and where members shared similar inflationary tendencies. Mobility of labour within the EU remains low (especially by comparison with the USA) and that is unlikely to change radically. Openness of goods markets may very well prevail but integrated stabilisation and political unification, or indeed similar inflationary tendencies are distant realities. Furthermore, members of the EMU will not constitute an optimal currency area unless the countries outside the Union *de jure*, act as *de facto* members of the Union. Unless, that is, countries outside the Union with trading and financial links with the EMU members, pursue economic policies compatible with those of the Union (Arrowsmith, 1995, p.84).

Within a single country there are substantial, often virtually automatic, transfers of income from the more prosperous to the less prosperous regions. The automatic elements come from the tax and social security system and other elements come through regional policy and allocation of funds to local government. Countries with federal structures have a significant proportion (say around half) of government expenditure at the national level with the national government having an ability to run deficits and operate fiscal policy, as well as to redistribute income between states. This is completely absent from the EU. Transfers from the operation of automatic stabilisers do not occur at the EU level and the discretionary transfers are relatively small. Hence the check on the decline of weak regions which emanates from these transfers is largely absent. Given the lower degree of labour mobility in Europe across national borders rather than within them, the complete loss of the exchange rate adjustment possibility requires an adequate policy of regional transfers through a Community fiscal policy to accompany the proposed common monetary policy. Such a common fiscal policy to be operated alongside and in co-ordination with the proposed common monetary policy is paramount.[8] The absence of such co-ordination, indeed the non-existence of fiscal policy at the EU level, implies that the interest rate variations necessary to achieve price stability, become highly uncertain. This raises concerns about the volatility of the euro in relation to the dollar and the Yen which is expected to be unusually high (Goodhart, 1998).

There are obviously many differences between the member countries of the EU, some of which are particularly significant for the adoption of a single currency. The variations in labour market institutions, notably over wage determination, mean that there are differing inflationary tendencies and different responses to shocks. The banking systems are at different stages of development with different characteristics where the capacity of banks to create credit depends on their stage of evolution. Banking systems in the peripheral countries (Greece, Portugal, Spain, Ireland) differ substantially from those in the core countries (and there are also important differences within the core countries, for example between the UK and Germany). Peripheral countries are characterised by weaker banking sectors, more uncertainty and higher liquidity preferences than in the core countries. These differences have a further and, in a sense, more serious implication. This is that the channels through which ECB monetary policies would affect other variables in the economy differ among the EU member states. This will inevitably have serious impacts on the performance of the EU countries, thus hurting rather harshly the integration process.

It is difficult to formulate criteria on inflationary tendencies, although there may be a temptation to say that if the criterion on convergence of inflation and of unemployment rates were simultaneously satisfied for a number of years, that would be the appropriate criterion for a country wishing to join the EU common currency. Goodhart (1996) has made a similar suggestion and argued that with the benefit of hindsight, it would 'have been desirable to supplement the inflation criterion with an unemployment criterion, for example, that no country could join without simultaneously having had inflation below 3 per cent and unemployment below, say 7.5% over the previous two years' (p. 246). As indicated above, we would argue for a much lower level of unemployment as part of the convergence criteria. Another proponent of these views is none other than the Governor of the Bank of England. In his evidence to the Treasury select committee, George (1998) argued for the exclusion of countries from the EMU with persistently high levels of unemployment. In fact, he had serious doubts whether all the eleven countries proposed to join the EMU should be allowed in, and this would include countries like France, Italy, Spain and Finland, which have unemployment rates above 12 per cent.

This leads us to the institutional and policy arrangements. On the monetary side, the key question is the role of the central bank. We would argue for the objectives of the bank to include the pursuit of full employment and economic growth as well as price stability (recognizing that there may be trade-offs between the objectives, although not necessarily in the manner suggested by the Philips curve). The central bank would also have the objective of the regulation of the financial system, with the further aim to provide an orderly functioning of the credit system. In this context there is also a requirement for more effective accountability, as argued above, which requires mechanisms of democratic influence (if not control) over the central bank from the European Parliament (and we would extend that to national Parliaments). This accountability would not affect the independence of the ESCB. It would reinforce the legitimacy of the institution and avoid at the same time dramatic conflicts between monetary policy and other EU objectives.

5. SUMMARY AND CONCLUSIONS

We have argued in this chapter that the transition to a single European currency entails essentially two serious problems. The first is that a number of countries, which are not strictly able to meet the Maastricht criteria comfortably, have been recommended to join the EMU. As a result, the ECB is expected to be more deflationary than otherwise. The second is that the attempt to meet these criteria has been accompanied by higher unemployment rates throughout the EU. We have also argued that the problem of unemployment will persist for countries even within the EMU and the single currency in view of the requirement not to deviate from the set criteria. In view of these problems we have suggested a more realistic New Maastricht. While this would retain the criteria proposed in the Maastricht Treaty, it would redefine them to include low unemployment rates. This would ensure that convergence will embrace economic activity in addition to the other criteria evident in the Maastricht Treaty.

NOTES

1. On 1 January 1999 the euro is planned to be launched only for inter-bank/business transactions. The ECB will formally take charge of monetary policy from the European Monetary Institute. On 1 January 2002 notes and coins denominated in euro begin to circulate across the EU and national currencies are withdrawn.
2. The Maastricht Treaty accountability requirements are twofold: the first is that quarterly and annual reports on the activities of the ESCB will have to be published; and the second is that members of the ECB's executive board will have to respond to questions posed by committees of the European Parliament.
3. There were also rounding-up rules which helped a number of marginal cases to be deemed to have met the criteria.

4. Germany reclassified hospital debt which took billions of marks of this debt out of the public sector (and, also, revalued her gold reserves); France included a one-off transfer of 'France Telecom' pension fund to public-sector accounts; Italy levied a repayable euro-tax; and Belgium sold some of her gold reserves. All of this 'inventive' accounting enabled countries to achieve the all-important budget deficit criterion, and keep it below the 3 per cent benchmark (see Dafflon and Rossi, 1998 for more details).
5. This is a real possibility in view of the repeated use by the Commission and the ECOFIN Council of the proviso that when judging the Maastricht criteria, the extent to which the debt/GDP ratio was sufficiently diminishing and approaching the reference value at a satisfactory rate, would be seriously accounted for. EMI also argued that countries with high debt/GDP ratios may need to achieve deficits smaller than 3 per cent of GDP, to demonstrate that their debt/GDP ratios are diminishing sufficiently.
6. This possibility of higher and more volatile interest rates following the introduction of the euro would add a certain degree of irony to the view that sterling joining the EMU would lead to lower interest rates in the UK (with the interest rate for euros being more towards the rate on the DM than on sterling), which would stimulate demand (especially in light of the role of variable rate borrowing in the UK). The Treasury takes the view that such demand stimulus would have to be offset by fiscal deflation with tax increases. But this could not be implemented due to the government's fear of being labelled a tax raising one. A further irony is that sterling is currently riding high on the foreign exchange markets as it is seen as a safe haven over the next few years when the euro may be brought into being without sterling being a member.
7. It should also be recognized that measured unemployment may not be a good indicator of the extent of slack in the labour market.
8. A new body, known as EURO-X, will have informal meetings of EMU members and is expected to play a central role in terms of policy issues within the euro area. It could turn out to be the main forum to co-ordinate economic policy for the EMU members.

REFERENCES

Arestis, P. (1997), *Money, Pricing, Distribution and Economic Integration*, London: Macmillan.

Arestis, P. and Sawyer, M. (1997), 'Unemployment and the Independent European System of Central Banks: Prospects and Some Alternative Arrangements', *American Journal of Economics and Sociology*, **56**(3): 353–68.

Arrowsmith, J. (1995), 'Economic And Monetary Union In A Multi-Tier Europe', *National Institute Economic Review*, **152**(2): 76–96.

Coakley, J. and Harris, L. (1983), *The City of Capital*, Oxford: Basil Blackwell.

Currie, D. (1997), *The Pros and Cons of EMU*, July, London: HM Treasury (published originally by the Eonomist Intelligence Unit, January 1997).

Dafflon, B. and Rossi, S. (1998), 'Public Accounting Fudges Towards EMU: A First Empirical Survey and Some Public Choice Considerations', *Public Choice*, **92**.

European Commission (EC) (1998), *EURO 1999, Convergence Report 1998*, The European Commission, Brussels.

European Monetary Institute (EMI) (1995), *Progress Towards Convergence*, Frankfurt: EMI.

European Monetary Institute (EMI) (1998), *The EMI's Convergence Report 1998*, Frankfurt: EMI.

George, E. (1998), 'Minutes of Evidence Taken Before the Select Committee on the European Communities', *House of Lords, Sub-Committee A*, 29 January.

Goodhart, C.A.E. (1996), 'The Transition to EMU', *Scottish Journal of Political Economy*, **43**(3): 241–57.

Goodhart, C.A.E. (1998), 'Minutes of Evidence Taken Before the Select Committee on the European Communities', *House of Lords, Sub-Committee A*, 13 January.

Miller, M. (1997), 'Eurosclerosis, Eurochicken and the Outlook for EMU', *Warwick Economic Research Papers*, no. 482, Department of Economics, University of Warwick.

4. External balances, internal growth and employment

Hubert Hieke[1]

I INTRODUCTION

Neoclassical supply-side growth models have dominated the research agenda during the last several decades. Neoclassical growth theory has been challenged, however, by the demand-oriented approach first suggested by Thirlwall (1979). Thirlwall argues that, for most nations, the rate of growth of domestic income is constrained by the balance of payments. Moreover, in contrast to neoclassical assumptions, the adjustment processes due to current account deficits generate considerable negative income effects. In the long run, a nation's rate of growth can be approximated by the rate of growth of exports divided by the income elasticity of demand for imports.[2]

Recently, several important theoretical contributions and extensions (McCombie, 1985, 1989, 1992, 1997; McCombie and Thirlwall, 1994; Thirlwall and Hussain, 1982) as well as empirical studies (Atesoglu, 1993, 1997; Bairam 1993a, 1993b, 1997, 1998; Blecker, 1992; Hieke, 1995, 1997) on Thirlwall's approach have appeared in the literature.[3] One of the issues debated in the literature concerns the extent to which Thirlwall's Law is applicable to the US economy (McCombie, 1997; Atesoglu, 1997; Hieke, 1997). Aside from some divergencies about the ability of the US to run longer-term balance of payments deficits, advocates of Thirlwall's Law seem to agree that the general impact of the unprecedented trade deficits of the US economy during the 1972–86 period can readily be explained, but not easily be incorporated or derived from Thirlwall's Law as commonly stated in the literature (McCombie, 1997; Atesoglu, 1997; Thirlwall, 1997), and that the actual rate of growth of US income during that period significantly surpassed the equilibrium rate implied by the Law.

Consequently, an attempt is made in the following sections to shed some light on this issue. Specifically, can the discrepancy between Thirlwall's Law, as generally understood in the literature, and the actual growth experience of the US economy be explained by capital flows and terms of trade effects?

Our findings, based on results derived from both export and import demand estimates, suggest that the extended version of Thirlwall's Law (Thirlwall and Hussain, 1982) does indeed provide a good approximation for the economic growth path of the US economy during the 1972–86 period. The US was in a position in the early 1980s to generate a domestically driven growth process which provided not only the US economy with a considerably higher rate of growth of output and employment, but offered its trading partners the opportunity to pursue (passive) export-oriented, low inflationary growth policies.

II   THIRLWALL'S LAW

Thirlwall (1979) derives a simple model for determining the long-term increase of the level of income. He starts out from the balance of payments equilibrium condition:

$$P_d X = P_f M \tag{4.1}$$

where P_d and P_f are export and import prices,[4] both expressed in domestic currency, and M and X are the quantities of imports and exports, respectively. In other words, P_d/P_f are the real terms of trade.[5] Equation (4.1) can also be expressed in rates of growth as:

$$p_d + x = p_f + m \tag{4.2}$$

where the lower case letters indicate rates of changes of the variables expressed in natural logarithms.

Furthermore, Thirlwall utilizes two standard import and export demand functions:

$$M = (P_f/P_d)^g Y^h \tag{4.3}$$

$$X = (P_d/P_f)^v Y^{*w} \tag{4.4}$$

where Y and Y^* are domestic and foreign (world) income, g and v are the price elasticities for imports and exports, and h and w are the income elasticities of imports and exports, respectively. g and v are assumed to be negative, h and w are positive.

Using natural logarithms and differentiating equations (4.3) and (4.4), the rates of growth of imports and exports may be expressed as:

$$m = g(p_f - p_d) + hy \qquad (4.5)$$

$$x = v(p_d - p_f) + wy^* \qquad (4.6)$$

where lower case letters indicate the rate of change of the variables.

Subsequently, Thirlwall substitutes equations (4.5) and (4.6) into equation (4.2), which gives the equilibrium rate of growth (y_b) as:

$$y_b = [(1 + v + g)(p_d - p_f) + wy^*] / h \qquad (4.7)$$

Thirlwall (1979, p.49) argues that if the assumption can be made that '...the Marshall–Lerner condition is just satisfied or if relative prices measured in a common currency do not change over the long run...',[6] equation (4.7) can be reduced to:

$$y_b = wy^* / h \qquad (4.8)$$

or, according to equation (4.6) and assuming relative stability of the terms of trade:

$$y_b = x / h \qquad (4.9)$$

Thirlwall (1979) tests the proposition stated in equation (4.9) for a number of industrialized countries for the Bretton Woods era and finds that '... the rate of growth of exports divided by the income elasticity of demand for imports gives such a good approximation to the actual growth experience of major developed countries since 1950 that a new economic law might possibly be formulated' (Thirlwall, 1979, p.46). In fact, his proposition has become known as 'Thirlwall's Law'.

Most previous empirical studies have relied on estimates of equation (4.9), partly because of data restrictions, but also because the empirical findings seem to provide more reliable estimates. Williamson argues, however, that the equilibrium rate of growth (y_b) should be calculated from wy^*/h rather than from x/h, because in the latter case, the rate of growth of exports (x), being an ex-post value, may already incorporate any effects resulting from changes of the terms of trade.[7] McCombie (1989) has responded to this criticism, showing empirically that regardless of whether equation (4.8) or (4.9) are utilized, the statistical results for alternative samples of countries appear to be quite similar. Nevertheless, this finding does not necessarily apply when individual countries are considered separately. Consequently, in order to highlight some of the potential empirical and conceptual differences, this study focuses on both the export and import demand elasticity approach.

III THE IMPACT OF THE TERMS OF TRADE AND CAPITAL FLOWS

Thirlwall and Hussain (1982) derive an extended version of Thirlwall's Law. Their model potentially allows for a quantitative assessment of the terms of trade effects and capital flows for nations which are able to finance balance of payments deficits by continuous capital inflows. These capital inflows provide the nation with the potential to grow at a rate beyond the limit determined by Thirlwall's Law as expressed by equations (4.8) and (4.9).

In deriving the model, Thirlwall and Hussain expand the balance of payments constraint expressed in equation (4.1) by adding net nominal capital inflows (CIN) to the l.h.s. of the equation to get:

$$P_d X + CIN = P_f M \qquad (4.10)$$

Taking rates of change, equation (4.10) can be expressed as:

$$(1 - l)\,(p_d + x) + (l)\,cin = p_f + m \qquad (4.11)$$

where lower case letters represent growth rates of the variables, and l the share of the value of net nominal capital inflows expressed as a proportion of the total import bill. Capital flows, defined in this way, always assert the export bill to be in balance with the import bill.

Substituting (4.5) and (4.6) into (4.11), Thirlwall and Hussain derive the following extended Harrod trade multiplier (y_{bb}):[8]

$$y_{bb} = \{[(1 - l)\,v + g]\,(p_d - p_f) + (p_d - p_f) \\ + (1 - l)wy^* + l\,(cin - p_d)\} \,/\, h \qquad (4.12)$$

The four terms on the r.h.s. of equation (4.12) describe the following: (a) the impact of terms of trade changes on the quantities of imports and exports; (b) the pure terms of trade effect on real income growth; (c) the exogenous export effect; and (d) the capital flows effect.

Thirlwall and Hussain stress several potential important divergencies between this extended version of Thirlwall's Law given by equation (4.12) and the basic Law described by equation (4.9). In examining the relative accuracy of y_{bb} and y_b, the authors distinguish among several primary cases where cin and l are both greater than or equal to zero. Accordingly, given initial balance of payments disequilibrium, Thirlwall's Law expressed by equation (4.9) will underpredict or overpredict the actual rate of growth (y), depending on whether the rate of growth of net capital inflows is greater or less than the rate of growth of exports.[9]

In fact, this crucial aspect has sometimes been overlooked in the literature. Bairam's (1998) estimates for the US economy during the 1970–85 time period, for example, appear to confirm Thirlwall's Law as stated by equation (4.9). However, capital inflows during this time period were not necessarily negligible and they also significantly surpassed the rate of growth of exports. Similarly, it is not the level but the rate of growth of capital flows, which needs to be considered. Consequently, findings which indicate an equilibrium rate of growth below the actual growth rate for a country that is confronted with sustained trade deficits cannot always be considered as consistent with Thirlwall's Law as suggested by Atesoglu (1995).

In this context it should be pointed out that the implications of the Marshall–Lerner condition, which conveniently applies for equation (4.7), is now somewhat altered by the extended version of Thirlwall's Law. This conclusion can be derived from a closer inspection of equation (4.12). Even if the absolute value of the sum of the import and export price elasticities g and v is equal to one, as long as the share of capital flows (l) is different from zero, i.e. if capital flows are significant, the impact of terms of trade changes on the quantities of exports and imports do not exactly balance with the pure terms of trade effect on real income growth. Therefore, even if the sum of the price elasticities is equal to one, the first two terms on the r.h.s. of equation (4.12) do not cancel out.

With respect to the question of how to incorporate capital flows into the empirical analysis, the suggestions by Thirlwall and Hussain have recently been further clarified by McCombie and Thirlwall.[10] Referring to the extended version of Thirlwall's Law outlined above, McCombie[11] points out that the weighted growth of real financial flows, i.e. real net capital inflows (ci), can be expressed as:

$$a(ci) = a \left[(ci_{t1} - ci_{t0}) / ci_{t0} \right] \tag{4.13}$$

where ci_{t1} and ci_{t0} are the average real rates of growth of capital inflows at the beginning and the end of a chosen time period and

$$a = ci_{t0} / (x_{t0} + ci_{t0}) \tag{4.14}$$

is the share of initial real capital inflows, relative to the total real import bill. The total import bill is equal to the sum of the rate of growth of exports, x, and ci. As McCombie points out, equation (4.13) is formally identical to

$$a(ci) = (ci_{t1} - ci_{t0}) / (x_{t0} + ci_{t0}) \tag{4.15}$$

In the following sections, McCombie's suggestion for integrating capital flows into the empirical analysis of this study is applied.[12] Accordingly, if terms of trade changes and capital flows are now accounted for in both the import and export demand function, the following two equilibrium rates of growth can be derived in conjunction with the analysis by Thirlwall and Hussain:

$$y_{bbb1} = \{+ g(tot) + (tot) + (1-a)\,x + a\,(ci)\}\,/\,h \qquad (4.16)^{13}$$

$$y_{bbb2} = \{[(1-a)\,(v+g)]\,(tot) + (tot) + (1-a)wy^* + a\,(ci)\}\,/\,h \quad (4.17)$$

where $[a(ci)]$ is the share of real net capital inflows times the rate of growth of real net capital inflows. Hereby, equation (4.16) is derived to provide an alternative quantitative measure on the extended law when data from the export demand function are not taken into account.

IV THE EMPIRICAL EVIDENCE

There seems to be no reason not to apply the extended Thirlwall's Law to industrialized countries and, in particular, the US economy. In fact, the primary reason why previous studies neglected this issue may be due to the following observation by Thirlwall and Hussain (1982). Referring to previous empirical evidence, the authors claim that '...so many advanced countries seemed to approximate this simple rule suggested that for most countries capital flows are relatively unimportant...and that relative price changes...play only a minor role....It is largely real income (and employment) that adjusts...' (Thirlwall and Hussain, 1982, p.498).

Similarly, McCombie and Thirlwall (1994) also have specifically addressed the impact of the significant US deficits on current account in recent years, but arrived at the conclusion, that '...even the U.S. was not immune from the balance-of-payments constraint' (p. 454). In view of the recent experience, the discussion of the size, impact, causes, and sustainability of persistent US trade deficits during the post Bretton Woods era, it seems reasonable to establish whether the extended version of Thirlwall's Law can provide insights of the relative importance of the terms of trade and capital flows.[14]

To estimate the US export demand function, the first task is to derive a proxy for real foreign income. An index of the level of foreign income (Y^*) is derived from data of the six major industrialized countries, Japan, Italy, United Kingdom, Canada, France, and Germany. It represents a weighted average of the six GDP volume indices, the weights representing the 1985 export shares of the six countries. The volume data are taken from OECD *Quarterly National Accounts*; trade weights are taken from *Monthly Statistics of Trade*. Choosing this proxy accounts for the relative importance of a country as a US trading partner. Previous studies have relied on similar data sets.[15]

The volumes of US import and exports of goods and services, (*M*) and (*X*), and the terms of trade (*TOT*)[16] are obtained from the *Survey of Current Business*. All data, except relative prices, are seasonally adjusted at source. The following export and import demand function in levels and using natural logarithms are utilized:

$$\ln X = a + v \ln(TOT) + w \ln Y^* \tag{4.18}$$

$$\ln X = a + w \ln Y^* \tag{4.19}$$

$$\ln M = a + g \ln [1/(TOT)] + h \ln Y \tag{4.20}$$

$$\ln M = a + h \ln Y \tag{4.21}$$

where *X*, *Y** and *TOT* are real US exports of goods and services, real foreign income, and the real terms of trade, respectively. *v* is the price elasticity for exports, and *w* is the income demand elasticity for exports. *M* and *Y* are real imports and real domestic income, respectively; *g* is the price elasticity for imports and *h* is the income demand elasticity for imports.

The cointegration procedure is applied to determine if long-term structurally stable relationships among the variables exist for the 1972–86 time period.[17] As the first step, unit roots tests for the 1972–86 period are performed on the levels of each data series, expressed in logarithms. The results of these tests are provided in Table 4.1.

Table 4.1   Unit roots test: the export and import functions, 1972–86

Variable	Level	First differenced
1972(1)–86 (4)		
$\ln Y$	–0.3894 (1)	–5.368 (0)*
$\ln Y^*$	0.3805 (4)	–5.000 (3)*
$\ln X$	–0.9622 (0)	–6.839 (0)*
$\ln M$	–0.1308 (1)	–6.176 (0)*
$\ln TOT$	–2.3250 (1)	–5.264 (0)*

Notes: *Significant at the 1% level; **significant at the 5% level; ***significant at the 10% level. Critical values are taken from Engle and Yoo (1987). Numbers in parentheses correspond to lags required to adjust for serial correlation.

The findings of Table 4.1 demonstrate that the series of the levels of US export and import volumes, the foreign income proxy, domestic income, and the terms of trade are all integrated of order one. Furthermore, all series are stationary, i.e. I(0), when first differenced.

Because all the data series are integrated of order one, OLS level regressions are performed on two export demand functions and two import demand functions, respectively. Subsequently, (augmented) Dickey–Fuller (DF/ADF) tests (Dickey *et al.*, 1986; Dickey and Fuller, 1981) are applied to determine possible stationarity of the estimated residuals of each of the four-level regressions.

Table 4.2   Cointegration test: the export and import functions, 1972–86

Cointegrating equation	slope coefficients					
	$\ln Y$	$\ln Y^*$	$\ln TOT$	D–W	R2	DF/ADF
1972 (1)–86 (4)						
$\ln M =$	2.2391			0.207	0.9206	−2.360 (0)
$\ln M =$	2.3868		−0.7384	0.806	0.9735	−4.721 (2)**
$\ln X =$		1.3384		0.139	0.8393	−2.606 (3)
$\ln X =$		1.1551	−0.8555	0.682	0.9638	−4.091(4)***

Notes: * Significant at the 1% level; **significant at the 5% level; ***significant at the 10% level. Critical values are taken from Engle and Yoo (1987). Numbers in parentheses correspond to lags required to adjust for serial correlation.

The results of the tests, provided in Table 4.2, show that the terms of trade are significant and need to be integrated into each of the cointegration equations in order to achieve stationarity of the residuals of the OLS-level regressions. The stationarity of the residuals is reflected by the DF/ADF statistics which demonstrate that inclusion of the terms of trade improves these values significantly. In other words, for the two-level equations ranging from 1972 to 1986 period, the DF/ADF statistics reject the null hypothesis of no cointegration at the 10% level for the export demand function and at the 5% level for the import demand function. As an additional indicator for the validity of this result, Table 4.2 shows that the Durbin–Watson statistics also rises considerably when the terms of trade are included, as compared to the bivariate OLS estimates.[18]

Including the terms of trade variable into the cointegrating regression leads to an increase of the income demand elasticity, compared to the non-cointegrated bivariate import function estimate. In the case of the export demand function, the opposite effect occurs. Consequently, according to our cointegration results, not including the price term into the respective demand equations may lead to considerable bias of the actual parameter values. More important, it also implies an incorrect, unstable model specification.

The absolute values of the import and export price elasticities for the 1972–86 time period are 0.7384 and 0.8555, respectively. The sum of these elasticities, stated in absolute terms, is 1.5939. Therefore, the Marshall–Lerner condition appears not to conform with the strict hypothesis implied by Thirlwall's Law (1979). Consequently, terms of trade changes may not only affect the volumes of exports and imports, but also the trade balance as a whole. On the other hand, it appears that relative prices would need to change dramatically in order to achieve significant effects on the US balance of payments.

Table 4.2 provides evidence that the US income demand elasticity for imports was about twice as high during the years 1972–86 as the income demand elasticity for US exports. According to Thirlwall's Law (McCombie, 1989; Davidson, 1990/1), this finding, *ceteris paribus*, would indicate the inability on the part of the US to grow at a rate as high as its trading partners without negatively affecting its balance of payments performance. In essence, the results in Table 4.2 demonstrate that both the import and export demand functions are cointegrated over the 1972–86 period when the terms of trade are included in the regression equations.

Table 4.3 gives the respective annual US equilibrium growth rates which can now be derived according to equations (4.8) and (4.9).[19]

Table 4.3   Equilibrium growth rates: the export and import functions, 1972–86

Variable	Actual average rate of growth (quarterly data annualized)	Equilibrium rates of growth (y_b)	
1972 (1)–86 (4)		x/h	wy^*/h
y	0.0262	0.0229	0.0151
y^*	0.0311		
x	0.0545		

In Table 4.3, the two r.h.s. columns give the US equilibrium rate of growth while the data column to the left gives the value of the actual average growth rate of US (y) and foreign income (y^*), and the actual average rate of growth of real exports of goods and services (x). The results show that the actual growth rate (y) lies considerably above the equilibrium growth rate (x/h) during the 1972–86 time period. With respect to the equilibrium rate derived from the export demand function, the difference between y and wy^*/h is even more striking, and US income actually rose considerably more than suggested by Thirlwall's equilibrium rate. Based on the results of Table 4.3, it appears that with respect to Thirlwall's Law, the actual US rate of growth forced the US into a balance of payments constraint.

Most empirical studies on Thirlwall's Law have not explicitly addressed the possibilities and potentially distorting impact of long-term external imbalances. In addition, no criteria for defining the condition(s) that establish evidence of current account imbalances other than the relative restrictive definition stated in equation (4.1) has been suggested. The integration of capital flows or, alternatively, justification for pursuing a study on Thirlwall's Law without taking capital flows into account, should, however, (always) be preceded by some test that provide at least some evidence about the validity of the balance of payments constraint, as stated in equation (4.1). If no such evidence for the balance of payments constraint can be established, net capital inflows may significantly impact on the equilibrium growth rate and should, therefore, be integrated into the empirical analysis.[20]

In order to determine, if the US was in a balance of payments equilibrium situation during the 1972–86 period, or, more accurately, if potential trade imbalances were kept within a limited range, the same cointegration test procedure as outlined above is applied. All quarterly data, seasonally adjusted at source, are taken from the *Survey of Current Business*.

Table 4.4   Unit roots test: the balance of payments, 1972–86

Variable	Level	First differenced
1972 (1)–86 (4)		
CIN	0.476 (0)	−5.109 (0)*
ln *EX*	−2.396 (3)	−5.184 (0)*
ln *IM*	−1.962 (1)	−6.082 (0)*

Notes: * Significant at the 1% level; **significant at the 5% level; ***significant at the 10% level. Critical values are taken from Engle and Yoo (1987). Numbers in parentheses correspond to lags required to adjust for serial correlation.

The results of the unit roots tests (Table 4.4) demonstrate that net nominal capital inflows (*CIN*) are integrated of order one, but stationary when first differenced. This finding indicates that the balance of payments constraint may not be valid for the US economy during the years 1972–86. Table 4.4 also shows nominal imports and exports of goods and services, (*IM*) and (*EX*), both to be integrated of order one, i.e. I(1) in levels, but I(0) when first differenced.

The results shown in Table 4.5. demonstrate that, irrespective of which way the OLS level regression between nominal exports and imports is run, the DF/ADF test results are significantly below the critical values. Accordingly the two series, ln *IM* and ln *EX*, may in fact not have moved along a common trend during the 1972–86 time period. Consequently, Thirlwall's balance of payments constraint, as expressed by equation (4.1) may not be applicable to the US during these years. It is, therefore, appropriate to integrate capital flow effects into the analysis.

Table 4.5   Cointegration test: the balance of payments, 1972–86

Cointegrating equation	slope coefficients				
	$\ln IM$	$\ln EX$	D–W	R2	DF/ADF
1972 (1)–86 (4)					
$\ln EX$	0.8490		0.158	0.9607	–2.309 (3)
$\ln IM$		1.1316	0.158	0.9607	–1.977 (1)

Notes: * Significant at the 1% level; **significant at the 5% level; ***significant at the 10% level. Critical values are taken from Engle and Yoo (1987). Numbers in parentheses correspond to lags required to adjust for serial correlation.

Table 4.6   Equilibrium growth rates: extended version of Thirlwall's Law, 1972–86

Variable	Actual average rate of growth	Equilibrium rates of growth
	(quarterly data annualized)	
1972 (1)–86 (4)		y_{bbb1}
y	0.0262	0.0284
x	0.0545	
tot	–0.0101	
1972 (1)–86 (4)		y_{bbb2}
y	0.0262	0.0253
y^*	0.0311	
x	0.0545	
tot	–0.0101	

The findings presented in Table 4.6 provide estimates for Thirlwall's extended version of the law, based on equations (4.16) and (4.17). The results clearly show that when capital inflows are integrated into the analysis, the actual US rate of growth during the 1972–86 period is well approximated by these two equilibrium growth rates. Obviously, according to Thirlwall's extended law, real net capital inflows allowed the US to grow faster than approximated by the basic Thirlwall's Law that does not take capital flows into account.

It must be emphasized that the terms of trade[21] have hardly any significance on these findings. The quantitative differences between the results stated in Tables 4.3 and 4.6 must be attributed to the unprecedented increase in the rate of growth of net capital inflows until 1986. In fact, almost half of value of the equilibrium growth estimate derived from equation (4.17) is due to net capital inflows during the 1972–86 period. And although this respective impact is somewhat lower when the analysis is based on equation (4.16), the effect is still considerable.

V   CONCLUSION

The extended version of Thirlwall's Law demonstrates the significant contribution of net capital inflows, and even though net capital inflows are sometimes considered as a residual outcome when import expenditures are not compensated by export revenues, the effect is nevertheless striking. In fact, our estimates indicate that the annual US rate of growth might have been only approximately 1.5 per cent, if the US had observed the basic balance of payments constraint and capital inflows had not accommodated the lack of export revenue during the 1972–86 era.[22] Consequently, Thirlwall's extended law provides a good conceptual framework even for industrial countries during shorter time periods, when export expenditure and import revenues are not balanced.

Godley and Milberg (1994) and McCombie (1997) have recently argued that the process of accumulating external imbalances cannot go on indefinitely and must soon (or at least in the foreseeable future) come to a halt. This may be correct, although previous, rather precise projections for such turning points have not always been accurate.[23] However, the expansionary, demand-oriented growth policy of the US in the first half of the 1980s has already proved to be a powerful stimulus to output and employment in the US (Davidson, 1992) and also among its principal trading partners.

NOTES

1.   The author is Research Fellow at the University of Mannheim. Part of the chapter was written while the author was visiting assistant professor at Arkansas State University. He wishes to thank Chris Brown, Karin Knaus, and Friedolin Bergstrasse for helpful comments.
2.   See Thirlwall (1979), and McCombie and Thirlwall (1994).
3.   This is not an exhaustive list of the literature. Excellent summaries of various aspects of Thirlwall's Law are provided by McCombie (1997) and McCombie and Thirlwall (1994, 1997). A brief history on the development of Thirlwall's approach is provided by Thirlwall (1997).

4. See also McCombie and Thirlwall (1994, p.234).
5. See Thirlwall and Hussain (1982, p.500, fn. 1), and Thirlwall and Gibson (1992, p.327).
6. In later versions of this paper, the statement referring to the Marshall–Lerner condition has been deleted, so that the focus has been on the assumption of relatively stable real exchange rates. See McCombie and Thirlwall (1994, p.236).
7. See also McCombie (1989), and McCombie and Thirlwall (1994).
8. Thirlwall and Hussain (1982, p.502–3).
9. For a discussion on various aspects of this issue see Thirlwall and Hussain (1982).
10. In private conversation, referring to the rate of growth of capital flows, Thirlwall suggests to 'take the change in capital flows over the whole period and divide by the number of years' (fax from Thirlwall, November 1994).
11. As expressed in private conversation (fax from McCombie, November 1994).
12. A detailed account of potentially arising problems in determining an appropriate procedure to integrate capital flows is provided by Hieke (1995).
13. From the import demand perspective, the equilibrium rate of growth cannot be assessed by applying equation (4.7). Rearranging equation (4.6): $(^*)\,wy^* = x - v\,(tot)$ and substituting equation $(^*)$ into (4.7) we get $(^{**})\,y_{bb} = [(1+g)\,(tot) + x]\,/\,h$ where $(^{**})$ is the equilibrium rate of growth based on the import demand function but including the terms of trade effect.
14. During the Bretton Woods era, the US external accounts were relatively balanced, although, as Helkie and Hooper (1987) indicate, net exports expressed in real terms showed a secular decline. During the flexible exchange rate era, the US merchandise trade balance, expressed in both real and nominal terms moved into considerable deficit. Net exports of goods and services followed the same pattern. Particularly, in the mid-1980s, the balance of goods and services reached record deficits. During these years, the US, previously the world's largest creditor, became the world's largest net debtor nation.
15. Rose and Jellen (1986, p.58), and Borkakoti (1992) also utilized data from the Group of Seven. Weights based on export shares have also been applied in previous literature (Borkakoti, 1992).
16. It should be emphasized that identical data for the terms of trade must be applied for both the export and import demand function.
17. Hieke (1995) has shown that the elasticity parameters of the US export demand function are not stable over the entire post Bretton Woods era.
18. The overall fit for the two regressions based on the trivariate data series also improves significantly.
19. The values for h and w are taken from the two cointegrated demand functions.
20. A test for determining the validity of the assumption of Thirlwall's approach has not been suggested previously in the literature.
21. If the total effects of terms of trade changes in each respective equation are considered.
22. This is the finding based on equation (4.17) and shown in Table 4.6.
23. Although, particularly for the US, as the world lender of last resort, it is probably impossible to quantify a precise limit for this process.

REFERENCES

Atesoglu, S.H. (1997) 'Balance-of-Payments-Constrained Growth Model and its Implications for the United States', *Journal of Post Keynesian Economics*, **19**, 327–35.

Atesoglu, S.H. (1995) 'An Explanation of the Slowdown in U.S. economic Growth', *Applied Economic Letters*, **15**, 507–14.

Atesoglu, S.H. (1993) 'Balance-of-payments-constrained growth', *Journal of Post Keynesian Economics*, **15**, 507–14.

Bairam, E.I. (1998) 'Balance of payments, the Harrod foreign trade multiplier and economic growth: the European and North American experience, 1970–85', *Applied Economics*, **20**, 1635–42.

Bairam, E.I. (1997) 'Levels of Economic Development and Appropriate Specification of the Harrod Foreign Trade Multiplier', *Journal of Post Keynesian Economics*, **19**, 337–44.

Bairam, E.I. (1993b) 'Income elasticities of exports and imports: a re-examination of the empirical evidence', *Applied Economics*, **25**, 71–4.

Bairam, E. (1993a) 'Static versus dynamic specification and the Harrod foreign trade multiplier', *Applied Economics*, **25**, 739–42.

Blecker, R.A. (1992) 'Structural Roots of U.S. Trade Problems: Income Elasticities, Secular Trends, and Hysteresis', *Journal of Post Keynesian Economics*, **14**, 321–46.

Borkakoti, J. (1992) 'On the US-Japan Trade Balance', in *External Balances and Policy Constraints in the 1990s*, C. Miller and N. Snowden (eds), St. Martin Press, pp. 144–77.

Davidson, P. (1992) *International Money and the Real World*, 2nd edn, Macmillan.

Davidson, P. (1990–91) 'A Post Keynesian positive contribution to "theory"', *Journal of Post Keynesian Economics*, **13**, pp. 298–303.

Dickey, D., *et al.* (1986) 'Unit Roots in Time Series Models: Tests and Implications', *The American Statistician*, **40**, 12–26.

Dickey, D.A. and Fuller, W.A. (1981) 'Likelihood Ratio Statistics For Autoregressive Time Series With a Unit Root', *Econometrica*, **49**, 1057–72.

Engle, R.F. and Yoo, B.S. (1987) 'Forecasting and Testing in Co-Integrated Systems', *Journal of Econometrics*, **35**, 143–59.

Godley, W. and Milberg, W. (1994) 'U.S. Trade Deficits: Recovery's Dark Side?', *Challenge*, November–December, 40–7.

Helkie, W.L. and Hooper, P. (1987) 'The U.S. External Deficit in the 1980s: An Empirical Analysis', International Finance Discussion Papers, no. 304, February 1987.

Hieke, H. (1997) 'Balance-of-Payments Constrained Growth: A Reconsideration of the Evidence for the U.S. Economy', *Journal of Post Keynesian Economics*, **19**, 313–25.

Hieke, H. (1995) Balance-of-Payments Constrained Growth: The Importance of Thirlwall's Law for the U.S. Economy during the Post World War II Era, Ph.D. dissertation, University of Tennessee.

McCombie, J.S.L. (1997) 'Empirics of Balance-of-Payments Constrained Growth', *Journal of Post Keynesian Economics*, **29**, 345–75. *Applied Economics*, 1992, p. 493–512.

McCombie, J.S.L. (1992) '"Thirlwall's Law" and balance of payments constraint growth – more on the debate', *Applied Economics*, **24**, 493–512.

McCombie, J.S.L. (1989) '"Thirlwall's Law" and the balance of payments constraint growth – a comment on the debate', *Applied Economics*, **21**, 611–29.

McCombie, J.S.L. (1985) 'Economic growth, the Harrod foreign trade multiplier and the Hicks' super-multiplier', *Applied Economics*, **17**, 55–72.

McCombie, J.S.L. and Thirlwall, A.P. (1997) 'The Dynamic Harrod Foreign Trade Multiplier and the Demand Oriented Approach to Economic Growth – An Evaluation', *International Review of Applied Economics*, **11**, 5–26.

McCombie, J.S.L. and Thirlwall, A.P. (1994) *Economic Growth and the Balance-of-Payments Constraint*, Macmillan, 1994.

Rose, A. and Jellen, J. (1989) 'Is there a J-Curve', *Journal of Monetary Economics*, **23**, 53–68.

Thirlwall, A.P. (1997) 'Reflections on the Concept of Balance-of-Payments Constrained Growth', *Journal of Post Keynesian Economics*, **19**, 377–85.

Thirlwall, A.P. (1979) 'The Balance of Payments Constraint as an Explanation of International Growth Rate Differences', *Banca Nazionale del Lavoro Quarterly Review*, **32**, 45–53.

Thirlwall, A.P. and Gibson, H.D. (1992) *Balance of Payments Theory and the United Kingdom Experience*, 4th edn, Macmillan.

Thirlwall, A.P. and Hussain, N.N. (1982) 'The Balance of Payments Constraint, Capital Flows and Growth Rate Differences Between Developing Countries', *Oxford Economic Papers*, 498–510.

Williamson J. (1984) 'Is There an External Constraint?', *National Institute Economic Review*, no.109, August, **34**, 73–7.

5. Thoughts on speculation and open markets

Paul Davidson

Since the United States abandoned the Bretton Woods exchange rate system in 1973, the exchange rate has become an object of speculation. With the removal of all restrictions on international capital flows in a world of flexible exchange rates, international financial transactions have grown thirty times as fast as the growth in international trade. In 1998, international financial flows dominated trade payments and exchange rate movements reflected changes in speculative positions rather than changes in trade patterns.

Since the 1970s, Nobel Prize winner James Tobin (1974) has been almost the only voice with significant visibility in the economics profession warning that free international financial markets with flexible exchange rates can have a 'devastating impact on specific industries and whole economies' (Eichengreen, Tobin and Wyplosz, 1995). Tobin advocates that governments constrain international flows via a 'Tobin tax'. Elsewhere I (Davidson, 1997, 1998) have explained why Tobin's assessment of the problem is correct but why the solution he proposes is wrong.

In this chapter I want to raise the issue of whether international (and/or domestic) financial markets are inherently fragile. Minsky (1986) has been characterized as a Keynesian pessimist who sees the financial market glass as half-empty and fragile. I have been characterized as the optimist who sees the glass as half-filled and surprisingly strong. In these days of Asian contagion and Russian bears, however, we are being haunted by the Minsky fragility syndrome and his frightening question 'Can "it" happen again?'

Bernstein (1998) notes that since World War II 'the number of stock markets around the world has grown from 50 to just over 125 – even the Chinese, nominally still socialists have seen fit to establish stock markets on their territory'. Accordingly, one might ask, if financial markets are so fragile, why have almost all economies turned to using them? The answer is that these markets provide investors with *liquidity*, a property that is especially important in economies whose future are very uncertain. The presence of liquidity encourages investors to provide finance to entrepreneurs that they might not do if the investment was illiquid. Bernstein (1998) notes that liquidity permits investors to have a very short time horizon by providing 'the ability to reverse a decision at the lowest possible transactions cost'. Market liquidity provides each investor with what Bernstein labels a 'quick exit strategy' the moment he/she is dissatisfied with the way matters are developing. (It also provides a quick entrance strategy the moment the investor is surprised how well matters are developing.)

Financial assets represent titles to potential future nominal income streams or what Keynes, following Marshall, called a stream of quasi-rents. Today's spot market price of any financial asset depends on 'the state of long term expectation' regarding this future stream of quasi-rents (Keynes, 1936, Chapter 12). Keynes, however, took a dim view of the belief that this state of long-term expectations could accurately forecast the future quasi-rent stream since the latter are uncertain in the nonergodic sense. In other words past and current market data on realized quasi-rent earnings do not provide a reliable statistical basis for forecasting future income streams. Deprived of any reliable foundation for forecasting future quasi-rents, today's market price of liquid assets is dominated by a convention.

> The essence of this convention – though it does not, of course, work out quite so simply – lies in assuming that the existing state of affairs will continue indefinitely, except if we have specific reasons to expect a change. (Keynes, 1936, p. 152)

In normal times, the conventional wisdom is that today's financial asset prices either directly reflect market 'fundamentals' such as current earnings, or at least have a high degree of built-in inertia relative to these fundamentals. In recent years, this simple-minded convention has been translated by a highly sophisticated econometric technology into the concept of a random walk down Wall Street. Of course, if the existing state of affairs does continue indefinitely, unless there is solid evidence of a change in what people call 'market fundamentals', then it should stand to reason that financial market activity should not be destabilizing or fragile. But doesn't uncertainty necessarily mean instability?

> Financial market instability is especially likely to be observed when the market's 'conventional valuation... is established as the outcome of the mass psychology of a large number of ignorant individuals, [then it] is liable to change violently as the result of a sudden fluctuation of opinion due to factors which do not really make much difference to the prospective yield.... In abnormal times in particular, when the hypothesis of an indefinite continuance of the existing state of affairs is less plausible...the market will be subject to waves of optimistic and pessimistic sentiment which are unreasoning and yet in a sense legitimate where no solid basis exists for reasonable calculation. (Keynes, 1936, p. 154)

Accordingly, whenever financial market activity is dominated by amateurs, or even professionals who are rewarded by short-term (i.e. quarter-to-quarter or even day-to-day) performance results, then any apparently ephemeral event can create uncertainty in market participants' minds. This rise in feelings of uncertainty can unleash the music for what I call bandwagon behavior that induces violent swings in market prices. If there is sufficient stampeding-herd behavior in the market, then such bandwagon behavior can be legitimate and self-justifying.

I CONVENTIONAL POLICIES TO REDUCE MARKET INSTABILITY

Many Keynesians[1] have been associated with the extreme view that because the future is uncertain, the financial system is inevitably fragile and this is the fundamental cause of economic instability. Accordingly, some Keynesian prescriptions, such as the Tobin Tax, have often been associated with public policies that attempt to constrain trading in financial markets. Old and New Classical economists, on the other hand, believe in the absolute robust efficiency of free financial markets where speculation is inherently stabilizing.

The conventional wisdom of New Democrats–New Liberal political leaders and their sycophant New Keynesian economists are attempting to occupy some middle ground between the Old Keynesian and the Classical schools. New Keynesians admit that late 20th century free-market capitalism has not quite yet attained the state of perfection claimed by their New Classical brethren. The New Keynesian conventional wisdom is that there is a role for a small army of skilled technicians (primarily enlisted from their former graduate students) who keep the free market machine from being pushed off its tracks by scoundrels, wastrels, shirkers, cronies, and fools. New Keynesians attribute financial market instability, especially in foreign nations, not to an uncertain future but rather to the actions of dishonest government employees, capitalist cronyism, and foolish investors who flourish in a world of asymmetric information.

For example, in a Levy Institute Report (1998, p. 3) on a conference in honor of Hyman Minsky on the 'fragility of the international financial system', Federal Reserve Vice-Chair Alice Rivlin's solution to the Asian financial crises is reported to lie in 'two key prescriptions, one relating to transparency' and the other 'increased supervision and monitoring of emerging financial markets'. Rivlin's key proposals imply that international financial market problems are entirely due to the 'other guy'; transparency and Central Bank regulation in the developed world's financial markets do not require any further policy fix. The Federal Reserve (and the Bank of England and the Bundesbank – but apparently not the Bank of Japan) one supposes has the situation well in hand.

At the same Levy Conference, Brookings Institution visiting scholar Martin Meyer attacks the lender of last resort function of *all* central banks. Meyer's solution is 'better accounting practices, increased transparency, and increased market discipline.... But the best hedge against crises is for central banks to end their unconditional support of the banking system and separate the banking system from the monetary system'. Would Meyer really welcome a return to the 19th century wild-cat banking era and possible bank runs in today's cyberspace?

This brief Levy Report may not do justice to the full Rivlin and Meyer position. Nevertheless, their conclusions about transparency, oversight, and market discipline as the primary ingredients necessary to solve our international financial market problems is the moral equivalent of being for motherhood and peace. No self-righteous person can be against motherhood, and by implication neither can one be against the provision of more costless information, i.e. transparency or market discipline (at least as opposed to market disorder[2]).

Keynes (1936, p.383) wrote that 'practical men ...are usually the slaves of some defunct economists ... [and m]admen in authority ... are distilling their frenzy from some academic scribbler of a few years back'. Of course this was written long before we had the instant communications revolution and the now common-place political injection of academic scribblers into high places at the Fed, the US Treasury, the World Bank, and the IMF. Academic scribblers today are often either power brokers themselves or the chief advisors on the staff of political power brokers. Consequently, academic concepts often are transformed into eight-second sound-bite code words for TV coverage.

The sound-bite word 'transparency', for example, is a canonization of the misleading and potentially devastating New Keynesian 'asymmetric information' concept. The latter implies that markets would always be Pareto-efficient in the short run except for the 'fact' that reliable information about the future is not free.[3] There is, therefore, a profit incentive to beat the crowd in finding and analyzing information. Such beat-the-crowd, asymmetric information-driven behavior is considered a prime cause of the current international financial market crises that have devastating real impacts. By implication, therefore, 'transparency' is a call for all the information to be disseminated widely and as freely as possible. In my recent invited lecture to a plenary session of the Royal Economic Society (Davidson, 1998), I developed why I believe this asymmetric information scenario is logically inconsistent as well as inapplicable to the world in which we live.

I sent copies of this RES lecture to friends for comment. An old friend, Allan Meltzer, who is known for his Classical-Monetarist leanings, responded as follows regarding the Tobin Tax policy advocated by Keynesians:

> I have never been able to understand two things about international economics. Why is it that price adjustment is good everywhere else but not when it comes to exchange

rates? Why is it that open trade in goods is a great idea, but open trade in financial assets is considered to be destabilizing? (Meltzer, personal letter dated May 22, 1998)

Meltzer asks an excellent rhetorical question and one which I hope to shed some light on in the following pages. But for those readers who cannot wait for the analytical development of my argument, my cryptic answer to Meltzer was: 'But I do not think that unfettered trade is, under all circumstances, good, nor do I think that open trade in liquid assets, under certain circumstances, is bad.'

The analytical problem is to determine the relevant circumstances, and the institutional arrangements, that will permit relatively open trade in goods and assets while simultaneously promoting full employment stability with a minimum of financial instability. With proper institutions, financial markets need not exhibit financial fragility. As I responded to Meltzer:

> if there is no institutional anchor for nominal prices of both goods and financial assets, then under circumstances that I call 'bandwagon' speculation (a behavior that is sensible in either a nonergodic stochastic system or a deterministic system where, in Savage's term, agents can not order all possible outcomes) open trade in either real goods or in financial assets can be terribly destabilizing.... All financial markets require an institutional anchor – a market maker to assure liquidity. The only question is how much of an anchor should this market maker provide. Here you and I would differ, not on the need for a market maker – although you see the market maker solely as a 'lender of last resort' and I see a market maker having a more active role. We both agree, I think, that some form of intervention in the financial markets is necessary when markets start becoming 'disorderly'. The question is when to start intervening and by how much. You take the Old Testament view that intervention should occur only after all the sinners are punished; while I believe that market discipline punishment of sinners in a case of a systemic disruption is likely to punish too many innocent bystanders and hence should be avoided at least until all the innocents are protected – even if that means some of the sinners avoid punishment.
>
> In the market for goods we are – and always have been since our days at Penn [the University of Pennsylvania], in disagreement. You see an institutional anchor in determining the rate of growth of the money supply. I see an institutional anchor in constraining money wage rate growth to productivity growth via an incomes policy. But again, I believe, neither of us would permit real unfettered trade in goods financed by some uncontrolled open banking system – similar to what some Austrians advocate.

(And now I would add that I surmise that Martin Meyer would not object to an Austrian-type uncontrolled but transparent banking system.)

> Of course, your rhetorical question regarding open trade in goods vs. open trade in financial assets would be well-placed if you were addressing Larry Summers or Joe Stiglitz. As I point out in my Royal Economic Society lecture – both Summers and Stiglitz (and Jim Tobin by inference as well) believe in the Pareto efficiency of open trade in goods but the destabilizing effects of trading in financial assets ... they are

logically inconsistent in their theoretical model by assuming open trade in financial assets can be destabilizing, while open trade in goods and services are Pareto-efficient. (I guess consistency is a the hobgoblin of a small mind – and no one ever accused these super Keynesians of having a small mind.) At least you, Friedman, and Lucas are being logically consistent in your views on open trade in goods and open trade in financial assets. Most Old and New Keynesians are not.

II   WHY DOES SPECULATION OCCUR?

Let us compare two economies, a CEE (Classical Ergodic Economy) where the future can be predicted with statistical reliability, and a KNEE (a Keynes NonErgodic Economy) where agents realize the future cannot be reliably predicted on the basis of any given existing market data (or what new Keynesians call information). In each economy there is a market for financial assets that are legal title to a future stream of quasi-rents.

In the CEE economy, today's spot price (p_s^{t0}) simply reflects the statistically reliable forecast of the discounted future quasi-rents (q) minus carrying costs (c) of the underlying real asset, i.e. $p_s^{t0} = \Sigma(q - c)(d_r)$, where ($d_r$) is the rate of discount used and Σ indicates the stream of ($q - c$) each time period are summed from period $t = 0$ to period $t = n$, where n indicates the period which marks the end of the economic life of the underlying real asset. The expected spot price in the $t1$ period (p_s^{t1}) is equal to $[p_s^{t0} - (q - c)_{t0}]$. In other words, in the CEE economy the spot market price of the asset in every future period will be reduced by the net quasi-rents earned in the previous periods.

In a CEE economy only irrational fools would take either speculative bull or bear positions, since everyone 'knows' that the spot market evaluation at any point of time is always (within statistical significance limits) the correct present value of the future income stream that the holder is legally entitled to receive. Only when the spot price randomly strayed (due to white noise) from the estimated statistical average might arbitrage traders (classical speculators) enter into the spot market to move the price back towards its (known) statistical average. Accordingly, in a CEE what might be called speculation is really arbitrage, and as such it is always stabilizing.

In the KNEE economy, however, the $\Sigma(q - c)$ remaining embodied in any real asset cannot be predicted with any statistical reliability. In a KNEE economy, the spot market price of any liquid asset in a well-organized, orderly free market can change over time in a nonpredictable fashion. Savers who are storing liquid claims on resources in financial assets must contemplate the possibility of an appreciation or depreciation in the financial asset's spot market price at any future date thereby affecting the market value of their portfolio. This potential capital gain or loss is obtained by subtracting today's spot price (p_s^{t0})

from the expected spot price at a future date (p_s^{t1}). When $(p_s^{t1} - p_s^{t0}) > 0$, a capital gain is expected from holding the asset until $t1$; if $(p_s^{t1} - p_s^{t0}) < 0$, a capital loss will be expected.

Offsetting the possible future capital loss on choosing to hold any liquid asset as a store of value today is the value of expected earnings $(q - c)$ over the time interval the asset is held until it is liquidated (sold). Bernstein (1998) has noted that the existence of liquid financial markets permits investors to shorten their time horizons for the holding period of assets to dramatically less than the potential economic life of the underlying durable assets. (Expected q and c should be measured in terms of their absolute monetary values for the brief period that holding is contemplated rather than as a realizable rate of return.) The values of q and c tend to increase with the length of the time interval the asset is held. There are also transactions costs (T_s) incurred in both buying and reselling any liquid asset. T_s is independent of the time interval and normally increases at a decreasing rate as the transaction value of the asset increases. If there are no expected capital gains (or losses) then for any given expected flow of $q - c$, T_s sets a minimum time interval that the asset must be held to prefer it to cash.

If, for any specific liquid financial asset the portfolio manager expects

$$(q - c) + (p_s^{t1} - p_s^{t0}) - T_s > 0 \qquad (5.1)$$

then the manager is a 'bull'. If it is expected that

$$(q - c) + (p_s^{t1} - p_s^{t0}) - T_s < 0 \qquad (5.2)$$

then the fund manager is a 'bear'. A portfolio manager will choose, *ceteris paribus*, to move her money into those assets that are expected to yield the highest positive values[4] and sell those assets that have negative perspective yields.

In the simplest case, if $(q - c)$ minus T_s equals zero, then if

$$[p_s^{t1}/p_s^{t0}] > 1 \qquad (5.3)$$

then the person is a bull, while if

$$[p_s^{t1}/p_s^{t0}] < 1 \qquad (5.4)$$

the person is a bear.[5] Since in the KNEE the future is uncertain, there is no 'firm' fundamental foundation for a stable relationship between spot price expectations over time in financial markets.

In today's floating exchange rate system, the exchange rate has become a potential object of speculation. Nations (or their central banks or currency boards) must hold significant foreign reserves as a buffer stock to encourage and support *orderly*, organized exchange markets. Orderliness is defined as when the next spot price does not vary significantly from the last executed price. Orderliness can be maintained even in the face of potential lemming-like international speculative portfolio flows until either:

(1) the foreign reserves of the nation suffering the outflow of hot money are nearly exhausted. Then the nation cannot maintain an orderly exchange rate market and fund managers who are latecomers cannot readily convert their holdings into foreign assets if at all[6] unless there is an international lender of last resort; or
(2) the country being drained of reserves increases its interest rate (i.e. the $q - c$ term) sufficiently to offset the expected potential capital loss from holding liquid assets denominated in its currency; or
(3) central banks (singularly or cooperatively) actively intervene in the exchange market in an attempt to change private sector expectations regarding $(p_s^{t1} - p_s^{t0})$; or
(4) some form of taxation is added to increase the value of the T_s term to offset the expected capital gain from an exchange rate change; or
(5) some form of outright prohibition of hot money portfolio-flows is successfully introduced.

All that is required to set off international speculative flows is an expected change in the exchange rate. If, therefore, an institution can be developed that assures portfolio managers that exchange rates will be stable over time, this will do more to inhibit speculative short-term round tripping than any small Tobin tax.

It was such considerations that led Keynes to suggest an outright prohibition of all 'hot money' international portfolio flows through the creation of a supranational central bank and his 'bancor' plan. At this stage of economic development and global economic integration, however, a supranational central bank is not politically feasible. Accordingly what should be aimed for is a more modest goal of obtaining an international agreement among the major trading nations. To be economically effective and politically feasible, this agreement, while incorporating the economic principles that Keynes laid down in his bancor plan, should not require any nation to surrender control of local banking systems and fiscal policies. I have proposed such a plan, the IMCU, in several articles and books (see Davidson, 1994, 1997).

III   DOES TRANSPARENCY REDUCE SPECULATION?

New Keynesians Stiglitz (1989) and Summers (Summers and Summers, 1989), following the lead of Old Keynesian Tobin (1974), have argued that an *ad valorem* tax on international financial market transactions is socially desirable in that it will reduce the observed volatility in our 'super-efficient financial markets'.

In efficient market theory, agents gather information about fundamentals to calculate reliable conditional probabilities regarding the future. Accordingly, the future is merely the statistical shadow of the past and, as our CEE model illustrates, this 'known' future determines today's market prices. New Keynesians believe that we live in a CEE economy but that information about the discounted future stream of net quasi-rents is very costly to obtain. Hence, the possibility of asymmetric information-driven behavior where each agent outraces others to calculate the actuarially reliable future. Beating the market 'affects how the pie is divided, but does not affect the size of the pie' (Stiglitz, 1989, p. 103). By asserting that 'production, in every state of nature, in every contingency is precisely what it would have been had the information not been available' to any individual agents, Stiglitz (1989, p. 102) is arguing that the future is immutably determined by market fundamentals. In other words, future real returns of the underlying real assets are the inevitable outcomes predetermined by today's fundamentals so that the total social return to real capital assets is predetermined and unalterable by human activity. Of course, this information will inevitably reveal itself (at least in the long run) in determining the secular trend of financial spot market prices.

All mainstream Keynesians as well as all Classical economists accept the efficient market hypothesis as the applicable description of financial markets. One logically inevitable conclusion of this efficient market hypothesis is that, as Stiglitz (1989, pp. 102–3) states, the most 'important social function' of financial markets is to correctly allocate capital among industries in accordance with *reliable* information about future rates of return determined by fundamentals.[7] Stiglitz (1989, pp. 105–7) claims that a small transactions tax has a strong deterrent effect primarily on short-term speculators.[8] The tax will not be a deterrent to long-term asset holders who are rational[9] market participants who 'base their trading on fundamentals...and are willing to wait a long time to realize a return' (Stiglitz, 1989, p. 105). Rational market participants therefore do not change their already optimal behavior if a transaction tax is imposed.

In Stiglitz's model, short-term traders consist of two groups: 'The noise traders and those who live off them' (Stiglitz, 1989, p. 106). Observed volatile asset price movements *away* from fundamentals-determined values are attributed entirely to the existence of 'noise traders', i.e. the speculators who *mistakenly* believe they know how the stock market works and therefore do not have to acquire the correct information regarding future outcomes from the fundamentals (Stiglitz, 1989, p. 105). Those rational traders who feed on these foolish noise traders ultimately return the market to its fundamental value. The 'mistaken belief of all speculators' that they can do better than the market by ignoring the fundamentals is Stiglitz's (1989, p.106) sole explanation of the horrendous speculative volatility that we observe in our world. A tax on such foolish speculators will save them from their own folly, and save resources for society, and is consequently socially desirable.

In an efficient market world, however, if all information about the future is made available, then there would be complete transparency and, as our CEE example showed, speculation would always be the equivalent of stabilizing arbitrage. The New Keynesian 'noise traders' argument, however, presumes that there is something different about financial markets *vis-à-vis* product markets in a CEE world. For example, Stiglitz (1989, p.102) accepts the argument that the imposition of a transaction tax in any product market will *distort* the Pareto-efficient price structure. Stiglitz argues that a similar tax in the financial markets, however, does not have such a deleterious propensity but rather 'such a tax may be beneficial' (Stiglitz, 1989, p.102).

If financial markets are efficient and immutable market parametric relationships (i.e. fundamentals) are the determinants of the future returns, then it follows that those irrational agents who make persistent errors will either become extinct via some Darwinian economic process, or will survive by learning how not to make persistent mistakes. Despite their belief in efficient financial markets, pragmatic Keynesians (e.g. Stiglitz, Summers, Tobin, Rivlin) recognize that after several centuries of significant volume of daily trades on financial markets – and daily global trading volume as well as the number of organized financial markets has increased dramatically in the last two decades – potentially disruptive speculation continues to exist *and* even increase. But how can persistently mistaken 'noise traders' continue to exist in an efficient market system where rational traders can gluttonously feed off of these fools?

To resolve this dilemma of the centuries-old existence of speculation in financial markets, Stiglitz (1989, p.106) appeals to authority – the ultimate free market authority and successful circus impresario – P.T. Barnum who said: 'There's a sucker born every minute'. This appeal to Barnum's authority implies that society continues to produce, even in the long run, fools who irrationally believe they can beat the market.

Faced with the contradiction between the implications of the efficient market hypothesis where those who make persistent errors are eradicated and his attribution of volatile financial markets to the persistent existence of foolish market participants, Stiglitz and these other Keynesians have done the only 'rational' thing possible. They have ignored this logical inconsistency. Instead Stiglitz (1989, p.106) buttresses his argument that 'irrationality is pervasive' by appealing to the facts that this ubiquitous, persistent irrationality exists even among Stiglitz's brightest economics students. If students at our most prestigious universities are such irrational dolts, then what can one expect of the average financial market participant bereft of exposure to any efficient market analysis?

These Keynesians either do not realize, or else ignore the idea, that if persistent 'pervasive irrationality' is necessary to explain centuries-long financial market volatility, then logical consistency requires them to admit that irrationality can persist and be pervasive in all product markets.[10] If Barnum's homily that there is a sucker born every minute is a necessary condition for one's market model, then one must reject the orthodox argument that all markets involve efficient Darwinian processes that, at least in the long run, eradicate persistent error making fools. If Barnum is correct (and he certainly understood the circus market), then orthodox theory cannot claim that *laissez-faire* markets will maximize the welfare of the community. Open market price adjustments are not necessarily always a desirable economic process.

In other words, we can respond to Meltzer, that only in the fictitious CEE world would open and free trade in markets induce price adjustments that are always stabilizing around the Pareto-optimal price vector. Actual price distortions would be attributable to social limitations to open and free trade in all markets. On the other hand, if we live in a KNEE world, where the future is not predetermined by existing fundamentals, then it is not true that 'price adjustment is good everywhere' or every time.

From a Post Keynesian perspective, the problem of Old Classical, New Classical, Old Keynesian, and New Keynesian analysis is that they traditionally confuse the logic of efficient financial market behavior in a CEE with financial market behavior in a KNEE where agents know they are dealing with an uncertain (nonergodic) future.

IV KEYNES, SPECULATION AND LIQUID FINANCIAL MARKETS

Keynes's (1936, pp. 161–3) explanation of the existence of speculative activity requires rejecting the restrictive ergodic axiom. Keynes argued that, at any point of time, the future is uncertain in the sense that the actuarial profit or a reliable mathematically based expectation of gain calculated in accordance with existing probabilities cannot be obtained from any existing data set. In 1937, Keynes emphasized the difference between his 'general theory' and orthodoxy. In the latter

> [f]acts and expectations were assumed to be given in a definite form; and risks ... were supposed to be capable of an exact actuarial computation. The calculus of probability ... was supposed capable of reducing uncertainty to the same calculable state as that of certainty itself.... I accuse the classical economic theory of being itself one of these

pretty, polite techniques which tries to deal with the present by abstracting from the fact that we know very little about the future ... [a classical economist] has overlooked the precise nature of the difference which his abstraction makes between theory and practice, and the character of the fallacies into which he is likely to be lead (Keynes, 1937, pp. 112–5).

In Keynes's analysis, therefore, even if 'fundamentals' exist that have determined today's financial market price and even if a market data set permits one to calculate today's (presumed to exist) objective probability conditional distribution, such calculations do not form a *reliable* base for forecasting the future. In other words, today's conditional objective probabilities are not a reliable actuarial guide to future benefits in either financial markets or goods markets.

In a KNEE economy in which we live, as John Hicks (1977, p. vii) argued, agents 'do not know what is going to happen and know they do not know' the future. In a KNEE system, *the primary function of financial markets is to provide liquidity* and not necessarily to efficiently allocate real capital spending. This liquidity function involves the ability to buy and resell assets in a well-organized, orderly market in order to obtain the medium of contractual settlement to meet one's nominal contractual liabilities when they come due.

Bernstein (1998) has properly argued 'An efficient market is a market without liquidity'. Creating liquidity in financial markets would not be an important social function *if markets are efficient*.[11] Logical consistency for those claiming financial markets are efficient requires the presumption that individuals can also plan their future spending on goods and services efficiently by buying and selling financial assets whose sales and maturity dates match the individual's life-cycle spending pattern stream *vis-à-vis* the individual's income pattern stream (e.g. as assumed in overlapping generation models). In a classical efficient market system, rational self-interested agents should never have any sudden need for liquidity to meet an uncertain, unpredictable contractual obligations over their life cycle.

In a KNEE system, however, one is always uncertain not only about future unforeseen contractual obligations coming due, but also about future financial asset market prices. Consequently there is always the potential fear that when liquidity is needed, in the absence of an active lender of last resort to support financial asset prices, the financial markets may be unable to provide sufficient liquidity, no matter how prudent the financial investor has been in the past.

Now a practical theory of the future [financial market prices is] ... based on a flimsy foundation. It is subject to sudden and violent changes. The practice of calmness and immobility, of certainty and security, suddenly breaks down. New fears and hopes will, without warning, take charge of human conduct. The forces of disillusion may suddenly impose a new conventional basis of valuation (Keynes, 1937, pp. 114–5).

In a world of instant communication, any event occurring in the world can set off rapid changes in one's subjective evaluation of the market value of one's portfolio. Speculation about the psychology of other market players can result in lemming-like behavior which can become self-reinforcing and self-justifying. In a nonergodic system, if enough agents possess the same 'incorrect' expectations (to use Stiglitz's phrase), the result can be that these faulty expectations actually create future outcomes (cf. Arestis and Sawyer, 1998, pp. 188–9). The first 'irrational' lemmings to hit the ocean of liquidity may not drown. They may survive to make more mistakes and lead more leaps into liquidity in the future.

V   LIQUID FINANCIAL MARKETS – OWNERSHIP vs. CONTROL

Financial markets furnish liquidity by providing an orderly, well-organized environment where financial assets can be readily resold for cash. The 'essential properties' of the underlying real capital assets (see Keynes, 1936, p.241) prevent them from possessing the attribute of liquidity.[12] In so doing, financial markets promote the separation of ownership and management (Keynes, 1936, pp. 150–1; Davidson, 1972, pp. 61–9; Bernstein, 1998).

In the absence of a liquid financial market '[t]here is no object in frequently attempting to revalue an investment to which we are committed' (Keynes, 1936, p. 151). If, therefore, capital markets were completely illiquid then there would be no separation of ownership and control. Once some volume of capital was committed, there could be no 'fast exit strategy' to use Bernstein's apt phrase, and therefore the owners would have an incentive to use the existing facilities in the best possible way no matter what unforeseen circumstances might arise. Perhaps then capital markets might behave and utilize capital more like the efficient markets of mainstream theory.

Financial fragility is usually associated with a boom where exuberant bullish sentiment dominates liquid financial markets. The result, it is claimed, encourages savers to provide funding that encourages entrepreneurial investors to spend inordinate sums on new investment projects that would not be justified by the maximum stream of quasi-rents that cooler heads would expect could be obtained in the future. The inevitability of this dominating bullish sentiment is the ultimate basis of Minsky 's financial fragility hypothesis. With an uncertain future, however, how can we ever know that the future stream of net quasi-rents cannot yield what in today's boom economy might be dubbed 'irrational exuberance' on the part of buyers of new capital facilities?

The basis for my optimism on this 'financial fragility' question lies in my (and Keynes's) view that policy makers, enlightened by *The General Theory* will pursue policies that induce a continuous near-full employment level of effective demand. As Keynes noted

> The remedy for a boom is not a higher rate of interest but a lower rate of interest. For that may enable the boom to last. The right remedy for the trade cycle is not to be found in abolishing booms and thus keeping us permanently in a semi-slump; but in abolishing slumps and thus keeping us permanently in a quasi-boom (Keynes, 1936, p. 322).

When fund managers' fear of the future increases, sufficient bear positions will begin to dominate financial markets. This excessive bearish desire to maintain one's liquidity can impede the production of new investment capital even when real resources are idle and therefore readily available to produce new real capital goods. Too great a demand for liquidity can prevent 'saved'(i.e. unutilized) real resources from being employed in the production of investment goods.

Unlike Old and New Keynesians, Keynes explicitly recognized that the introduction of sand in the wheels of liquidity-providing financial markets via a transactions tax is a double-edged sword. Keynes (1936, p. 160) noted that a financial transactions tax 'brings us up against a dilemma, and shows us how the liquidity of investment markets often facilitates, though it sometimes impedes, the course of new investment'.

Keynes explained the circumstances that create price stability in open financial markets when he noted that 'it is interesting that [asset price] stability ... and its sensitiveness ... should be so dependent on the existence of a variety of opinion about what is uncertain. Best of all that we should know the future. But if not, then, if we are to control the activity of the economic system ... it is important that opinions differ' (Keynes, 1936, p. 172). In other words, the 'best of all' possible worlds for financial market stability would be an ergodic (i.e. CEE) system where the future can be known with statistical reliability. Then the future can be reduced to actuarial certainty, i.e. 'we should know the future' and market efficiency would be assured as long as agents operated in their 'known' self-interest. If the system is nonergodic, however, then actuarial certainty and the possibility of rational probabilistic risk spreading, which New Classicals and New Keynesians claim is the essential characteristic of efficient financial markets, is impossible.

There are two possible solutions for maintaining stability and therefore liquidity in financial markets in a KNEE system. One is to encourage substantial numbers of market participants to hold continuously differing expectations about the future so that any small upward change in the market price brings about a significant bear reaction, while any slight downturn induces a bullish reaction. If it was possible to maintain a broad market with continuously different bull–bear expectations, then the effect would be to maintain spot financial market (resale) price trend stability over time and therefore the market will maintain a high degree of liquidity. In a nonergodic world, however, the expectations of either the bulls or the bears cannot be described as either rational (in the Lucas sense) or *ex ante* correct. Accordingly, market stability requires a continuous (and dense) spectrum of bull and bear expectations – the more participants in this spectrum, the less, *ceteris paribus*, volatility. To believe that there will always exist a broad diversity of opinions in a free financial market, however, is wishful thing.

Alternatively, society can provide an institution – a *creditable market maker* – who guarantees that spot price movements over time will always be orderly. This alternative is attainable via deliberate public policy that builds such a creditable institution.

VI IRRATIONAL EXUBERANCE AND BANDWAGON BEHAVIOR

Increased volume in rising financial markets is sometimes associated with the 'irrational exuberance' behavior once mentioned by central banker Alan Greenspan. What Greenspan was implying was that many similar thinking 'irrational' participants were suddenly dominating the market. The implication was that more rational persons would recognize the overvaluation of financial assets and push the price down. If there was a sudden swing in opinion that created a bandwagon consensus of a large market downturn, i.e. if there was abruptly a lack of broad market participants *with differing (not rational) expectations about the future*, then market liquidity would dry up until there was a sufficiently large decline in the market price to break down this bearish bandwagon mentality and restore a broad market with differing bull–bear expectations.

To avoid potentially large changes (swings) in the secular trend of market prices, a market maker institution with sufficient financial resources is required to assure market price stability. The market maker must announce that it will swim against any developing bandwagon consensus view of a change market psychology. It is 'bandwagon' movements in financial markets and not daily white noise volatility that causes the liquidity problems that are potentially destabilizing to the real economy.

A bandwagon effect occurs when a consensus view suddenly congeals regarding the possibility of a severe change in the future spot market price of financial assets. Accordingly, the bandwagon concept implies that there suddenly appears a preponderance of participants only on one side of the market (whether it be in the bull or bear position). In the absence of a market maker with sufficient financial asset resources to stem the bandwagon tide, enterprise becomes the bubble on the whirlpool of speculation (Keynes, 1936, p. 159). Keynes's whirlpool of speculation analogy is not a description of a daily (or hourly?) volatility around a long-term stable secular trend. Rather, disruptive speculation involves unpredictable sharp and profound changes in the *ex post* moving average secular trend due to anticipating market psychological swings.[13]

In our world of experience, conventional wisdom is that as long as it is expected that the psychology of the market is not changing there will be an inertia in the trend in market valuations.[14] It then follows that any policy that involves reducing if not eliminating the possibility of disruptive speculation in financial markets must involve building institutions that assure market participants that the 'correct' market psychology is a belief in a persistent, stable (moving average) trend in market prices over time.[15] If, for example, market participants believe that a market maker exists who can guarantee an unchanging spot market price (or changing only within very small boundaries) over time under preannounced and readily understood rules of the game in an orderly and well-organized market, then the existence of a creditable market maker, who takes an active market position, provides an anchor for 'market psychology'. For participants to believe in the market maker's ability to maintain the target spot (resale) price, however, the market maker must have a 'sufficient' inventory of money and that item that is being sold in the relevant market. In a foreign exchange market for example, this implies that the domestic monetary authority has creditability (and a sufficient inventory of foreign reserves or easy access to additional reserves) and has announced that it will use its reserves to maintain an orderly market at the 'proper' exchange rate. That is the explanation of why currency boards with reserves equal to the domestic money supply can fix the exchange rate (but not simultaneously the domestic interest rate).

To prevent disruptive speculation in any specific market, therefore, requires a buffer stock policy practiced by a market maker. If the majority of market participants believe in the market maker's ability to maintain sufficient buffer stocks to fix the spot price, the only speculators that would exist would then be fools, i.e. a small group of offsetting bulls and bears, who disagree with the vast majority of market participants but whose actions cannot affect market movements. Provided there is an effective buffer stock market maker, there should be no disruptive speculation and enterprise can continue at its current steady stream towards an unknown future.

NOTES

1.   Minsky is a founder of this financial fragility view. Although others often have classified Minsky as a Post Keynesian, he himself never accepted this classification, if by Post Keynesians one meant the followers of the Weintraub–Davidson branch of American Post Keynesianism. Minsky thought of himself allied with economists such as Tobin, Samuelson and Solow in the

mainstream Old Keynesian school and saw perpetual government deficits as an essential stabilizing policy. Minsky was against such Post Keynesian anti-inflation policies as incomes policies.
2. The 'lender-of-last resort' function however is designed precisely to prevent market disorder.
3. In other words, reliable information about the future exists today. Consequently, the future could be reliably predicted except that it is so costly to find (despite the Internet) and analyze today's existing information.
4. If we permit unlimited borrowing to finance asset holdings, then since the cost of borrowing is included in computing c, the portfolio manager will buy all available assets as long as they meet inequality (5.1). If fund managers are limited in their ability to borrow, then they will choose those assets with the highest values for inequality (5.1).
5. In a closed economy, if one holds money as a liquid store of value, then there is no future net income [$(q - c) = 0$], no capital gain or loss [$(p_s^{t1} - p_s^{t0}) = 0$], and no transactions costs [$T_s = 0$]. If bank demand deposit money provides some positive interest income each day that it is held, then the q in our equations would have to be redefined as daily income in excess of what could be earned by holding demand deposit (cf. Keynes, 1936, p. 167n). In principle nothing is lost by ignoring this complication.
6. The fear of this occurrence can, in itself, induce a panic among fund managers similar to that which occurs when someone yells 'fire' in a theater.
7. The underlying Walrasian equations ground out a secular trend of financial market prices that are Pareto-efficient.
8. Unfortunately, if asset holders are presumed to be wealth maximizers, then, as I have demonstrated (Davidson, 1997) this claimed differential impact of a transactions tax on short-term holders *vis-à-vis* long-term asset holders can be demonstrated to be mathematically incorrect.
9. Note that the term rational only makes sense in an ergodic world.
10. Especially durable goods where the expected stream of utility will be obtained in the future.
11. Stiglitz recognizes that market participants may want liquidity, i.e. may want to exchange money for securities or vice versa, and that such financial market exchanges (free of tax) are Pareto-efficient (Stiglitz, 1989, p. 104). With asymmetric information however, those possessing less information about the future are (by definition) trading 'based on *incorrect expectations*'. Consequently, Stiglitz suggests, it is not obvious that a transactions tax that will make trading on incorrect expectations more expensive lowers social welfare.
12. Keynes (1936, p. 241n) argues that the 'attribute of "liquidity" ' is by no means independent of the presence of two essential properties, namely that the asset is not reproducible via the employment of labor and it is not substitutable for the producible output of industry.
13. The dictionary defines secular as 'lasting from century to century'.
14. *Ex post* one can always calculate a moving average for any time series of market prices and, if one accepts what Samuelson has called the ergodic hypothesis, the resulting market valuation over time can be attributed to being determined by some underlying 'fundamental'.
15. In fact, all markets in liquid assets require the institution of one or more credible 'market makers' who follow some preannounced rules of the game to assure orderliness in the market. The more orderly the market maker keeps the market, the less the moment-to-moment volatility. It is only when market makers fail in their responsibility to maintain orderly markets that volatility becomes disorderly and speculation can have real disruptive effects.

REFERENCES

Arestis, P. and Sawyer, M. (1998) 'Keynesian Economic Policies for the New Millennium', *The Economic Journal*, **108**, 181–95.
Bernstein, P. (1998) 'Stock Market Risk in a Post Keynesian World' *Journal of Post Keynesian Economics*, **21**, Fall 1998.
Davidson, P. (1994) *Post Keynesian Macroeconomic Theory*, Edward Elgar, Cheltenham.

108   *Full employment and price stability in a global economy*

Davidson, P. (1997) 'Are Grains of Sand In the Wheels of International Finance Sufficient To Do The Job When Boulders Are Often Required?', *The Economic Journal*, **107**, 671–86.

Davidson, P. (1998) 'Volatile Financial Markets and the Speculator', *Economic Issues*, **36**.

Eichengreen, B., Tobin, J. and Wyplosz, C. (1995) 'The Case for Sand in the Wheels of International Finance', *The Economic Journal*, **105**, 162–72.

Hicks, J.R. (1977) *Economic Perspectives*, Oxford University Press, Oxford.

Keynes, J.M. (1936) *The General Theory of Employment Interest and Money*, Harcourt Brace, New York.

Keynes, J.M. (1937) 'The General Theory', *Quarterly Journal of Economics*, reprinted in *The Collected Writings of John Maynard Keynes*, vol. XIV, edited by D. Moggridge, Macmillan, London, 1973.

Levy Economics Institute of Bard College (1998), *Report*, **8**, no. 2.

Minsky, H.P. (1986) *Stabilizing an Unstable Economy*, Yale University Press, New Haven.

Stiglitz, J.E. (1989) 'Using Tax Policy To Curb Speculative Short-Term Trading', *Journal of Financial Services*, **3**, 101–113.

Summers, L.H. and Summers, V.P. (1989) 'When Financial Markets Work too Well: A Cautious Case for a Securities Transactions Tax', *Journal of Financial Services*, **3**, 163–88.

Tobin, J. (1974) 'The New Economics One Decade Older', *The Janeway Lectures on Historical Economics*, Princeton University Press, Princeton.

6. Financial market behavior: rational, irrational, or conventionally consistent?

Andrea Terzi[*]

In this chapter I discuss and compare three ways of modeling financial market behavior. More specifically, it is the purpose of this chapter to highlight the problems with two models of financial asset pricing, summarize how the understanding of the behavior of financial markets is changing and contribute to delineate a third alternative interpretation.

Modern financial theory considers market rationality its cornerstone hypothesis. This is that asset prices always equal the rational expectation of 'fundamentals', i.e. the best assessment of the present value of the asset that is currently justified by the foreseeable, expected impact of available information upon future profitability. Yet, private investors as well as international organization representatives and public officials from governments or central banks periodically express concerns that market prices may at times be dramatically at variance with economic rationale. This is the older, but still alive, view that markets have a tendency to generate bubbles, which finally burst. Markets producing booms and busts are a disturbing element that causes unwarranted instability, and eventually compels authorities to carry out, somewhat reluctantly, emergency rescues.

There is hardly anything new with economists facing the same set of empirical studies, and yet holding diverging views of how financial markets behave. One can, at the same time, bump into a passionate defense of the belief that 'the market interprets economic fundamentals with sufficient perceptiveness and speed,' and that a few unexplained anomalies do not justify the adoption of 'the caricature of the market popularized by Keynes' (Keane, 1991); or, into an equally firm statement of opposite sign, that 'the existence of significant inefficiencies suggests that fundamentals do not play as central a role in market performance as has been thought' (Fortune, 1991). In fact, a number of studies have challenged, from different perspectives, the validity of mainstream efficient market models; have argued against the belief that financial market prices are optimal estimates of the underlying investment value; and have revived Keynes's notion of 'conventional behavior' in the stock market.

In what follows, I provide an account of three distinct views of financial market behavior in a stylized fashion. Each is found in some form in today's debate, and is worth being carefully isolated. These views do not pretend to capture the specific ideas of selected authors, but rather aim at presenting three different paradigms: the *boom-and-bust* (irrationality) view, the *market rationality* view and a *conventional market consistency* view. The former two views are largely popular. The third view is emerging from a number of contributions that go beyond the dichotomy between rationality and irrationality. Though rooted in Keynes (1936, Chapter 12), this third view goes beyond the 'animal spirits' hypothesis, as it is commonly understood.

Each view will be considered with respect to its tenets about three closely related questions, yet useful to be listed and discussed separately: the variability, the predictability, and the significance of asset prices. The question of *variability* is the question of the theory of price formation in financial markets: one controversial issue is whether the movements of the prices at which investors trade assets reflect rational or irrational behavior, fundamentals or irrational fads. The question of *predictability* had long been confined to professionals, and has come under the spot of economic models with the empirical literature on market efficiency. Is there a scope for forecasting financial market prices? And, if so, what strategies have value? The question of *significance* is the question of what is the information content of market prices: do they provide a guide to private economic decisions as well as to economic policy? Or, rather, are prices influenced by the institutional and social context, and responsive to economic policy initiatives?

A convenient grid at the end of this chapter (see Figure 6.1, p. 120) summarizes each view's tenets on variability, predictability and significance of asset prices.

The three views here considered also differ with respect to the type of economic policy that best fit market behavior. It is today commonly understood that financial markets have become too important for economic policy makers for them to afford ignoring them when formulating their policies. But the extent to which policy ought to consider financial markets as a constraint is highly dependent on the way we understand how financial markets behave.

THE BOOM-AND-BUST PARADIGM

According to this well-known, popular view, the prices of financial assets not uncommonly diverge from their 'fundamental' value. Investors' decisions are not only driven by (rational) economic behavior: they are also driven by the moods and whims of human behavior. Changes in psychological sentiment drive prices at levels inconsistent with economic rationale. Deviations of price from value will, sooner or later, be corrected. Adjustment may happen gradually, thus creating market trends, or violently, through a sudden market reversal. Although asset prices reflect values in the long run, equality between price and value is the exception rather than the norm.

The boom-and-bust paradigm has prompted a variety of models. Kindleberger (1978) provides a historical account of speculative manias, and models market behavior using Minsky's financial instability hypothesis, where an initial human error sets herding behavior in motion that will finally end in panic. Ultimately, it is crowd madness that generates instability: as financier Bernard Baruch wrote in the introduction to Mackay (1932 [1841]) 'anyone taken as an individual is tolerably sensible and reasonable – as a member of a crowd, he at once becomes a blockhead'. In a different formulation, Robert Shiller (1984) has modeled markets being populated by non-optimizing investors, whose time and natural intelligence is limited, and where psychology matters.

There are two problems with markets that are periodically and inherently subject to the boom-and-bust syndrome. First, the significance of stock prices is sub-optimal: they do not fully express the fundamental value of the underlying assets. Second, large price swings result from cumulative movements of market sentiment, and when deviations from value are ultimately recognized, adjustment tends to happen violently. Thus, for reasons that remain largely unexplained, the market is inherently unstable: something called 'crowd madness', or 'people's irrationality', is the only *ex post* account.

The boom-and-bust view explains the variability of financial prices (see Figure 6.1) as a result of a mixture of influence of changing economic value (p^*) and an irrational element reflecting the uncontrolled moods of investors (m). It admits the possibility that when the market divorces from fundamentals, the most skilled and judicious investors (i.e. those who can recognize p^* from m) will take advantage of the opportunity to earn above average returns. Skilled traders who study the divergence of p^* from m ('fundamentalists'), or learn how to recognize patterns of m ('chartists'), will act to anticipate market movements. Within this paradigm, irrational investors (i.e. those who do not take advantage of the divergence of price from value) remain the majority: if this were not so, then the market would not be subject to the booms and the busts in the first place.

Until some 40–50 years ago, in the age of 'Keynesians' versus 'Monetarists', financial markets were seen through the lenses of this model: differences in views regarded the size and the duration of the deviation of price from value. Monetarists argued that the market selection process of profit-making speculators who stabilize prices in their own interest is enough to guarantee that prices remain substantially meaningful. In the Monetarists' free market, liberist, view, it was emphasized that speculation was not necessarily a bad word indicating 'casino' activities of dubious economic value: for Friedman the market must ultimately be driven not by the capricious, but rather by the best traders who anticipate future prices. This requires that the action of skilled speculators influences the market, and is thus beneficial as it compensates the disturbance of irrationality. This is Pareto's as well as Friedman's idea of the role of speculation. If markets operate freely and monopolistic and fraudulent behavior are prevented, then in the long-run competitive equilibrium only the skilled traders will, by natural selection, succeed, their profit being instrumental to assign financial market prices the best value.

'Keynesians', on the contrary, leant towards the idea that financial markets may divorce from true value significantly and for relatively long periods, thus markets should not be relied upon as meaningful pricing mechanisms. For 'Keynesians', and for English neoclassical authors like Marshall and Lavington, even professional speculators find it difficult and risky to go against the crowds. Rather than seeing booms and busts as being tempered by professional speculators who ultimately drive the market towards equilibrium, 'Keynesians' saw no automatic adjustment mechanism that guaranteed that periods of irrationality are short-lived, and that judicious investors beat the market on average, thus helping market prices to converge towards values. Such investors may just be harmless when facing crowd manias, and booms and busts may easily be amplified.

The speed of adjustment of price to fundamental value matters for economic policy. If deviations from value are excessive and long, with adjustment to fundamentals expected to happen in the distant future, then the significance of market prices is low and markets do not work as meaningful pricing mechanisms. To the extent that prices are not meaningful for business decisions, as well as for policy makers, some form of regulation or restriction of market activities is justified to avoid they become a source of instability. Economic policy would be justified if it tried to modify the process of price formation. Largely influenced by Keynes's image of capitalism as the 'by-product of the activities of a casino', and pointing towards the several historical anecdotes of financial bubbles, 'Keynesians' advised regulation of stock markets, and containment of financial flows. The financial sphere of the economy could only become a source of instability and problems. The sources of economic growth were to be found elsewhere in the real capital accumulation process.

In the 'Monetarist' perspective and to the extent prices converge sufficiently quickly towards value, financial markets play a role in the public interest: deviations from fundamental value are physiological, and will ultimately be corrected with no need of policy interference. Policy makers who attempt to stabilize markets may in fact send the wrong signals, which may trigger instability. For 'Monetarists', untimely policy actions could temporarily fool markets and generate excess reactions, for example by generating a bubble from excessively expansionary monetary policy until the burst of the bubble ends the attempt to influence the market outcome. In their view, the booms and the busts originate predominantly from active policy interference.

In any event, and whatever the causes of the market swings may be, the boom-and-bust paradigm provides a framework for studying financial market instability through price deviations from value. In *The General Theory* Keynes partly adopted the 'boom-and-bust' view when he argued that stock market evaluations (i.e. Keynes's 'speculation') may largely differ from entrepreneurial evaluations (i.e. Keynes's 'investment'), and thus markets may become a disturbing element of a true entrepreneurial environment. He even indicated drastic measures to tame the market monster, although he found them impractical. But the boom-and-bust view clearly pre-dates Keynes's analysis of the stock market:[1] it was a largely held belief at the time Keynes wrote his famous Chapter 12 that stock price movements have a psychological, as well as a rational, dimension. For example, Withers (1910) writes that stock 'price movements are chiefly a psychological question' and that 'there is nothing by which the valuation can be tested'. Considering that stock evaluation depends on public opinion (and anticipating one of Keynes's propositions in Chapter 12), he wrote, 'it is often dangerous to be too clever and far-seeing concerning the influences that may be expected to improve or depress prices'.

THE RATIONAL MARKET PARADIGM

The story of the emergence of the 'efficient market hypothesis' is well known. When the technological progress in data processing and computing opened up new possibilities for managing financial transactions and developing forecasting techniques, the question of predictability emerged in a different light. Statistical analysis of price series would reveal the pattern of market movements, be those of a wild psychological market behavior (the 'Keynesian' wing), or of a milder divergence from the long-term equilibrium value (the 'Monetarist' wing). Yet, academic researchers had hard trouble finding any fixed rules to predict those movements: published quantitative analysis seemed powerless to shed light on market price movements. Analytical tools failed to provide evidence of price series regularities that could be exploited: no clear signal of divergence of price from value, no formula to find 'market inefficiencies', no break into the 'secrets' of market behavior. Markets suddenly seemed much less predictable than had been thought. And yet, portfolio managers claimed they could earn higher than average returns consistently. Economists started asking whether professional investors could be overselling their forecasting abilities.

It is then that the liberist, free-market, wing of the 'boom-and-bust view' meets rational expectations. When market traders hold rational (homogeneous) expectations of future companies' earnings and discount them appropriately, trade must happen at prices that fully reflect everything traders know. Nobody will be in a position to earn abnormal returns from information arbitrage, because no piece of information of what is known publicly remains unexploited. So, price changes are determined by changes in 'fundamentals', and are thus unpredictable, because they only change when investors learned something new about the economy, the industries, and the companies, and this makes sense, being a stochastic phenomenon.

In fact, efficient market theorists do not want us to believe this 'strong' form of the hypothesis. As Fama (1991) put it, 'the extreme version of the market efficiency hypothesis is surely false'. Information translates into prices as a result of trade based on information, and if information and trading costs are positive, then prices must 'reflect information to the point where the marginal benefits of acting on information ... do not exceed the marginal costs'. There is value in overall market activity in that prices converge towards value, except for information and trading costs. Portfolio and fund managers' abilities to earn above average returns, however, are limited to that short time interval when asset prices respond to stochastically generated information. The movements of stock prices are explained by the rational reactions of investors to information, i.e. new evidence interpreted in the light of the best available knowledge. Rather than spending resources on forecasting techniques, portfolio and fund managers should focus upon the relationship between risk and return in an efficient market and learn how to manage 'optimal portfolios'.

If this model captures stock market price behavior, a number of consequences follow in terms of the questions of variability, predictability and significance (see Figure 6.1). Rational markets are markets where information is quickly incorporated into price. This means that the signal transmitted by the price is identical (except for information and trading costs) to the implications derived from available information: no information arbitrage is possible. Even what may at times appear as being ruthless price variability of markets, is in fact rational. As far as predictability is concerned, there is dubious scope in forecasting activity of financial market prices, since these respond quickly to new pieces of information that are, by definition, statistically unpredictable. In fact, superior performance, even by market professionals, is rare, and should be carefully measured. In terms of significance, stock market prices provide a meaningful guide to private economic decisions as well as to economic policy actions. Business decisions are optimally guided by stock market prices. If markets are rational, policy makers should listen to their message, and avoid trying to influence their performance towards unsustainable goals. Policy makers will better listen to markets, when it comes to take action, or markets will veto unsound decisions that cause a long-term welfare loss. Economic policy decisions should be taken in conformity with, and be respectful of, financial markets.

How did the rational market paradigm improve our understanding of market behavior? It is critical that we distinguish the attempts to measure market rationality from the empirical results in this literature. The former remains inconclusive: as Fama (1991) put it, 'precise inferences about the degree of market efficiency are likely to remain impossible'. The latter have largely centered on the statistical properties of stock price series and on the speed by which prices adjust in response to specific events, like newly released information about companies. In particular, 'event studies' have strengthened our beliefs in the hypothesis that stock market prices adjust quickly to 'information', but they remain inconclusive as to whether price adjustment is 'rational'. As Andersen (1983–4) and Glickman (1994) have argued, 'information' is not a well-defined concept in this literature.

Fama (1991) has candidly admitted that 'market efficiency per se is not testable': we cannot test whether price equals value if we cannot agree on how to model value appropriately. This did not prevent Fama from arguing that despite its logical and empirical problems, the market-efficiency hypothesis, with its related empirical literature, has improved our understanding of financial markets in one respect: stock prices adjust quickly to information, that is, private information among investment mangers is rare. An undoubtedly healthy demand for performance evaluation has indeed emerged as a result.

The rational markets literature has effectively spread the message that prices adjust quickly to the release of information, that opportunities to exploit a publicly available information advantage are rare, and investors should carefully monitor portfolio risk, rather than wasting resources into techniques aimed at exploiting differences between price and value. If divergence can hardly be detected and exploited, then there may not be any divergence at all, and market prices may just be varying with value, with no such thing as a mood, or fad, component.

TOWARDS A NEW PARADIGM: CONVENTIONAL MARKET CONSISTENCY

Where do we stand today? Each of the two explanations surveyed above give us a different key to the understanding of market behavior, and yet each seems to grasp only half of the picture, leaving some important questions unanswered.

The irrational markets view leaves it unexplained why investors trade assets at prices they should know differ from real value, and why they only later recover from madness. Why aren't booms recognized before they bust? Is not there a mechanism that stops overoptimism before it builds up and gets too dangerous? If markets do not behave rationally, how do they behave? And if we cannot trust markets, should markets be closed down, or, their activity be restrained to impose non-market equilibrium prices? Or, as it is the case when policy makers adopt this view (and assuming the case of euphoria followed by panic is more common than unjustified depression followed by adjustment), should central banks keep liquidity scarce to avoid markets embarking on 'asset inflation' followed inevitably by a crash? And, most importantly, is full employment hindered by the danger that financial markets may become intoxicated if economic growth is too strong?

The rational market view also leaves a number of questions open. If prices converge quickly, they must converge, by assumption, towards fundamentals, but the concept of fundamentals is ambiguous. Following Glickman (1994), this notion of fundamentals reflects an objective view of information as if it existed 'in the physical world awaiting discovery'. Indeed, every time we observe large swings in market prices that cannot be explained (not even *ex post*) by changing fundamentals, we are left with the (inconclusive) joint-hypothesis problem: should we accept the 'irrational hypothesis', i.e. investors have temporarily ignored fundamentals? Or the 'rational hypothesis', i.e. investors have followed fundamentals that nobody could predict (nor explain *ex post*) better than the market did?

The boom-and-bust and the rational market paradigms also share, surprisingly, some common ground. First, they share the central role of fundamental value within their analysis. The difference is that for the latter, adjustment takes place very quickly, or even instantly: prices are at all times determined by the existing set of available information, and are thus, at all times, equal to fundamental value. The former, although sharing the same conceptual framework of a homeostatic system where equilibrium is the vector of fundamental values, leaves the question of stability and speed of adjustment to the psychological attitudes of traders: although there exist well-defined fundamentals, traders have sometimes reasons for ignoring values, temporarily. So, in one case prices reflect immediately, and in the other with delay, the true value of underlying assets.

Second, both the rational and the irrational views assume that prices at which market participants are willing to hold assets reflect market participants' expectations (rational or irrational that they may be) that have formed exogenously to the market process. In rational markets, it is the information available to investors (no matter how slippery this concept may be) that determines the value of the asset: if expectations are rational, price will reflect value. In irrational markets, it is the psychology of investors that rules, at least until traders recover from their madness. And if investors' expectations are sensitive to changes in mood, price will reflect manias and panic. In both cases, however, price is determined by a process that remains external to the market, not differently from the way the general equilibrium price vector is determined by exogenously given preferences and technology.

A third common element can be found in the policy consequences. If markets are inefficient and inherently unstable, and in the absence of severe restrictions that limit their movements, economic policy should be carefully managed to avoid that the wrong signals awake the market 'monster'. If policy makers cannot muzzle markets with enough regulation, markets remain powerful in restricting the realm of decisions by policy makers. From both the rational and the irrational views, therefore, there follows an indication for policy makers that limit active policy, either because markets are 'too smart', and thus policy intentions backfire, or because they are 'too crazy', and thus they tend to amplify policy inputs. Either way, policy may be destabilizing.

A variety of authors, dealing with behavioral hypotheses in economics and in financial markets specifically, have challenged both paradigms. And a third paradigm is now under construction, where market equilibrium does not result from rational investors maximizing expected utility, nor from irrational deviations of individual behavior from a rational norm.

Differently from the former two views, comparison of market price with an objectively determined fundamental value is here meaningless, and convergence towards an equilibrium value is in fact convergence towards a conventionally-held belief. The difference between price and value is here blurred: one could argue that fundamental value no longer exists as a point of reference, or, alternatively, that any price may become fundamental value as long as traders agree to consider it such. Current market prices are not seen as something to be compared with value, but rather as something reflecting and transmitting signals to other traders.

Modern contributions pointing towards this direction include models of behavioral finance, herding behavior, information cascades, recognition of investors' different time-horizons, etc. The attempt that follows aims at indicating some distinguishing features of this 'conventional market consistency' approach.

(a) *Conformity*. Market participants' actions are not irrational, when 'irrational' is a decision to choose an option that is known not to be optimal in the choice context. Yet, this does not imply that investors can always solve an optimization problem in terms of expected utilities. Behavioral finance applies theories of human behavior from other social sciences. Among these theories, recently surveyed by Shiller (1998), prospect theory finds evidence that people show a distaste for uncertainty, and this explains human choices that would otherwise seem irrational. Since it is a fact that the success of a trading strategy in any speculative market depends, by definition, on how well one conjectures what the market will expect (and what capitalization rate will be applied) at some future date, then investors facing uncertainty will have an incentive to *conform* to others' behavior. Facing the task of estimating the prospective yields of stocks in the (theoretically infinite) future, as well as the best capitalization rate, investors can only adopt models as a result of a behavior of conformity of judgment. It is in the interest of investors that they converge towards a commonly held set of beliefs. Keynes's 'conventional' behavior maintains its validity. As Froot, Scharfstein and Stein (1992) have put it, in Keynes's view of the stock market a trader is better off if other traders act on the same information. The opposite is true in a rational market, where a trader is worse off if a vast number of traders study the implications of a single piece of information (because information arbitrage, and thus profit opportunity, is thereby reduced by competition). Judgment conformity is what Keynes called a 'convention', a socially accepted evaluation of companies' prospects, by its very nature precarious, and subject to sudden and potentially large revisions. The 'beauty contest' was Keynes's effective metaphor, meaning not that anything can happen, but, rather, that investors tend to herd collectively towards some generally accepted model of interpretation of information. But why would investors conform – the rational market representative keeps asking – when they 'know' that the market is wrong?

(b) *Double nature of price*. In fact, in an uncertain environment perceived by traders as being non-ergodic in Davidson's (1991) sense, traders never 'know' that the market is 'wrong'. They see prices not simply in comparison with their own (uncertain) estimation of value, but also as a source of information of what other market participants believe. Not simply a barometer that (more or less well) reflects news, price is a channel of communication among traders. Hicks's (1946) concept of elasticity of expectations, Hayek's (1937) notion of the market as a dynamic process, and George Soros's (1987) concept of reflexivity matter here. While for both the boom-and-bust and the rationality views price is the barometer of aggregate traders' beliefs, in the 'conventional market consistency' view market dynamics unfolds in a way that market prices are not simply signals of current market sentiment, but they also contribute to form market sentiment as well. The price observed is itself a determinant of the *position* of the demand schedule of financial assets. The idea that the greater the amount of information available, the closer the convergence between price and value, no longer holds here, since there exists no calculable market valuation that differs from market price. In fact, it is possible that more information will destabilize the current conventional equilibrium, as Banerjee (1993) has shown in a theoretical model.

(c) *Anchors*. The dynamics among traders lead them to converge, or conform, temporarily, around some commonly held belief, that functions as an 'anchor' for their expectations (Keynes's 'convention'). Market equilibrium price, that at which the bullish and the bearish sentiment offset each other, will settle not in response to exogenous information or moods, but rather *at* some commonly agreed anchor ($p^{@}$). Conventional market equilibrium is robust when the 'anchor' for investors' beliefs is strong. It becomes fragile when investors lose confidence in the common anchor, and starts searching for another. Birkhcandany, Hirshleifer and Welch (1992) have developed a model where it is optimal for individuals to disregard their own information and follow the actions of other traders, thus creating an informational cascade, a herding movement, that can be shattered violently by a small bit of information. One interesting empirical result is to be found in the empirical studies of the microstructure of financial markets, revealing the complexity of tick-to-tick trade. If price adjustment in financial markets were the result of an objective interpretation of information by all, or most, traders, then prices would adjust with large trading volume. Rather, as Goodhart and O'Hara (1997) explain in their survey, it is the rate of trade, not volume, that moves the market. Indeed, if traders mutually test their understanding of information in search of a conventional interpretation, and conform towards a price level that will be gradually defined in the process of convergence, this is what one would expect to find empirically.

But – the rational market representative keeps asking – can investors predict such changes? If they cannot, if nobody knows where the market will be heading next, then the market is efficient for all practical purposes.

(d) *Search for patterns*. Indeed, if there is no divergence from, or convergence towards some inherent value, then no pricing errors can be spotted, and no (more or less prompt) information arbitrage is possible. In this sense, the market is 'consistent'. And to the extent that prices converge towards a conventional equilibrium price, the market is 'conventionally consistent': market traders tend to conform, take the price as an information signal of other investors' sentiment, and search for a commonly held belief about future profitability.

The statistical characteristics of price changes under the 'conventionally consistent market hypothesis' are not obvious. In fact, there is no reason to expect that this complex search for an anchor generate purely random price changes. Under 'conventional market consistency', a fundamentalist is not someone who attempts to get a better estimate of value, but rather someone who conjectures how the commonly held convention will change next. And a chartist is not someone who traces the regularities of human irrationality, but rather someone who traces the dynamic internal process of conventional price formation.[2] Viewed from this perspective, resources spent on market forecasting are not necessarily the wastes that efficient market theory indicates. As Goodhart and O'Hara (1997) have argued, 'detailed analysis of the micro-structure of asset markets ... has given rise to a greater willingness to believe in the possibility of certain complicated regularities, and with it the possibility that some of the trading rules of technical analysis might be applicable'. If financial markets live in a non-ergodic environment, however, forecasting techniques are likely to succeed temporarily, not permanently: talented portfolio managers are ready to recognize the limitations of their models and develop new ones.

(e) *Conventionally consistent markets and economic policy.* What are the policy consequences of theories of market behavior? The boom-and-bust and the rational market paradigms leave little choice between introducing stringent controls of markets and let markets go their way. Conventional wisdom has it that governmental institutions or central banks should aim at well-specified stability objectives (such as price stability) without interfering with markets. Monetary policy is considered valuable when it adapts to the market view.

But if it is true that markets are stabilized by conventional, precarious behavior anchored to some form of long-term confidence, then policy makers should develop a different approach to financial markets. They should neither take market judgment as necessarily optimal (thus undergo market vetoes), nor try to correct market judgment through compensating actions (slowing down activity to cool off 'market exuberance', for example). If market stability depends on the strength of the anchor, then policy makers should carefully consider what consequences their decisions have on markets' beliefs, and what kind of action is required to strengthen investors' confidence.

In a conventionally consistent market, prices depend on the search for a conventional equilibrium. Rather than being subdued by market judgment, and hesitate giving markets a signal that differs from markets' expectations, policy makers may find a better option in providing markets with a stronger anchor. Markets need directions, and they have in several historical circumstances converged towards the political consensus, if this is sufficiently credible. Domestic public policy actions, as well as international institutions and agreements have an impact upon markets' perceptions. Rather than suggesting that markets are 'too crazy' or 'too smart', domestic and international institutions should make a greater effort in giving markets a better confidence in future stability.

	Boom-and-bust	Rational markets	Conventional market consistency
Variability	$p = p^* + m$ (value and mood)	$p = p^*$ (value)	$p = p^{@}$
Predictability	separate p^* from m	no information arbitrage	search for patterns
Significance	suboptimal	optimal	conventional

Figure 6.1   Financial market behavior

NOTES

* Funding from the Centro Nazionale delle Ricerche, Italy, is gratefully acknowledged.
1. Although Keynes is commonly attributed the 'animal spirits' hypothesis of stock market behavior (i.e., the view that stock markets are led by the subjective waves of misplaced optimism and overpessimism that drive investors' actions through booms and busts), he used the phrase 'animal spirits' in the different context of real (not financial) investment. Indeed, configuring Keynes's position as the 'animal spirits hypothesis', as Summers (1986) and Merton (1987) do, disregards Keynes's richer analysis, which may better be captured by the third view below.
2. See Terzi (1994).

REFERENCES

Andersen, T.M. (1983–84) 'Some Implications of the Efficient Capital Market Hypothesis', *Journal of Post Keynesian Economics*, Winter, 281–94.
Banerjee, A.V. (1993) 'The Economics of Rumours', *Review of Economic Studies*, **60** (2), 309–27.
Birkhcandany, S., Hirshleifer, D. and Welch, I. (1992) 'A Theory of Fads, Fashion, Custom, and Cultural Change in Informational Cascades', *Journal of Political Economy*, **100** (5), 992–1026.
Davidson, P. (1991) 'Is Probability Theory Relevant for Uncertainty? A Post Keynesian Perspective', *Journal of Post Keynesian Economics*, **5**, 129–43.
Fama, E.F. (1991) 'Efficient Capital Markets: II', *Journal of Finance*, **46** (5), 1575–617.
Fortune, P. (1991) 'Stock Market Efficiency: An Autopsy?' *New England Economic Review*, March–April, 17–40.
Froot, K.A., Scharfstein, D.S. and Stein, J.C. (1992) 'Herd on the Street: Informational Inefficiencies in Market with Short-term Speculation', *Journal of Finance*, **47** (4), 1461–84.
Glickman, M. (1994) 'The Concept of Information, Intractable Uncertainty, and the Current State of the "Efficient Markets" Theory: A Post Keynesian View', *Journal of Post Keynesian Economics,* Spring, 324–49.
Goodhart, C.A.E. and O'Hara, M. (1997) 'High Frequency data in Financial Markets: Issues and Applications', *Journal of Empirical Finance*, June, 73–114.
Hayek, F.A. (1937) 'Economics and Knowledge', *Economica*, **4** (N.S.), 33–54.
Hicks, J.R. (1946) *Value and Capital*, 2nd edn, Oxford: Oxford University.
Keane, S.M. (1991) 'Paradox in the Current Crisis in Efficient Market Theory', *Journal of Portfolio Management*, Winter, 30–4.
Keynes, J.M. (1936) *The General Theory of Employment, Interest, and Money*, New York: Harcourt Brace.
Kindleberger, C.P. (1978) *Manias, Panics, and Crashes: A History of Financial Crises*, London: Macmillan.
Mackay, C. (1932 [1841]) *Extraordinary Popular Delusions and the Madness of Crowds*, with a Foreword by Bernard Baruch, New York: Dutton.
Merton, R.C. (1987) 'On the Current State of the Stock Market Rationality Hypothesis', in *Macroeconomics and Finance: Essays in Honor of Franco Modigliani*, R. Dornbusch, S. Fisher and J. Bossons, eds, Cambridge, MA : MIT Press.
Shiller, R. (1984) 'Stock Prices and Social Dynamics', *Brookings Papers on Economic Activity*, **2**, 457–98.

Full employment and price stability in a global economy

Shiller, R. (1998) 'Human Behavior and the Efficiency of the Financial System',
Working paper no. 6375, National Bureau of Economic Research, January.
Soros, G. (1987) *The Alchemy of Finance*, New York: John Wiley and Sons.
Summers, L.H. (1986) 'Does the Stock Market Rationally Reflect Fundamental Values?',
Journal of Finance, **41** (3), 591–601.
Terzi, A. (1994) 'Is There an Economic (Non-Neoclassical) Explanation for the Magic
of the Technical Analysis of Stock Markets?', in *Employment, Growth and Finance:
Economic Reality and Economic Growth*, P. Davidson and J.A. Kregel, eds, Aldershot:
Edward Elgar.
Withers, H. (1910) *Stocks and Shares*, London: Smith, Elder.

7.   On banks' liquidity preference

Fernando Carvalho*

I   INTRODUCTION

Hyman Minsky once stated that '[t]he essential liquidity preference in a capitalist economy is that of bankers and businessmen ...' (Minsky, 1982, p. 74). Jan Kregel (1984/5, p.152), criticized '[s]upporters of endogenous and exogenous monetary creation' for not realizing that 'banks are also profit maximizers with liquidity preferences'. In fact, Keynes himself, in 1937 pointed out that an excess demand for money could raise interest rates 'if the liquidity preferences of the public (as distinct from the entrepreneurial investors) *and of the banks* are unchanged ...' (Keynes, 1937b, p.667, my emphasis)

The need to take banks' liquidity preferences in consideration seems perplexing for many. If money is *the* most liquid asset of an entrepreneurial economy and most of it is constituted by banks' own liabilities, demand deposits, why should banks have a liquidity preference and how would it be expressed? What could satisfy banks' liquidity preferences? An intuitive answer to the latter question, actually assumed in many models of the banking firm, would point to reserves created by the central bank. However, for those post Keynesians who believe that central banks freely supply reserves at a given interest rate the idea of banks being concerned with reserves to the point of actually having liquidity preferences may sound strange indeed since liquidity, in this sense, could be obtained in unlimited amounts. Under these conditions, why should any bank care whether they are short of liquidity?

Of course, this latter view, part of the horizontalist approach to money endogeneity, although very popular among post Keynesians, is not unanimously accepted in this school of thought. Money can be endogenous in different senses and for different reasons. The banks' liquidity preference approach suggests that banks pursue active balance sheet policies instead of passively accommodating the demand for credit. However, most of the authors who have used the concept did it in a rather suggestive manner, refraining from offering more rigorous definitions.[1]

The object of this chapter is to define and to explore the concept of banks' liquidity preference. To do so, it is divided into four sections, besides this introduction. As the expression *liquidity preference* may be, perhaps, vague for many, in section 2 I try to give a precise definition of the concept that is compatible with the post Keynesian notion of a monetary economy. Section 3 briefly examines how neoclassical theories of the banking firm dealt with a similar concern and how the question was first introduced more explicitly in the post Keynesian literature by Dymski in a 1988 paper published in the *Journal of Post Keynesian Economics*. Section 4 develops a liquidity preference approach to banks' decisions that draws on Keynes's views in the *Treatise on Money*, and on works by other post Keynesian economists. Finally, a concluding section summarizes the findings and identifies some of the implications of this theme to issues such as the debate on the endogeneity of money.

II LIQUIDITY PREFERENCE

Liquidity preference theory, in *The General Theory*, consists in the statement that 'the rate of interest at any time, being the reward for parting with liquidity, is a measure of the unwillingness of those who possess money to part with their liquid control over it. (...) [The rate of interest] is the 'price' which equilibrates the desire to hold wealth in the form of cash with the available quantity of cash...' (Keynes, 1964, p. 167). The reasons to have a preference for liquidity were discussed in chapter 15 of *The General Theory*: one needs money because one has expenditure plans to finance, or is speculating on the future path of *the* interest rate, or, finally, because one is uncertain about what the future may have in store so it is advisable to hold some fraction of one's resources in the form of pure purchasing power. These motives became known as transactions, speculative and precautionary motives to demand money.[2] On the other hand, in the world of *The General Theory* the quantity of money in existence is one of the 'ultimate independent variables ... determined by the action of the central bank' (pp. 246–7). Accordingly, most of the Keynesian literature took liquidity preference to mean demand for money and liquidity preference theory as a theory whereby *the* rate of interest is determined by demand and supply of money.

   This narrow interpretation of liquidity preference theory is debatable though. An alternative view is that it is a theory of asset choice. In fact, as Keynes emphasized in his debate with Ohlin in 1937, liquidity preference was a theory of choice between holding money idle and holding loans, being the role of the rate of interest to equalize the 'attractions' of both (Keynes, 1937a, p. 250). To restrict asset choices to only two possibilities, money and interest-paying bonds, however, is not essential to the theory but results from the aggregation structure adopted in *The General Theory*.[3] *The* interest rate was the reward for parting with liquidity in a model where there were only two classes of assets: short-term liquid capital-risk-free assets, called *money*, and long-term illiquid assets called *bonds*. One could, however, easily extend the argument for a situation where a greater variety of classes of assets existed, or at least so thought Keynes (Keynes, 1964, p. 137fn). In fact, such an extension was actually offered in Chapter 17 of *The General Theory* where a different, more detailed, aggregation structure is adopted.

In that chapter, Keynes argued that assets are characterized by four attributes: the generation of incomes to their possessor (profits, interest rates, dividends, rents, etc.), q; their carrying costs, c; their liquidity premia, l; and the appreciation or depreciation of their market values, a.[4] Wealth-owners would demand each class of asset according to their own-rate of interest, given by the expression:

$$a + q - c + l$$

For a given state of expectations, those assets with higher than average own-rates of interest would face heavier demand and their current market prices would rise, while the prices of those offering lower-than-average returns would fall. In equilibrium, asset prices would be such as to equalize those rates of return. In this approach, the theory presented in Chapter 13 of *The General Theory* should be seen as a special case in which there are only two assets, 'money' and 'bonds', and only one kind of risk is considered, the risk of capital losses on bond portfolios caused by a rise in interest rates. Liquidity preference would be reflected, in this highly aggregated model, in the terms of the tradeoff between monetary returns $(a + q - c)$ and the liquidity premium of money (l). The liquidity premium was defined as the rate of monetary returns one would be willing to forego in exchange for 'the power of disposal over an asset during a period [which] may offer a potential convenience or security' to its owner (p. 226). Of course, the 'power of disposal' of an asset is not measured only in terms of how easily one can sell a given asset but also in terms of how large a capital risk would have to supported when contemplating this possibility.[5] Money had a maximum liquidity premium because it could be disposed of very quickly and still be exempt of such losses in capital value. When there is uncertainty as to when a given portfolio may have to be disposed of a high degree of liquidity may be specially valuable, so asset-holders that value liquidity may be willing to pay a high premium, in the form of foregone returns, to remain liquid. Thus, a rise in perceived uncertainty, which increases the ex-ante value of being liquid, would imply, *for given stocks of each class of assets*, that liquidity preference would cause shifts of the demand schedules for the different types of assets, causing the prices of assets demanded mainly for their liquidity premium to rise compared to earning but less liquid assets. For reproducible assets, these shifts in demand should bring about changes in available stocks, favoring those in heavier demand.

Only a few of Keynes's followers realized what chapter 17 of *The General Theory* was about. Kaldor, in 1939, derived from the own-rates of interest model an approach to the problem of speculation, focusing on the relation between spot and forward prices of assets (Kaldor, 1980). Joan Robinson, on the other hand, was one of the first Keynesian economists to adopt the view of liquidity preference as a more general theory of asset demand. In her 1951 paper, *The Rate of Interest* (Robinson, 1979), Robinson offered a richer list of risks than that considered by Keynes in the *GT*, including inconvenience (or 'illiquidity in the narrow sense'), capital uncertainty, income uncertainty, and lender's risk ('that is, the fear of partial or total failure of the borrower').[6] Robinson argued: 'These qualities of the various types of assets are differently evaluated by different individuals ... The general pattern of interest rates depends upon the distribution of wealth between owners with different tastes, relatively to the supplies of the various kinds of assets. Each type of asset is a potential alternative to every other; each has, so to speak, a common frontier with every other and with money. Equilibrium in the market is attained when interest rates are such that no wealth is moving across any frontier. Prices are then such that the market is content to hold just that quantity of each type of asset that is available at the moment.'[7]

Thus, Chapter 17 shows that if the 'money-rate of interest ... is nothing more than the percentage excess of a sum of money contracted for forward delivery, e.g. a year hence, over what we may call the "spot" or cash price of the sum thus contracted for forward delivery[, i]t would seem ... that for every kind of capital-asset there must be an analogue of the rate of interest on money' (Keynes, 1964, p. 222). In this context, money is special because its own-rate of interest is stated to fall more slowly than the own-rates of other assets when their availability increases, for reasons that do not directly concern us here. What does concern us, on the other hand, is the proposition that assets are differentiated according to the *combinations* of monetary return and liquidity premia they offer, not because one of them is entirely liquid and others entirely illiquid. Liquidity is a matter of degree.

Post Keynesian economists, like Paul Davidson, combined both the Robinsonian and the Kaldorian strands of the 'Chapter 17 school' to present a model where speculation problems are treated within a model of capital accumulation (Davidson, 1978, Chapter 4). Post Keynesians have, in fact, taken this analysis one step further, approaching liquidity preference as a theory of *portfolio* choice, rather than a theory of *asset* choice. Although Keynes himself had not addressed the question of how individuals financed their purchases of assets, it was not very difficult for post Keynesian authors, like Minsky, to generalize the approach focusing on the tradeoff between monetary returns and liquidity premia to portfolio decisions as a whole, involving both the evaluation of assets and the decision to issue liabilities of various forms.[8] To do it, Minsky adapted the meaning of the own-rate of interest equation to relate to entire portfolios rather than to individual assets. In his 1975 book, Minsky redefines the asset attributes to make q to mean the rate of cash inflows generated by a given portfolio, c the mainly financial costs of carrying out that portfolio, that is the cash outflows implied in the liabilities issued to finance the holding of that portfolio, and l the proportion of the assets held by the individual in the form of money or of very liquid assets (cash-kickers). Among the latter group one could also include pre-agreed lines of backup finance supplied by financial institutions and the possibility of using assets as collateral to support debt issuance.

While Keynes emphasized the value of being able to change one's collection of assets if and when unpredicted events took place to define the attractiveness of liquidity, Minsky specialized his concept of liquidity in terms of the ability to pay one's debts. In particular, Minsky is concerned with the differences in time profiles of cash in and outflows resulting of a given list of assets and liabilities in one's balance sheet that may create the need to borrow or to liquidate assets in order to honor contractual commitments. Liquidity, thus, becomes the ability to honor contractually fixed cash outflow commitments. In this case, the 'power of disposal' over an asset is only one of the forms through which liquidity can be provided. The possession of an asset of a given class affects the liquidity of the portfolio to an extent that depends on how certain are the cash inflows it is expected to generate, on the 'power of disposal' over it, that is, its marketability, and on the possibility of becoming a collateral to debt issuance. Under these conditions, the 'liquidity premium' of a given collection of assets, that is, *the value recognized by the asset-holder* of the power of disposal over it, depends very much on the nature of the liabilities issued to finance its purchase. Committed cash outflows pattern the needs that will have to be satisfied by earnings from or by the sale of assets. Provided liquidity is understood in this broader sense, the fundamental statement of liquidity preference theory remains the same: an asset's expected rate of return has to be such as to compensate for its degree of illiquidity given the degree of uncertainty felt by asset-holders that determines its liquidity premium, that is, the amount of monetary returns agents are prepared to give up in exchange for that liquidity. Therefore, in equilibrium, how agents evaluate the illiquidity of a given asset is reflected in its expected rate of return[9] and, thus, in its current market value.

III LIQUIDITY PREFERENCE OF BANKS: MODELS OF DEMAND FOR RESERVES

One cannot say that neoclassical theory has been oblivious to the problem discussed here. In fact, orthodox models of the banking firm have traditionally focused on the problem of a bank's choice between a representative earning asset, *loans*, and a liquid asset, *monetary reserves*. Most commonly, these models take the amount of deposits made at the bank as given.

The standard formulation of the problem can be found in Baltensperger (1980). With its amount of deposits determined exogeneously, a bank has to choose between reserves, R, and loans, L, that are remunerated by the interest rate, r. X is the value of outflow of deposits, with probability $f(X)$. The cost of an eventual deficiency of reserves is the penalty rate p. To avoid this penalty, the bank constitutes reserves R, at the opportunity cost of rR. If the bank decides to lend, its losses are given by

$$\int p(X - R)f(X)dx$$

The optimizing solution is to divide its resources between loans and reserves in the proportion that is determined by the condition

$$r = p\int f(X)dx$$

Losses are then minimized when the marginal loss on keeping reserves, given by lost interest revenues at the left side, is equal to the expected value of losses for insufficient reserves, described at the right side. The choice of R affects the probability of a reserve deficiency.

The model can be generalized for a more diversified collection of assets and for different kinds of deposits. One can also extend it in another direction considering monopolistic elements that would allow the bank to have some control of the amount of deposits and, thus, on its size. Finally, one can also work with other kinds of costs, such as operational costs. Generally solutions will consist in determining collections of assets and types of deposits that respect the condition that marginal returns are equalized for the various assets being held and are also made equal to the marginal costs involved in the financing of that position.[10]

A general feature of these models is that liquidity preferences are reflected in the demand for reserves (actually free reserves) to cover for possible net deposit outflows, and are determined by the costs of carrying insufficient reserves and by the probability of facing higher-than-average outflows.

A similar concern was introduced in the post Keynesian literature by Dymski (1988). The focus of that paper was 'on banks, which are obliged to supply liquidity on demand while making new loans and funding loan contracts of lengthy duration' (p. 511). Dymski's model goes beyond standard neoclassical theory of the banking firm in many respects. Deposits are no longer given but, at least in part, result from the loan decisions of banks themselves. This makes the model more realistic but does not essentially change the nature of the decision problem for banks: '[t]he more credit banks create to satisfy loan demand, the fewer funds are available for redistribution to meet depositor demands for liquidity' (p. 516). Dymski's approach is also more flexible in that he considers both the possibility of lending out excess reserves and of borrowing in the interbank reserves market. The explicit consideration of calendar time, however, in his model does not seem to represent any fundamental change when compared to Baltensperger's treatment, whereas the bank faces a similar challenge as Dymski's bank: the decision as to how much to lend in the present, given future demands for cash by depositors that cannot be presently known with certainty.

Dymski's 1988 paper triggered a debate in the JPKE that centered, however, mainly on issues other than the banking firm itself.[11] From the point of view being offered in this paper, however, the main limitation of that work may be its view of the choices open to banks, still focusing on two alternative assets, each endowed with exclusive attributes. A liquidity-preference-of-banks approach should, in contrast, stress choices of a different nature.[12]

IV LIQUIDITY PREFERENCE OF BANKS: A POST KEYNESIAN APPROACH

The emphasis on the dichotomy reserves versus loans seems to be an inadequate starting point for two main reasons. Empirically, the accumulation of reserves does not seem to be, or to have been, the way in which liquidity needs are actually satisfied. Keynes, in the *Treatise on Money*, had already observed that, 'save in exceptional circumstances, all banks use their reserves to the hilt; that is to say, they seldom or never maintain idle reserves in excess of what is their conventional or legal proportion for the time being' (CWJMK, Volume 6, p.47). The 1930s seemed to have been of those 'exceptional circumstances'. Morrison (1966) had shown that American banks did accumulate excess reserves during the depression, displaying that kind of behavior that Friedman called 'absolute liquidity preference'.[13] Other cases of excess reserve accumulation during periods of heightened uncertainty are known.[14] In fact, Keynes himself had analyzed one of these situations in detail in his youth.[15]

The second, and most relevant, point was made by Keynes in the following-up to that quotation above:

> The problem before a bank is not how much to lend ... *but what proportion of its loans can be safely made in the relatively less liquid forms* (p. 47, my emphasis).

According to Keynes:

> what bankers are ordinarily deciding is, not *how much* they will lend in the aggregate (...) but in *what forms* they will lend – in what proportions they will divide their

resources between the different kinds of investment which are open to them. Broadly there are three categories to choose from – (i) bills of exchange and call loans to the money market, (ii) investments, (iii) advances to customers. As a rule, advances to customers are more profitable than investments, and investments are more profitable than bills and call loans; but this order is not invariable. On the other hand, bills and call loans are more 'liquid' than investments, i.e. more certainly realisable at short notice without loss, and investments are more 'liquid' than advances (CWJMK Volume 6, p. 59, Keynes's emphases).

The point being made is that, in accordance with the generalized liquidity preference approach being proposed here, one should not think of dichotomies between liquid versus illiquid assets, but of *degrees of liquidity*, associated to the various assets at the reach of banks. The question is not how to compensate the accumulation of earning but illiquid assets with the holding of completely liquid assets that do not pay anything to their holder. These are not the choices considered by banks (in fact, by anybody), at least under normal conditions.

Keynes argues that 'bankers are faced with a never-ceasing problem of weighing one thing [profitability] against another [liquidity]'. Finally, it is important to notice that these evaluations change according to the degree of uncertainty felt by bankers: '[w]hen, for example, they [bankers] feel that a speculative movement or a trade boom may be reaching a dangerous phase, they scrutinise more critically the security behind their less liquid assets and try to move, so far as they can, into a more liquid position' (*ibid*. pp. 59–60). The expression 'liquidity preference' was still to be created, but one can hardly find a more vivid explanation of its influence on banks' decisions.

Although Keynes clearly recognized that, *for the banking system as a whole*, the total amount of demand deposits were largely a result of the banks' own decision to extend loans, the situation would be more complex when dealing with individual banks, since any given bank could not be sure that the deposits it created would not be diverted to another bank.[16] In fact, according to the liquidity preference of banks' approach, one should expect the amount *and type* of liabilities to be issued by a bank to be jointly determined with the amount and type of assets being purchased. This, however, is certainly a very difficult decision to model when we cannot rely on some simple criterion like the equality between marginal revenues and marginal costs, for example.

If, for the moment, we take demand deposits to be the only type of liabilities issued by a bank (Keynes also mentions savings deposits), its balance sheet should be as follows:

Assets	*Liabilities*
Bills of exchange/Call loans	Demand deposits
Investments	
Advances to customers	

Liquidity preference of banks would be reflected, in this case, in the specific basket of assets chosen by the bank. Given the nature of demand deposits, as Minsky once observed, the bank had to act as if all its liabilities had to be refinanced every day: 'they are virtually refinancing their position daily by offering terms that are attractive to their depositors' (Minsky, 1982, p. 140). Its choices as to how much liquidity it would keep, by sacrificing higher earnings, would depend on its assessment of the risks of depositors being willing to cash those liabilities. Any demand from depositors would be satisfied through one or more of the four following possibilities: the proceeds of earning assets; the sale of earning assets; the issuance of new debt; or the depletion of liquid reserves. If one excludes for the moment the creation of new debts, since it is not reasonable to assume that a bank could pay back deposits or fulfill payment orders in favor of other banks by creating new deposits, we see that there are in fact two choices to generate cash inflows: the incomes generated by the earning assets or the proceeds from the disposal of assets.[17] If incomes inflows generated by assets are not enough to pay for the deposits being lost, some assets will have to be liquidated. It is in anticipation of this possibility that banks should be willing to partially forego profitability in favor of liquidity when choosing assets to purchase. Now, the 'power of disposal' over an asset becomes its most important quality. Therefore, the composition of the asset side of the balance sheet will depend on the expectations of bankers as to the possibilities of such contingencies taking place in which assets have to be liquidated. As already observed in section II, the *value* this power of disposal over an asset assumes in the eyes of the banker depends on the nature of the bank's liabilities. In this case, since we are only considering demand deposits, a potentially very risky kind of liability, liquidity premia associated to liquid assets should be very high.

If uncertainty increases (that is, the degree of confidence on one's expectations decreases), liquidity preference will rise and asset demands will be biased toward more liquid but less profitable assets. In this case, the supply of credit advanced to customers should decline, even though they are not necessarily replaced by reserves in the balance sheet. Therefore, liquidity preference of banks determines the value, that is, the market price of those assets that can be purchased by them. These market prices depend on the present value of expected monetary returns from each class of assets, on their liquidity premia and on the available stocks of each asset. One important qualification to be made is that, in the case of banks, advances to customers can be increased when their own-rates of interest are higher than those of other assets. Nevertheless, that advances to customers can be easily 'reproduced' does not invalidate in the least the scheme, quite the opposite. It is the situation in which this kind of asset is in heavier demand that its value goes up, inducing the bank to purchase more of these assets, thereby extending credit.

Summing up the argument so far, for a given state of expectations, that includes the prospective returns of each class of assets, the degree of confidence on those calculations and an evaluation of the power of disposal of each type of assets, and their liquidity preferences, on one hand, and the nature of their liabilities, on the other, banks will not ('save under exceptional circumstances') choose between idle reserves and loans, but will distribute their investments between the various kinds of assets and determine their prices. *For a given state of expectations, banks' liquidity preferences will determine the desired profile of the assets they purchase and their prices, that is, the rate of returns each type of asset must offer to compensate for their degree of illiquidity.*

Thus, we can read banks' liquidity preferences from their balance sheets. In Keynes's times attention was mainly given to the types of assets being purchased, given their assumed narrow choice of liabilities.

Besides the risks represented by their potential volatility, bank deposits are (or were) also usually subjected to reserve requirements that increase the costs of these liabilities to banks, particularly in periods of tight money when those requirements can be raised by the monetary authorities. In the liquidity preference approach, the same kind of concerns that explains how investments are distributed among the different categories of assets may lead to a diversification of sources of funds as well. Thus, liability management practices developed under the stimuli provided both by attempts by central banks to restrain deposit expansion in inflationary periods and by the creation of substitutes for demand deposits by competing institutions that attracted resources away from banks. In fact, *liability management* is as natural an element of the liquidity preference approach to the banking firm as *asset management* was in Keynes's original description. Minsky's well-known classification of investors as hedgers, speculators or Ponzi shows how holding a given collection of assets could be financed through different combinations of financial costs and risks.[18] The central insight remains that liquidity preferences are read in the profiles of balance sheets and the values of each class of assets. Generally, if safety is a factor, the profile of debts issued by an agent has to have a crucial influence on his decision as to what combination between expected returns and risks to buy.

In this case, we could consider a richer balance sheet structure, as in the following example:

Assets	*Liabilities*
Cash	Demand deposits
Treasury bills	Time deposits
Bills of exchange/call loans	Interbank borrowing
Interbank loans	
Longer-term securities	
Loans to customers	

The most important difference between this balance sheet and that presented earlier is the variety of liabilities types in this case. From the liquidity preference standpoint, we have a similar choice to what we have defined before, with signs reversed. We can still think of a tradeoff between interest rates and safety. Now, however, interest rates measure directly how much the bank is willing to pay to reduce the possibility of being surprised by an untimely demand for payment from its lenders, including depositors.

The liquidity preference approach would naturally explain the *balance sheet strategy*, rather than choices of individual assets or liabilities, according to the perception of risks and profit opportunities by banks. As in the preceding example, above, the supply of bank credit, in this approach, is not passively determined by borrowers. It would rather depend on each bank's assessments not only of the specific credit risks each borrower represented, but also on the nature of the liabilities issued by the bank, the need to be ready to meet the contractual cash outflows even under adverse conditions and the own-rates of interest of the other classes of assets.[19] Assets have to be evaluated not only by their expected returns, but also by their liquidity premia, the latter meaning, now, both its marketability and its potential use as collateral in debt-issuance by the bank.[20] One should notice, in any case, that having dated liabilities in its balance sheet reduces the uncertainty for the bank as to cash outflows, reducing the *value* of liquidity as attribute of assets. In this case, one should expect that banks would invest more in profitable assets and less on those assets whose main quality is liquidity.

Finally, it is important to notice that the 'power of disposal' over a given asset can vary not only because of expected changes in market conditions but also because of 'structural', permanent, factors. As Kaldor (1980) and Davidson (1978) have shown, an asset's liquidity is largely determined by the permanent characteristics of its markets. Liquidity is not a natural quality but results from the creation of specific market institutions. The creation of a market is costly and viable markets are those sufficiently dense to allow those costs to be shared by those who operate in it. Density of markets depends on features of the commodity that is being transacted. In particular, standardization is a crucial requirement because it makes all items close, if not necessarily perfect, substitutes for one another. Standardization, thus, allows markets to be created increasing the liquidity premium of that commodity and altering its value in the eyes of the investor. If, for some reason, expected returns from a given class of assets begin to fall, it is possible to keep it attractive to investors if its liquidity characteristics are also altered. The success of securitization, that is now reaching bank loans, is an example of this kind of change. In fact, securitization changes the nature of the operation performed by the bank. Its liabilities are reduced so the risks the bank is subjected to are lowered. It is all made possible because the loan that is securitized becomes very liquid; in fact it becomes so liquid that the bank can simply sell it right away. Again, balance sheet profiles should reflect these structural changes in liquidity premia.

Among the recent structural changes that have affected banks' choices as to liquidity and expected return perhaps the more important is the rapid development of derivatives markets that is in fact still going on. To a large extent, derivatives markets satisfy a similar demand as secondary markets. They are devices that allow a reduction of the risks associated with any specific asset position. Since any portfolio decision implies a specific bet on expected returns and identifiable risks any bank balance sheet strategy can be portrayed and analyzed according to options theory, including, when it happens, the accumulation of reserves, as Kregel (1997) has shown. Options theory, still beginning to be accepted in larger circles, is amply compatible with the liquidity preference approach presented here.[21]

V   CONCLUSIONS AND IMPLICATIONS

The banking industry has been undergoing a process of deep transformation. The classical type of institution that limited itself to create demand deposits and made short-term loans to finance working capital seems to be either disappearing or being gradually confined to a marginal and secondary role in the financial industry. The traditional approach to the banking firm that phrased its decision problem in terms of deposits, loans and reserves is disappearing with it, if it was ever entirely adequate.

Banks, however, are changing, not disappearing (Kregel, 1997). Liquidity preference theory, as a theory of balance sheet determination, allows us not only to portray banks' decision problems in a more precise way but also to understand the nature of the changes that are taking place in this industry. Its starting point is that every asset offers a mix of expected monetary returns and a liquidity premium in opposition to the traditional approach in which an asset gives only monetary returns and the other only liquidity. On the other hand, each mix of liabilities implies a different combination of costs of servicing debts and of risks of being unable to roll them over if needed. Liquidity preference determines which mix of assets and liabilities is acceptable to each individual agent, be it a person or an institution, like a bank. Therefore, liquidity preferences will be shown in the collection of assets an agent chooses, their market values and his/her collection of liabilities. So a bank's decision problem is how to distribute the resources they create or collect among these different items that offer specific combinations of expected monetary returns and liquidity premia, instead of just choosing between reserves and loans or of passively supplying whatever amount of credit is demanded. *Banks' liquidity preferences describe their balance sheet strategies, not their demand for money, not even their demand for outside money. On the other hand, banks with liquidity preferences will not accommodate passively the demand for credit but will compare expected returns and liquidity premia of all purchasable assets.*

There are many important implications to be drawn from this approach. Two of them will be mentioned in this concluding section. First, it offers a possible explanation for the cyclical turning points that transform an expansion into a contraction of the economy. A booming economy requires a growing concentration of a bank's investment on 'advance to customers', to use Keynes's language. This is made easier by the fact that until the last moments of a boom safety is not a good in heavy demand, neither by borrowers nor by banks, since in a rapidly growing economy practically any project seems to be potentially successful. On the other hand, its lower liquidity, when compared to more liquid investments, such as call loans, bills, etc., is compensated by its higher profitability. As Minsky and Keynes show, this implies a growing exposure of banks to illiquidity risks. Even if the monetary authorities do not take any measures to force banks to reduce their exposure, a limit will be reached when more liquid assets become so rare in banks' balance sheets that they will try to redress the balance between returns and liquidity. A turning point in the economy will result from the reduction or deceleration in the growth rate of credit resulting from the reshuffling of assets in the balance sheets of banks. A financial crisis ensues when banks try to retreat to more liquid positions.[22]

A second area where this approach has some important implications is, as Kregel suggested in his 1984/5 paper, the question of the endogeneity of money. A large part, perhaps most, of the literature about the endogeneity of money focus their argument on the power of the central bank to resist banks' demand for reserves to validate the latter's previous creation of deposits. In particular, the contenders take the debate to be defined in terms of what instruments, if any, are really under the control of the monetary authority, the monetary base (for the 'verticalists') or the interest rate (for the 'horizontalists'). To consider the liquidity preference of banks allows us to discuss whether or not money is endogenous independently of the different question of which variable is controllable by the central bank. Endogenous variables are those whose values are determined in the solution of a model. A liquidity preference approach to banks' decisions has money, that is, deposits determined in the model, thus an endogenous variable, because money is created as a result of private decisions of banks, independently of whether the central bank controls the monetary base or the interest rate. In fact, this approach allows us not only to consider money as largely endogenous (which does not mean a 'horizontalist' view) but also to follow the impact of banks' decisions on the economy. Using again Keynes's language, when banks decide to make call loans or to buy bills or other securities (what Keynes meant by 'investment'), they are directing the deposits they create or control to the *financial circulation*. When making 'advances to customers' they are pouring deposits into the *industrial circulation*. Only the latter is directly related to the demand for goods. The first two categories direct money to the circulation of assets that have no definite relation to the demand of goods.[23] Thus, to consider banks' liquidity preferences allows us to go further than the mere discussion of *how much* money is created to discuss what proportion of it is directed to support income-generating activities, which is a dichotomy that the endogenous/exogenous money debate seems to have unfortunately ignored. A fuller exploration of this point, of course, is not possible in the limits of this paper.

NOTES

[*] This chapter was prepared for the Fifth International Seminar on Post Keynesian Economics, Knoxville (TN), June 1998. The author is grateful to the participants of the Money and Financial Systems Research Project at the Institute of Economics/UFRJ. I also want to thank my friend and colleague Fernando N. Costa for raising the question that led me to write this paper. Comments by Gary Dymski, Steve Fazzari, Nina Shapiro and Philip Arestis were most welcome. Financial support from the Brazilian National Research Council (CNPq) is gratefully acknowledged. E-mail: carvalho@ie.ufrj.br

1. See, for instance, besides Kregel's paper already quoted, Dow (1996), Dow and Dow (1989), Chick (1983), Chapter 12. I have also used the idea in Carvalho (1992) and (1995), in both occasions suggesting the usefulness of the concept rather than working it out. Kregel (1997) goes much beyond the suggestion to consider bank balance sheet strategies but presents his argument mostly in terms of options theory rather than liquidity preference, although these may be seen as alternative ways of presenting similar views rather than opposing approaches.

2. Keynes later added a fourth motive to demand money, the finance motive, in anticipation of discretionary spending, like investment spending. See Keynes (1937a, 1937b).

3. A detailed examination of Keynes's choices as to aggregate structures given in Leijonhufvud (1968).

4. All these attributes are measured by a rate in which the denominator is the current spot price of the asset.

5. 'The power of disposal over an asset involves, in a monetary economy, the expectation of being able to exchange the asset for the medium of exchange cheaply and readily in a continuous spot market at money price which is never very different from the well-publicized spot prices of the last few transactions. For any asset which is simultaneously the medium of exchange and the store of value, the power of disposal must, by definition, be the greatest' (Davidson, 1978, p.62).

6. Robinson (1979, p.140).

7. Robinson (1979, p.143). Kahn, three years later, also took liquidity preference of interest rates to mean a more general asset pricing theory. His argument, however, was closer in form to Keynes's, focusing margins of indifference between assets of different maturities in terms of capital risks. See Kahn (1972, p.73).

8. As Minsky put it: 'Each economic unit makes portfolio decisions. A portfolio decision has two interdependent facets. The first relates to what assets are to be held, controlled, or acquired; the second relates to how the position in these assets – i.e., their ownership or control – is to be financed.' According to Minsky, Keynes's discussion of these decisions in chapter 17 was 'flawed because he [did] not explicitly introduce liability structures ...'(Minsky, 1975, pp.70 and 79). I thank my graduate student Gustavo Braga for locating these quotations.

9. That is the ratio between expected quasi-rents net of carrying costs and capital gains and the market price of the asset.

10. Besides Baltensperger (1980), another useful reference is Santomero (1984), both of them being surveys of existing models to those dates.
11. See Wray (1989) and Dimsky (1989).
12. Actually, Dimsky, in his paper presented to the last post Keynesian seminar, pointed out that his 1988 model could be seen as obsolete in important respects, mentioning specifically the treatment of liquidity restrictions on the behavior of banks. See Dimsky (1996).
13. In fact, Morrison's work was originally a PhD thesis written under Milton Friedman's supervision.
14. In the second semester of 1995, a banking crisis in Brazil was generally seen as highly probable. Because of that, banks with excess reserves refused to supply interbank loans to institutions that were considered risky. As a result, 'liquidity puddles' were formed and forced the Central Bank to reactivate rediscount windows that had fallen into disuse in the recent past. For a discussion of bank difficulties in that period, see Carvalho (1998).
15. According to Keynes, right after the outbreak of World War I, business in the London exchange was interrupted given the international nature of most of its deals. Brokers could not honor their contractual debts, particularly with banks. The Bank of England tried to relieve the situation by injecting liquidity into the banking system, but banks chose to retain this increased liquidity instead of circulating it to other institutions. See CWJMK, Volume 11, pp. 100 ss.
16. According to Keynes, 'deposits are created either against the receipt of cash or a payment order from an individual depositor or when it purchases an asset paying for it by establishing a credit against itself. In both cases the bank creates the deposit' (CWJMK, Volume 5, p.21). Keynes added that 'the rate at which the bank can, with safety, actively create deposits by lending and investing has to be in a proper relation to the rate at which it is passively creating them against the receipt of liquid resources from its depositors' (*ibid.*, pp.21–2). What is important, then, is '[e]very movement forward by an individual bank weakens it, but every such movement by one of its neighbor banks strengthens it; so that if all move forward together, no one is weakened on balance. Thus the behaviour of each bank, though it cannot afford to move more than a step in advance of others, will be governed by the average behaviour of the banks as a whole ...' (*ibid.*, p.23). This question was explored in some detail during the 21 February 1930 session of the MacMillan Committee of which Keynes took part. See CWJMK, Volume 20, pp. 87 ss.
17. Keeping in mind that liquid assets include not only cash itself but also 'cash-kickers'.
18. But Minsky reminded us that a 'commercial bank cannot be a hedge-financing unit' (Minsky, 1986, p.207).
19. As Dow (1996) stated, the decision to supply credit may depend on the 'mood' of the financial institutions when deciding whether or not collaterals are acceptable. Dow and Dow (1989) had already stressed that the choice between advances to customers and liquid assets influenced the supply of credit.
20. This latter meaning of liquidity is particularly important with the growth of repurchase operations in recent times.
21. The increasing complexity of ways and means to satisfy liquidity preferences of banks is described in Federal Reserve Bank of New York (1990).
22. As in the classical discussion by Keynes (Keynes, 1963, Part II, Chapter 7), 'The consequences to the banks of the collapse of money values'.
23. The deflationary influence of a diversion of deposits from the industrial circulation to the financial circulation is mentioned many times in the *Treatise on Money* (CW JMK, Volume 6, Chapters 23 and 37).

REFERENCES

Baltensperger, E. (1980) 'Alternative approaches to the theory of the banking firm', *Journal of Monetary Economics*.

Carvalho, F. (1992) *Mr Keynes and the Post Keynesians*, Cheltenham: Edward Elgar.

Carvalho, F. (1995) 'Post Keynesian developments of liquidity preference theory', in P. Wells (ed.), *Post Keynesian Economic Theory*, Boston: Kluwer.

Carvalho, F. (1998) 'The real stabilization plan and the banking sector in Brazil', *Banca Nazionale del Lavoro Quarterly Review* **51**, (206), September, 291–326.

Chick, V. (1983) *Macroeconomics After Keynes*, Cambridge, MA: MIT Press.

Davidson, P. (1978) *Money and the Real World*, 2nd edition, London: Macmillan.

Dow, A. and Dow, S. (1989) 'Endogenous money creation and idle balances', in J. Pheby (ed.), *New Directions in Post Keynesian Economics*, Cheltenham: Edward Elgar.

Dow, S. (1996) 'Horizontalism: a critique', *Cambridge Journal of Economics*, **20**, 497–508.

Dymski, G. (1988) 'A Keynesian theory of bank behavior', *Journal of Post Keynesian Economics*, **10** (4), Summer 499–526.

Dymski, G. (1989) 'Keynesian versus credit theories of money and banking: a reply to Wray', *Journal of Post Keynesian Economics*, **12** (1) Fall, 157–63.

Dymski, G. (1996) 'Banking in the new financial world: from segmentation to separation?', Manuscript.

Federal Reserve Bank of New York (1990) Funding and liquidity. Recent changes in liquidity management practices at commercial banks and securities firms, Staff Study.

Kahn, R. (1972) 'Some notes on liquidity preference', in *Selected Essays on Employment and Growth*, Cambridge: Cambridge University Press.

Kaldor, N. (1980) *Essays on Economic Stability and Growth*, New York: Holmes and Mayer.

Keynes, J.M. (1937a) 'Alternative theories of the rate of interest', *The Economic Journal*, June, 241–52.

Keynes, J.M. (1937b) 'The 'ex-ante' theory of the rate of interest', *The Economic Journal*, December, 663–9.

Keynes, J.M. (1963) *Essays in Persuasion*, New York: Norton.

Keynes, J.M. (1964) *The General Theory of Employment, Interest and Money*, New York: Harcourt, Brace, Jovanovich.

Keynes, J.M. (1971/1983) *The Collected Writings of John Maynard Keynes*, London: Macmillan. Volumes are referred to as CWJMK, followed by volume number.

Kregel, J. (1984/5) 'Constraints on the expansion of output and employment: real or monetary', *Journal of Post Keynesian Economics*, **7** (2) Winter, 139–52.

Kregel, J. (1997) *The Past and Future of Banks*, Manuscript.

Leijonhufvud, A. (1968) *On Keynesian Economics and the Economics of Keynes*, New York: Oxford University Press.

Minsky, H. (1975) *John Maynard Keynes*, New York: Columbia University Press.

Minsky, H. (1982) *Can 'It' Happen Again?*, Armonk: M.E. Sharpe.

Minsky, H. (1986) *Stabilizing an Unstable Economy*, New Haven: Yale University Press.

Morrison, G. (1966) *Liquidity Preferences of Commercial Banks*, Chicago: The University of Chicago Press.

Robinson, J. (1979) *The Generalization of The General Theory and Other Essays*, London: Macmillan.

Santomero, A. (1984) 'Modeling the banking firm', *Journal of Money, Credit and Banking*, November.

Wray, L.R. (1989) 'A Keynesian theory of banking: a comment on Dymski', *Journal of Post Keynesian Economics*, **12** (1) Fall, 152–6.

8. Financial globalization and housing policy: from 'Golden Age' housing to 'Global Age' insecurity

Gary Dymski and Dorene Isenberg

1 INTRODUCTION

Two interlocking structural shifts combined to support a 'golden age of capitalism' in Europe and North America for two decades after the second World War. The first was a series of 'social contracts' between governments, capitalists, and working classes (Glyn *et al.*, 1990). Under these implicit arrangements, workers gained rising real wages and employment security, while owners and managers enjoyed stable profit rates and rising productivity. The second was the Bretton Woods system, which linked national currencies to a US dollar convertible to gold. During the years of the dollar shortage and the Marshall Plan, the Bretton Woods system generated relatively steady macroeconomic expansion; this, together with labor peace, permitted governments to undertake fiscal and regulatory policies which provided for their citizens' needs.

The formerly warring countries all made sustained efforts to enhance social welfare, an implicit *quid pro quo* for the many sacrifices of the war years; foremost among these was the need to either rebuild or expand the available pool of available housing. So the social contract in each nation encompassed the provision of adequate housing (Feldman and Florida 1990; Harloe 1995). Given the large scale of housing outlays relative to income levels, making the new and existing housing supply affordable also required special mechanisms for housing finance. Each nation solved the linked problems of housing supply and finance uniquely, using some combination of dedicated instruments and institutions, transfers, and subsidies.

Things have changed dramatically in the past 20 years. In the US and in many other nations, the system of housing supply and housing finance has been shifting irrevocably from a need-based to a market-based approach since the 1970s, when the fixed exchange rates of the Bretton Woods system fell apart. The wild swings in exchange rates, macroeconomic growth rates, and current-account balances in the post-Bretton Woods era have fed and been fed by financial volatility and global capital shifts. Technological advances have further eased cross-border capital flows.

For many analysts, these changes mean that marketization is now inevitable: in an environment of international financial instability and instantaneous communications, all national economies must compete for financial capital; and this means reducing social expenditures, especially those requiring long-term financial commitments. In this view, government efforts to direct large-scale resource flows – such as those for housing – are futile. The crisis of the Asian model apparently demonstrates that governments can channel resource flows in directions not applauded by global financial interests only at their peril. So fiscal policy aimed at enhancing social welfare is necessarily a thing of the past; and in the view of many, good riddance, since the market-driven outcomes replacing government initiatives are necessarily more efficient.

This chapter explores three core features of global marketization in the form of three questions about housing supply and financing. First, does global marketization necessarily generate more efficient resource allocations? Second, does marketization mean the shrinkage of state involvement in economic outcomes? Third, is the marketization of formerly state-directed activities an inevitable byproduct of financial globalization? This chapter investigates these questions by comparing the transformation in US housing finance with concurrent changes in the United Kingdom, France and Germany.

To anticipate our conclusions, we find that global financial integration *per se* has not dictated the pace and character of the marketization of housing in these countries. At least as important has been another kind of globalization – governments' global financial deregulation, and their global retreat from supplying housing to needy households. National deregulations have affected the character of mortgage financing flows far more than has the actual or threatened movement of funds across borders. Further, we find that marketization does not mean government withdrawal from housing finance: instead, current efforts to develop sophisticated mortgage-based financial markets depend on continued governmental underwriting and subsidies. Housing prices have not been cleansed of governmental distortions; they reflect a different pattern of subsidies and guarantees. Finally, the emerging market-based systems are not clearly more efficient than the old ones. We develop a social notion of efficiency, which adds households' shelter-related 'life-cycle risks' to the standard roster of financial risks, and conclude that housing-finance innovations have ambiguous net efficiency effects. Marketization has not reduced risks, but shifted them: intermediaries' financial risks have been reduced by parallel increases in households' life-cycle risks.

Section 2 summarizes the transformation of US housing and housing finance as a benchmark for analysis, since the US is often viewed as a paradigm for the marketization wave. Section 3 then takes a critical look at the efficiency effects of the US marketization. Section 4 explores other countries' experience. Section 5 concludes.

2   HOUSING AND MORTGAGE TRANSFORMATION IN THE UNITED STATES

Housing policy in the US emerged in New Deal legislation and in subsequent policies put in place after the war. This policy has always been ambiguous. On one hand, many mechanisms facilitating households' purchase of homes were established. Federal guarantees were used to make cheap financing at low rates and with low down payments widely available; a dense network of thrift institutions, dedicated to home loans and underwritten by federal support, provided the required credit. Housing construction in suburban areas was implicitly supported through the federal government's massive highway-construction program. Most of the risks of the long-term mortgage instruments required to permit the spread of homeownership were borne by financial intermediaries and by government. On the other hand, the right to housing was never ceded. Further, even in the halcyon days of the US welfare state, a right to adequate housing was never established, and the supply of social housing for lower-income households perpetually lagged behind demand.

Worsening macroeconomic instability in the 1970s and the erosion of the 'social contract' between capital and labor have combined to assault the generalized household prosperity of the 1950s and 1960s. In the subsequent three decades, US government policy has shifted from social guarantees to household risk-bearing in many policy areas. In the area of housing, government has gradually retreated from supplying social housing by building or subsidizing the construction of lower-income residential units; and it has shifted toward income-based programs (especially Section 8) that supplement the housing purchasing power of qualifying households by providing them with rental vouchers.[1] Recent administrations have even encouraged homeownership by selling public-housing projects to their occupants. This restructuring of government's role in housing provision has shifted costs from the state and toward lower-income families. Tax codes have been made less progressive, and subsidies for the dependent poor and working poor have been cut while middle- and upper-class subsidies have been spared.[2] Deep reductions in the federal social housing budget (Dymski and Isenberg, 1997) demonstrate this retreat.

The private market has for its part been slow to build lower-income rental housing, largely due to binding credit-market constraints (Dymski and Veitch, 1992) on non-profit builders. The result has been a rapid erosion in the number of lower-cost rental units, even as many lower-income households have been formed, and even as the stock of higher-priced units has grown rapidly.[3] In consequence, a gap between the supply and demand of affordable housing has grown steadily; Newman and Schnare (1988) estimate that in 1985 there were 9.3 million households with $8000 or less in annual income, and only 5.3 million housing units affordable for this income class (of which one million were substandard). The very poorest face the real risk of being squeezed out of any housing unit and made homeless.

The same macroeconomic pressures that helped shift government housing policy put the US banking and housing-finance systems under pressure. High nominal interest rates in the late 1970s and early 1980s led to negative cash-flow and insolvency for many depository institutions, especially the mortgage-holding savings and loans which had supplied most housing finance. Banking acts in 1980 and 1982 used deregulation as a tool for restoring depositories' viability: in exchange for non-banks entering financial product-lines previously reserved for banks and thrifts, banks and thrifts were allowed more freedom in setting prices and selecting product lines. Large commercial banks quickly became embroiled in the LDC debt crisis. And in the *laissez-faire* environment of the Reagan years, many savings and loans used their new powers to engage in speculative projects; by 1989 Congress had to act again to provide more systematic oversight and to bail out the savings and loan industry.

As the savings and loan industry imploded, new methods and sources of housing finance were found. Floating-rate mortgages became common. Expanded government underwriting of mortgage sales led to the rapid growth of mortgage securitization, which in turn opened up new sources of credit supply to replace lost thrift lending capacity. Increased mortgage securitization, in turn, required increased government (and private) underwriting of mortgage sales, and the use of standardized mortgage eligibility criteria in lieu of the earlier system of 'relationship' lending.

3   DOES THE NEW HOUSING FINANCE REGIME ENHANCE EFFICIENCY?

These events in the US are part of a global shift away from government-determined outcomes and toward market-determined outcomes. Does this global shift reduce government involvement, and does it increase efficiency? Many economists and policy analysts hold that shifts of this kind do clearly increase efficiency. Those who propound this view of housing finance, such as Diamond and Lea (1992a) and Wachter (1990), base their ideas on the efficient-markets model of financial allocation: resources are allocated best when allocation is done with minimal governmental intervention and when all relevant information is incorporated into prices determined in decentralized markets without entry barriers. In housing finance, this view implies that countries with the most 'open and competitive markets' and with the fewest public subsidies will deliver mortgage finance at the lowest adjusted spreads – that is, most efficiently. It also implies that the freer are loanable funds to move from one asset to another around the globe, the more efficient the outcome.

This approach regards financial globalization, which eliminates both government interference in pricing and market-entry barriers for offshore buyers and sellers, as an unmitigated good. But this view deserves hard scrutiny. Globalization is a more complex phenomenon than this interpretation permits: far from freeing market forces from their embedded historical roots, globalization reflects the historical circumstances of the late 20th century.

For those not predisposed to equate the modern state with Hobbes' Leviathan, the notion of governmental incompetency is, to say the least, inconsistent with welfare states' great achievements in providing for their citizens' security during the Golden Age. The view that markets are more competent than governments in allocating resources has gradually become more dominant in the past several decades. A slow transformation of political discourse has undoubtedly played a role in this process. In the economic realm, the notion of the limited capacity of domestic policy is due to growing external pressures; and the signal event in the rise in external pressure was the demise of the Bretton Woods fixed-exchange regime.

So the stress point for the pressures that built up under the fixed-exchange rate period was the United States, which served as guarantor of the Bretton Woods arrangement. It is not possible here to detail the decline of Bretton Woods in detail; see Guttman (1994) and Davidson (1982). It is sufficient to mention the overall pattern. Initially a dollar shortage in Europe and elsewhere permitted the US to run current-account deficits as a means of restoring international liquidity; however, by the mid-1960s the dollar shortage had become a dollar overhang, and the US imposed capital controls to reduce pressure on the dollar. As Europe and Japan grew stronger, however, and the US got more involved in the Vietnam War, the dollar became increasingly overvalued. Finally President Nixon suspended convertibility in 1971 and then allowed the dollar to float in 1973.

This heightening pressure on US hegemony was paralleled by the growing importance of transnational institutions, including global banks and transnational corporations. Of particular interest is the rise of the Eurodollar markets.[4] Ironically, the federal government encouraged acquisition-minded US transnationals to borrow Eurodollars in the 1960s as a means of reducing pressure on the US current account. However, the pool of what Machlup termed 'stateless money' grew quickly; by the early 1970s economists were debating the inflationary consequences of Eurodollar repatriation.

The Eurodollar market was further institutionalized as the principal mechanism for recycling 'petrodollars' during the two 1970s oil-price shocks. Over time, small principalities created offshore low-tax platforms for the growing pools of financial wealth outside national boundaries. These havens and a globe-girdling network of financial centers permitted freedom of movement for global banks' and institutions' invested funds. This dense network of havens and financial centers provided the infrastructure for financial speculation; the instability of co-respective exchange rates and interest rates in the post-Bretton Woods world provided the requisite motivation. The presence of the Euro-markets, cash-rich speculators, offshore tax havens, and overseas financial centers all have put pressure on governments to reduce taxes on financial wealth, and to ease restrictions on its movement.

In effect, the balance of power between domestic governments and stateless money and wealth and corporations has swung decisively toward the latter in the last two decades. This is the context for the widespread view that localities that over-regulate capital risk being capital-starved. Starvation occurs as the owners of capital attempt to evade controls by shifting their funds out of the country. This action legitimizes the efficient-market views that resources are allocated best when government intervenes least and that prices are most efficient when freest of government interference. The efficient-markets theory presents as a desideratum a state of affairs which global capital would like government policy-makers to regard as a necessity.

3.1 Financial Internationalization versus Financial Globalization

In light of this ongoing struggle between government prerogative and global financial freedom, what exactly is globalization? Two prevailing approaches can be identified. One is to measure the degree of globalization on the basis of financial prices. Fukao and Hanazaki (1987), for example, find that interest and exchange rates are increasingly being determined in world, not national markets. A common approach investigates the uniformity of prices in terms of uncovered interest parity and financial-price equalization. A second approach examines macroeconomic evidence of financial globalization by examining whether the correlation between national savings and national investment has been weakening over time – the Feldstein–Horioka test. However, recent studies find little evidence that financial globalization, as these two approaches define it, has arrived; see Mussa and Goldstein (1993) and Epstein and Gintis (1994), among others.

So while innumerable financial contracts *could* be traded electronically around the world at volumes that would eliminate interest-rate and exchange-rate inconsistencies and uncouple national investment/savings relationships, financial contracts are *not* in the main being so traded. Why not? Is financial globalization overrated? The answer, like the question, is complicated. One problem is that price- and macro-based measures of financial globalization may, because of the (perhaps inherent) incompleteness of options markets and the volatility of exchange rates, be misleading. We suggest a third approach, based on the character of financial instruments. We begin with Cerny's argument (1994) that globalization consists above all else of organizational changes: the development of both integrated world-wide market structures and of firms with the organizational capacity to center their activities on these markets.

We build on Cerny's insight by offering a distinction between internationalized and globalized markets. A financial market is *internationalized* when assets with idiosyncratic risk/return characteristics – that is, whose risks and returns are unique to the regulatory and banking structure of the country of origin – are sold offshore as well as domestically. A financial market can be considered truly *globalized* when it involves the continuous exchange in financial centers around the world of assets whose risk/return characteristics are independent of national regulatory and banking structures. Internationalized markets are integrated to the extent that prices are identical across national borders. Fully integrated markets are globalized markets. In effect, globalization is the endpoint of a process cleansing financial asset of idiosyncratic characteristics derived from their countries of origin.

3.2 An Efficient-Markets versus a Social Efficiency Approach

Financial markets are typically considered more efficient the more well defined and predictable are the returns and risks of traded instruments, and the more transparently these instruments' prices reflect these factors alone. An efficient outcome then requires that agents holding instruments, directly or indirectly, do so in full recognition of the risk/return combination they have chosen. And when multiple instruments compete for portfolio-owners' wealth, the only way to attract more wealth is to improve return holding risk constant, or to reduce risk with return constant. Efficient-market analysts like Diamond and Lea applaud the implementation of policy changes in the US and elsewhere that improve the fit between market interest rates and the cost of housing finance, and which improve the risk–return characteristics of housing finance paper. The key problems with the previous system were that gaps frequently opened up between market and housing-finance rates, and risks were not explicitly priced.

One way to understand this argument for housing-finance transformation is by thinking of the risks associated with the creation and holding of a financial asset during its lifespan. These are readily identified. Default risk, created with the instrument itself, arises because the borrower may be unable to meet the agreed repayment terms on time. Further, any instrument entitling its holder to fixed payments exposes its holder to interest-rate risk, since market interest rates (and hence the costs of holding this instrument) may rise or fall over time. Liquidity risk arises because it may be impossible to sell this instrument on demand at par. Prepayment risk may also arise. These risks are brought into being with the creation of the agreement between borrower and lender; which party bears these risks then depends on the structure of this agreement. In the old US system, all these financial risks, were borne by lenders. But a defining feature of the new housing finance system is the shifting of risks from the intermediaries making loans onto other parties. Interest-rate risk is shifted onto households when flexible-rate mortgages are created; when fixed-rate mortgages are created, interest-rate risk is borne by the pension funds, overseas investors, and insurance companies that end up holding them. The intermediaries making these loans then must hold risks down if they are to place this paper. In the US, this is, in turn, accomplished in two ways: either by allowing only conforming households to borrow, or by relying on government underwriting to dampen overall risk levels. It is immediately clear that government underwriting is precisely a means of eliminating idiosyncratic risk from housing-finance paper and insuring a global market for this paper. Government funding also underlies this market revolution in that the mortgage interest deduction is a crucial factor in maximizing the size – and hence depth and liquidity – of mortgage-based markets.

This brings us to our alternative approach to efficiency. Is anything wrong with this picture? Not if our only concern is with making financial assets safe for world-wide investors. But what if we consider not just the risk characteristics of financial assets, but those of the households seeking to generate these assets so as to buy housing. Households financing homes are exposed to risks in housing markets, just as intermediaries are. And like intermediaries, households are long-lived, and their success requires that they adapt to shifting market environments. But unlike intermediaries, the individuals comprising households have a life-cycle: two dependent phases in which no income is earned, bracketed around a middle phase of income-earning. This life-cycle is punctuated by occasional geographic relocation and occupational transition. We can describe households' risks in housing markets as follows.

Life-cycle risks of households:

(a) *Entry risk*. Any given individual, when she singly or jointly starts her own household, faces the risk of not finding adequate housing when entering the housing market; in the extreme, entry into the housing market must be deferred.
(b) *Tenure risk*. Once a given household has acquired an adequate housing unit, it faces the risk of being unable to stay in that unit. This is tenure risk.[5] This has several causes, including earnings instability, increased rental or

financing costs, and the demolition or conversion to non-residential use or unobtainable tenure of one's housing unit.

(c) *Re-entry risk*. Finally, there is the risk that a unit vacating a housing unit will be unable to find an adequate replacement unit within its means. This risk depends on two factors – the existence of an available supply of housing at some market price, and income and wealth levels that are adequate to allow a household to purchase rental services.

Table 8.1 illustrates the two-sided character of housing-related risks: households' chronic attachment to housing units is replete with risks, just as is wealthowners' chronic attachment to financial assets. Household and financial risks clearly interact. As a tighter creditworthiness test is used to screen potential homeowners, households' entry and re-entry risks rise, but asset holders' default risks decline. When interest-rate risk is borne by homeowners, their tenure risk increases, while asset holders' risk decreases. The following simplified depiction provides further insight into life-cycle risk, using $Li(x)$ to denote the likelihood of event x:

Li(household formation) = Li(homeownership) + Li(rentership | not a homeowner) + Li(home-sharing | not a homeowner or renter)

Li(homeownership) = Li(supply of affordable homes exists)[Li(household can meet downpayment) + Li(household income can support monthly payments | downpayment)]

Li(rentership) = Li(supply of affordable apartments exists)[Li(household has security deposit) + Li(household income can support monthly rent | security deposit)]

Li(household shelter security) = Li(sustaining ownership | have achieved owner status) + Li(sustaining rentership | have achieved renter status)

These likelihoods are crude and merely suggestive of complex, open-ended social processes. In effect, entry risk $\cong$ $(1 - Li(\text{household formation}))$ and tenure risk $\cong (1 - Li(\text{household shelter security}))$. Re-entry risk is the same as entry risk, with the additional condition that either owner or renter status has to be obtained given the household-wealth and credit-rating consequences of leaving or losing previous shelter arrangements. And life-cycle risk = entry risk + tenure risk + re-entry risk. Note that reducing entry risk by permitting households to use more of their monthly income for mortgage or rent payments leads to increased tenure risk and re-entry risk. Life-cycle risk embodies a simple idea: if a household unit from a given country was chosen at random, what are the chances that this unit can find and maintain an adequate, affordable

148   *Full employment and price stability in a global economy*

Table 8.1   The two-sided character of housing risk

	Household seeking affordable housing and secure shelter:	Portfolio investor seeking maximum return and minimum risk:
Initiation of household unit		
Threshold requirements	Wealth and income base sufficient to initiate new household, plus an available and affordable housing unit	
Risks	Entry risk – possibility that net wealth and income do not permit household launch, and/or that no affordable units are available	

Initial acquisition of housing asset

Homeownership: creation of financial claim (mortgage) and transfer of real asset (home). This occurs when would-be homeowner pre-commits a portion of her anticipated cash-flow to servicing this financial claim, and the would-be mortgagor accepts the attendant nonpayment risks.

Risks	Tenure risk – possibility that income and net wealth be insufficient to meet servicing pre-commitments; may be exacerbated by interest-rate risk	Borrower default or partial-payment risk, compromising the promised cash-flow to asset owner (lender); may bear interest-rate risk

Sale of existing housing assets and acquisition of new assets

Secondary markets	Households seeking to move must find home buyers for their current homes	Mortgage holders seeking to sell them off need to find asset buyers
Risks	Re-entry risk – possibility that established unit seeking a different affordable housing will be unable to do so given their net wealth and income position	Borrower default risk on new home, and on old home if not sold off
	Liquidity risk – inability to unload prior home by finding timely buyer at a market price that does not entail capital loss	Liquidity risk – inability to unload mortgage asset to timely buyer at price that does not entail capital loss

housing unit as a basis for carrying out its other social and economic activities? In a society with large wealth and income inequalities, an answer to this question should account for the experience of different portions of the social aggregate, and not simply measure societal averages.

The notion of life-cycle risk opens up a broader assessment of the efficiency effects of changes in housing systems. Clearly, any system of supplying and financing housing generates different levels of both life-cycle and financial risks. From households' perspective, housing and housing-finance markets and policies are efficient if they generate an adequate, affordable housing stock; any market innovation or policy change that reduces life-cycle risk increases 'efficiency' in this sense. From wealth-holders' perspective, efficiency means minimization of financial risks given promised return. Social efficiency then can be defined suggestively as follows:

$$\text{Social efficiency} = (1 - \text{life-cycle risk})) + (1 - \text{financial risk})$$
$$\text{household efficiency} + \text{financial-market efficiency}$$

When more fully developed, these broader efficiency concepts may permit quantitative assessments of policy changes that give equal weight to households' and asset-owners' objectives. Even without quantification, however, a social efficiency assessment comes to a more skeptical conclusion about the effects of the housing-policy revolution in the US than the assessments mentioned above. The federal government's reduced provision of public and lower-income housing units, combined with the overall shortage of rental units, has substantially increased entry and tenure risks for lower-income, lower-wealth, and non-traditional households, even while the proliferation of mortgage brokers has reduced entry risk for middle- and upper-income households hoping to buy homes. At the same time, the reduced downpayments and higher debt service/income ratios that lenders have tolerated to push down entry risks have increased tenure risk. The adoption of flexible-rate mortgages reduces interest-rate risk for mortgage holders, but increases tenure risk for households. Institutional shedding of the placement function and the use of securitized instruments has given some households more financing choices, but it has also raised the implicit risk to government of systemic defaults in a downturn. In effect, making housing-finance instruments conformable with the requirements of globalized asset markets has in the United States meant a reorientation of the public support of housing.

In sum, changes in the housing finance market have reduced financial risk for asset-owners primarily by increasing subsidies and guarantees supporting the middle- and upper-income end of the housing market; but this has come at the expense of government support for housing for lower-income households. And many households have obtained homes with secularly increasing levels of tenure risk. So the social efficiency effects of housing marketization are, at best ambiguous.

4   HOUSING FINANCE AND RISK-BEARING IN THE UK, FRANCE AND GERMANY

Our discussion of the US case has suggested some tentative answers to the three questions posed above about housing marketization: marketization has not, in the US, reduced public involvement in housing resource allocation; it has ambiguous efficiency effects; and it is not driven by financial globalization, but by a sustained economic crisis and political reconsideration of the prior system of housing provision and finance. This crisis can be traced in part to inconsistency between domestic economic policies and the international economic order; but it was not driven by capital flight. Are these tentative answers generally valid? This section extends our analysis to the recent housing experiences of the UK, France, and Germany.

Emerging from World War II, all the European nations urgently needed to rebuild decimated housing stocks for returning troops and civilians. Over time, more prosperous households moved into owner-occupied units; social housing was left to a lower-income constituency, including an increasing number of immigrants and ethnic minorities. Then, as macroeconomic growth stalled and revenues tightened, the increasingly troubled social housing programs became a political target (Prak and Priemus, 1985). The political push against social housing, however, has had to face the organized political power of the organizations and localities that had put this housing in place. Indeed, this section will show that while all these countries have moved in the direction of less housing provision, fewer subsidies for lower-income housing, less market segmentation, and less protection of financial customers, their housing finance systems remain distinctly different. Financial globalization *per se* is not the transformative force behind housing-policy decimation and housing-finance marketization; the principal impetus remains with these nations' governments.

4.1   Housing Policy and Finance in the United Kingdom

Prior to World War I, 10 per cent of all households were owner-occupiers and 90 per cent were private renters. A United Kingdom housing policy took shape after the war, spurred on by an active working-class labor movement. Public housing was introduced in 1919; it expanded in the post-World War II period, with the commitment to public housing holding firm until the end of the 1960s. Meanwhile the annual targets for housing production rose steadily – from

300000 dwellings a year in 1951 to 500000 by 1970 (Malpass, 1986: 6). Many of these new units were private and intended for homeowners (Leather and Murie, 1986: 43). The state's activities produced a change in tenure distribution: by 1970, 50 per cent of all households were owner-occupiers, 20 per cent were renters from private landlords, and 30 per cent rented from local authorities and new towns (Malpass, 1993: 71; Figure 3.1, 72).

By the end of the 1970s the UK commitment to public housing had succumbed to a stagflationary economy and the neo-liberal ideology of Margaret Thatcher, elected Prime Minister in 1979. During her legendary term she promoted the rule of the market in place of socially equalizing government policies. In the realm of housing policy and finance Thatcher oversaw institutional deregulation, cuts in social housing production, and the sale of social housing into the private sector. Institutional lenders diversified their product lines and mortgages acquired market prices. Public housing production fell and was in short supply. These policy shifts were not tenure or risk neutral. By 1989, tenure distribution was 69 per cent owned, 10 per cent rented from the private sector, and 22 per cent rented from local authorities (Maclennan, 1995: 665). Indebtedness had skyrocketed and foreclosures had almost tripled (Whitehead, 1993).

Housing finance. Marketization changed both the types of institutions providing mortgages and the financial instruments they used. Building societies had a virtual monopoly on housing finance until the middle of the 1980s, just as thrifts did in the US; but building society problems similar to those of thrifts permitted banks and centralized lenders (mortgage banks) to break the building societies' cartel. Endowment mortgages supplanted self-amortizing mortgages, and securitization along with access to wholesale funds promoted the dominance of market-determined capital flows and prices for housing finance.

Compared with the self-amortizing mortgages primarily used before the mid-1980s, endowment mortgages put borrowers at greater financial – and hence tenure – risk. When issued an endowment mortgage was combined with a life insurance policy: the mortgage covered only the interest on the loan, while the insurance policy paid off the principal of the loan when the policy matured.[6] The endowment mortgage, like its self-amortizing predecessor, carried a variable interest rate. But interest rates were no longer set by the building society cartel; they now fluctuated with the increasingly volatile money market rates.[7] The impact of increased interest-rate risk on homebuyers is described in a Council of Mortgage Lenders analysis (quoted in Malpass, 1993: 91): 'the steep increase in interest rates meant that repayments which had been just affordable at the point of purchase became very much heavier.'

What did these shifts mean for financial and tenure risk? With domestic capital markets opened up to international players the result was more volatile interest rates. By creating an endowment mortgage with a flexible interest rate financial institutions successfully shielded themselves from interest-rate risk – all of which was shifted onto borrowers. Additionally, lenders now had an insurance policy for the house against which the loan was made. Effectively, the default risk once borne by the lender was shifted from the mortgage originator to the insurance company.

Mortgage lenders came to rely heavily on the capital market (wholesale funds) instead of the traditional deposit base. Building societies raced to include wholesale funds among their funding sources; meanwhile, centralized lenders floated bond issues in these markets to obtain loanable funds. Beginning in 1987, lenders bundled their floating-rate mortgages and sold them off into these markets (Bradt, 1991).[8] Wholesale markets did afford lenders greater flexibility in meeting loan demand. But these bonds are unsecured; and the use of shorter-term securities to finance housing assets created maturity mismatches. And heavier use of these markets increased volatility in mortgage rates.

The marketization of lending practices and financial deregulation have also added to the life-cycle risks of borrowers by increasing their indebtedness. Instead of requiring 20–25% equity for a home purchase, lenders began requiring as little as 10%. Additionally, lenders fostered the growth in second mortgages (home equity loans) which allowed homeowners to borrow against their equity. These changes increased homeowners' tenure risk.[9] Consequently, foreclosure and arrears rates rose substantially. In 1980, the foreclosure rate stood at 0.06%, the 6–12 months arrears rate stood at 0.25%, and the 12+ months rate at 0.08%. By 1989, these rates were 0.17%, 0.73% and 0.15%, respectively. At the same time, eased access to housing credit pushed house prices up in the late 1980s. Then volatile interest rates and an economic contraction in the early 1990s pushed up foreclosure and arrears rates even more, to 0.77%, 1.87% and 0.93%, respectively (Whitehead, 1993), and created a situation in which 'falling house prices reinforced the downturn. Payment arrears quickly matured into possessions, and by 1994, 250 000 owners had lost their homes and 150 000 households still had arrears exceeding 12 months. Possession sales further fed house price drops, and negative equity affected an estimated 1.5 million owners' (Maclennan, 1995: 687).

Housing policy. In the Thatcher period, Britain's avowed housing policy was owner occupancy and reduction in state provision of social housing (Kleinman, 1996: 19–28). Promotion of these policies led to the privatization of social housing, reduced construction of social rental housing, and reliance upon private housing rentals. In 1980 the Right to Buy policy had established the right of council housing and housing association tenants to purchase their homes at large discounts from market prices with automatic local authority financing. By 1987, a Tory White Paper scathingly attacked public housing providers and voiced a new policy of support for the private rental sector (Malpass, 1993: 81–2). The

1988 Housing Act then forced housing associations to rely primarily on private finance for new housing construction; this caused rents to more than double in some cases (Kleinman, 1996: 40). By the 1990s, the desired result was achieved: Britain has the highest rate of owner-occupation among the OECD nations; meanwhile, social housing houses only those too economically incapacitated or too poor to afford market-provided housing. Social housing has been reduced to the tenure of last resort (Malpass, 1993; and Maclennan, 1995).

These policy changes have increased entry and tenure risk for newly-formed households, the unemployed, single-head households, and the elderly. These households' life-cycle risk depends to a large extent on the quality, affordability, and availability of rental housing. But as data drawn from Boleat (1985) and Whitehead (1993) indicate, the number of the public and private rental units declined by almost 2 million between 1979 and 1990, while rents skyrocketed: local authority rents rose from £401 to £1237 between 1980 and 1990 while dwelling prices moved from £23 000 to £64 357 forcing private rental rates up along with them. In this same time period, the proportion of income spent on rents moved from 9% to 15% and on housing, 12% to 19%. The combination of higher rents and more expensive dwellings has increased life-cycle risk for most Britons.

4.2 Housing and Housing Finance in France

France has a long history of state intervention in housing and financial markets; the French government has subsidized low-income housing since 1912, primarily through a system of locally controlled housing organizations (HLM). Established by 19th-century philanthropic *communes*, the HLM were taken over by local governments and construction interests in the early 20th century.

After World War II, war damage, a disorganized financial system, and population increase created a vast housing shortage, which drove rental prices rapidly upward for usable units, pushing life-cycle risks to politically dangerous levels. The French government responded by implementing its distinctive approach to housing policy: it focused its resources and subsidies directly or indirectly on households in need of assistance, relying primarily on a variety of imperfectly coordinated categorical programs, while taking steps to encourage housing construction and the revival of market-based housing.[10]

To combat tenure risk, the French government endorsed rent controls on existing rental units in the 1948 Rent Act and provided a rental assistance program to some households in unaffordable housing (the *Allocation Familiale de Logement*, or *AL*). Participation in *AL* was not universal, but instead was available to certain household categories, such as families with children (Wood, 1990). To combat entry and re-entry risk, 'the greater proportion of state aid to housing has, since the war, been directed toward the construction of dwellings ... with little discrimination in allocation of funds between income groups' (Pearsall, 1984: 12).

To encourage housing construction, the 1948 Rent Act decreed that no rent controls would apply to newly-built units. Housing construction was financed by a 1% corporate tax for housing and by government subsidies. The HLM were used as the principal conduits for a surge of social-housing construction aimed at low and moderate-income households; their projects were financed at 2% interest repayable over 65 years. Many subsidized private dwellings were also built. By 1970, social housing accounted for 15% of French housing stock, but 60% of all rental units. (Boleat, 1985).

French policy concern has always centered on how to finance market-based housing despite the relatively thin French capital markets. Historically, long-term mortgages could not be supported, and state policy has not encouraged them.[11] As of 1965 the government allowed households to put tax-free deposits into savings banks, at below-market rates, against future home purchases. All households also have the right to establish tax-protected savings accounts for every individual (including children) and to borrow against these accounts for housing-related purposes. The end of the Bretton Woods system only enhanced the financial constraints on the French system; in 1972 severe pressure on the Franc led to credit controls which remained in effect for 15 years. These controls barred commercial banks from making loans of more than 10 years' maturity, thus effectively preventing banks from financing mortgages.

Rising personal incomes and public willingness to absorb higher housing costs led to a 1977 reform act which further encouraged market-based financing and home ownership (Boleat, 1985: 165–6). Housing finance was opened more thoroughly to general intermediaries. A relaxation of the loan-maturity ceiling on commercial banks encouraged banks to enter the mortgage market; and a secondary market facility was established. This law also created two new categories of loans: the unsubsidized contractual loan (the *prêt conventionne* or *PC*), provided by private banks, which entitled recipients to participate in the housing allowance program; and a new category of subsidized homeowner loan, the *prêt aidé à l'accession à la proprieté* (*PAP*), provided by the publicly owned *Crédit Foncier de France*. These new loan programs were designed to supplement the older housing-savings system. By 1982, the *PC* and *PAP* constituted 15% and 19%, respectively, of outstanding homeowner loans, with housing-savings loans constituting another 19%, and conventional mortgage loans just 19% (Boleat, 1985: 165).

The 1977 reforms also signalled a shift away from 'bricks and mortar' subsidies: the *sector aidé* loans were radically cut. To compensate for reduced public support for housing supply, the government created a supplement for lower-income households, both renters and homeowners, termed the *aidé personnalizée au logement* (*APL*). While the *APL* is an income-related housing subsidy, it supports units, not households. By 1984, 19% of owner-occupants were receiving either *APL* or the older *AP* assistance, versus 24% of tenants in private rental housing, and 41% of those in social housing (Wood, 1990). Over time, the concentration of *APL* aid in social housing, combined with the increased ownership opportunities for financially able households, has led to the concentration in social housing of lower-income households, a disproportionate number of whom are ethnic minorities (Harloe, 1995).

Marketization in France. Diamond and Lea describe France as moving 'from a heavily segmented, subsidized, regulated system toward a market-driven system' (1992a: 39). There is no doubt that this system is undergoing a transition much as the US and UK did some years earlier. The rent controls imposed by the Socialist government in the early 1980s were relaxed in 1986 (Gyourko, 1990). Securities markets and mutual funds have been growing rapidly, as corporations have begun accessing money and capital markets directly, as in the US – *monetaires* now total 60% of banks' liquid deposit total. Some housing finance is being provided directly in financial markets; indeed, a significant proportion of these free-market housing loans have been supported by guarantees known as *cautions*, in a system closely resembling FNMA underwriting (see Stone and Zissu, 1992). *Cautions* are provided indirectly by *Crédit Foncier* against a mortgage lien in the event of default, for the lowest-risk loans; the implicit government subsidy has permitted a liquid resale market for these securities. Further, a financial modernization act passed on July 1, 1996 opened up French financial markets and permits financial intermediaries to engage in a broader set of activities. These innovations have pressured French banks, who traditionally relied on long-term relationships with customers for whom they provided comprehensive services (including housing finance). Initially, French banks responded to the new competitors by taking risks and lending at low margins. To meet the new Basle capital-adequacy standards, many of these banks have subsequently had to take steps to improve their balance sheets – including the strategic use of loan securitizations, pursuant to a 1989 law providing for closed-end securitized loan pools.

But evidence is also plentiful that the French embrace of marketization has been tentative at best. For one thing, the French government has continued to take actions to reduce household life-cycle risks stemming from financial risk. In particular, many households that obtained loans in the 1981–85 period did so at very high (fixed) nominal interest rates, in booming real estate markets. Subsequently, many of these households' loans generated unsustainable tenure risk for low- and middle-income owners. The *Crédit Foncier* stepped in to help these households renegotiate these loans at terms more suited for the subsequent low-inflation environment of the late 1980s and 1990s. In addition, the 'Law

Scrivener' has protected lower-income households against excessive indebtedness. And most mortgage financing still enjoys either explicit subsidies (for *PAP* and *PC* loans) or implicit subsidies (for mortgages financed at depositories paying below-market rates). A large share of the mortgage securities sold in financial markets are placements for subsidized *PAP* loans by the *Crédit Foncier*.[12] Loan securitization has not come to dominate French housing finance as in the US and UK, for two reasons. First, rates of return are difficult to calculate, in part due to the absence of data on prepayment risk, and in part because French law makes it difficult for lenders to foreclose on non-performing housing loans. Second, French mortgages are often made at below-market rates as part of the *quid pro quo* for households' pooling of savings to purchase homes. The large proportion of below-market-rate loans makes it impossible to fund housing-loan pools with funds paying market rates.

In sum, the French system historically has put many public subsidies and guarantees in place with the aim of minimizing households' life-cycle risks and intermediaries' financial risks. They have continued to intervene strategically in housing-finance outcomes even at the expense of reduced access to global financial markets. French markets continue to feel the effect of financing constraints. Competitive mortgages are primarily fixed-rate instruments for 10–20 years with a loan-to-value ratio in the range 60%–80%; as such, they are insufficient to fully fund most households' home purchases. Thus, households still rely on multiple loans to obtain housing; and some of the supplemental loans – notably the *plans d'épargne-logement* (PELs) and the *comptes d'épargne-logement* (CELs), which are provided in conjunction with contract and household savings plans – are subsidized.

In the meantime, financial risks have grown. Liquidity risk, especially that borne by banks, is high due to the undeveloped character of secondary markets and the growth of *monetaires*. Intermediaries also bear high levels of repayment and interest-rate risk, though their default risk is minimal because of French laws which protect lower-income households against default. The patchwork of protections and marketization efforts has had uneven effects. For example, France's mutual, savings, and state-owned banks have arguably had difficulty selling equity shares because of their low profit margins, which can be traced to free entry plus the large share of below-market mortgage and deposit rates on their balance sheets. Despite such difficulties, the French have thus far avoided the widespread risk-shifting observed in the US and UK. Whether protections against life-cycle risk will be maintained for all households, however, is unclear due to the increasing social divide between homeowners and those in social housing – a divide that some have not been slow to exploit for political gain. The multi-ethnic French team's World Cup victory aside, the growing association of low-income status with minority ethnicity may challenge the long-standing French commitment to *'égalité, liberté, fraternité.'*

4.3   Housing Policy and Finance in Germany

After World War II the German government implemented a housing policy aimed at rationing the existing housing stock and stimulating the construction of new rental housing. Throughout the post-war period the government has played a central role in housing the nation. Even when the Conservative-Liberals controlled the government in the 1980s and encouraged more market-based allocation in housing, the active role of government was never questioned.

Housing policy. German housing policy and other social programs start from the widely held premise that its citizens' social welfare should not be left entirely to the market. This philosophy, *soziale Markwirtschaft*, means the market must be socially responsible. In response to the decimated state of available shelter after World War II, the 1950s' housing programs strove to increase housing supply and keep rental costs down. As in France, subsidies for new housing construction and rent control on both new and old housing formed the heart of these programs.

Germany had a booming economy in the 1970s, unlike other OECD nations; and this boom spurred housing construction. In the 1980s the Conservative-Liberals ascended to power. Thinking the housing shortage problem solved, they dismantled rent controls, cut back on construction of social housing, and implemented a housing allowance (Tomann, 1990; Kleinman, 1996). That is, they acted like the conservatives in power in the UK and the US.

By the mid-1980s, a new housing crisis had emerged in the form of widespread housing shortages. In response to increased demand, prices rose, and private investment in housing increased. At the same time, government responded by building more social housing. At its nadir in 1987 social housing accounted for only 19% of new housing; but between 1990 and 1992 it rebounded to 30% (Kleinman, 1996:108–109). Even though there was a resurgence in social housing construction, it has not played the same role in the 1990s as in earlier times. Like Britain, France and the US, this housing is increasingly being used to house the poor, not a cross-section of the working population. Unlike these other countries, however, the owner-occupier is not the dominant form of tenure, so private rental housing retains a more pivotal political and social role.

Housing finance. The housing finance system in Germany funds both social and private housing, hence both rental and owner-occupied dwellings. This lack of distinction is important since most German households are renters. In 1967, only 32% of the population were owner-occupiers, and at the height of owner-occupancy, the 1980s, only 43% claimed that tenure. By 1995 owner-occupation fell to 38%, and social housing renters accounted for 26% of the population (Balchin, 1995: 11).

Housing finance is provided by a large set of financial institutions, each component of which has historically specialized in one aspect of lending. German mortgage origination normally involves a first mortgage, historically emitted by a mortgage bank, and a second mortgage, provided by a Bausparkassen. The first mortgage is legally limited to 60% of building value; a second mortgage can cover an additional 20% of its value. As housing prices and interest rates rose in the 1970s, a third, unsecured mortgage became a common feature of home-purchase transactions; third mortgages are limited to 10% of home value. The 1970s also saw the historically important lenders – savings banks, mortgage banks, and Bausparkassen – joined by commercial banks engaging in a new form of universal banking, *Allfinanz*.

The system's transformation via mergers and acquisitions resulted not in new financial institutions or instruments, but in heightened competition within product lines. By 1983, after the advent of *Allfinanz*, commercial banks originated almost 7% of first mortgages and over 15% of second mortgages – double their 1970 share of these asset markets. With the exception of mortgage banks, whose share of second mortgages gained 1%, the historical lenders all lost market share in this time period (Ball, 1990: 171).

Financial risk. The German financial depository system even with its universal banking structure is governed by strong prudential regulations (Kregel, 1993). Financial institutions are supervised closely and must adhere to strict rules of operation governing balance sheets: maturities must be matched for assets and liabilities; loans must not exceed a certain size and a certain proportion of deposits; capital must be adequate; and loan risk-levels are tightly controlled (Kregel, 1993: 671–2).

Institutions that rely on funds from capital markets – such as the mortgage, commercial, and savings banks, which use bank bonds or collateralized mortgage bonds to fund their loans – are still subject to these same prudential regulations (Ball, 1990: 183; Kregel, 1993). These regulations underlie the highly liquid market for third mortgages, since these are unsecured. The third mortgages originated by savings and commercial banks are both reviewable rate (variable rate) and renegotiable (fixed-rate for one to ten years, usually less than 5 years). So institutions' interest rate risk is attenuated, but borrowers' default risk is increased. Regulators have watched market developments carefully, incorporating new financial instruments into their regulatory requirements (Kregel, 1993: 672). Beyond the regulatory net also lies the confidence that the central government would intervene to prevent a major bank failure (Ball and Martens, 1990).

The ownership structure of German financial institutions also prevents innovations from necessarily increasing the individual or systemic level of risk. The majority of financial institutions are publicly or cooperatively owned. Savings banks are publicly owned and operate only within the geographic limits of the jurisdiction of their regional public authority. Mortgage banks and Bausparkassen also are at least partially owned by public authorities. This public ownership has led to cooperative rather than competitive relationships (Ball and Martens, 1990: 177).

Household risk. Have the risks borne by German households increased with the changes in housing policies and the financial structure? Borrowers in the restructured system bear the same risks they had before – default risk, tenure risk due to variable-rate mortgages, and entry risk due to high equity requirements. But have the financial and housing policies' changes produced higher risk levels? And how have renters been affected?

The 1980s' push to homeownership found many buyers defaulting or in foreclosure and arrears. Between 1980 and 1985 defaults increased from an average of 0.1% to 0.5% (Diamond and Lea, 1992b: 98), and foreclosures doubled (Ball and Martens, 1990: 174). These trends produced increased tenure and re-entry risk. At the same time, both private and social-housing construction declined in the 1980s; the number of housing units actually decreased in net terms. Those who defaulted thus experienced rising re-entry risk. The government did respond to housing-market changes by replacing its 'bricks and mortar' policies with the housing allowance, but the shortages persisted.

Overall, life-cycle risk is less prevalent in Germany than in either the US or UK. Entry, tenure and re-entry risks are attenuated by a robust rental sector. However, this statement should not be misconstrued. The social-housing sector experienced sell-offs in the 1980s and declines in construction that diminished its capacity (Harloe, 1995). While the 1990s saw a resurgence in social-housing construction, new problems of *de facto* segregation by race, income, and ethnicity have changed the nature of life in social housing (Kleinman, 1996). The question of whether the government's legacy of investment in housing will survive Germany's efforts to meet European Monetary Union admission criteria also looms unanswered.

5 CONCLUSION

Financial internationalization is here, but the era of financial globalization has not yet arrived. Housing finance systems have not become homogenized and standardized in OECD countries. The claim made by many (such as O'Brien, 1992) that financial innovations have necessitated the homogenization of housing-finance systems is wrong. There is little evidence that capital has moved across borders to purchase mortgages or mortgage-backed securities, in large part because European countries have been unable or unwilling to replicate the characteristics of US mortgage-backed securities.

The widespread moves toward market-based allocations of housing resources have not been uniform; and they have by no means created standardized financial instruments with uniform risk characteristics. The interweaving of market risks with national policies and (national) budgetary commitments makes even instruments that are similar on the surface very different in practice. Consider the very different procedures that accompany homeowner default in the countries examined here: except in the US, homeowners are cushioned – but how much depends on governmental commitments which are not written in stone. Further, our cross-country comparison has shown that marketizing housing finance doesn't make housing systems more socially efficient. Indeed, some of the nations faced with the most desperate housing-supply and housing-affordability gaps have moved most rapidly to market-oriented systems of finance.

The proponents of marketization have predicted that globalization would homogenize allocation processes and lead to price convergence. But a unified world market has not emerged, and none is in view. Instead governments have, of necessity, continued to play vital roles in allocating national resources; and market arrangements have continued to reflect the historical, social, and cultural mores of their society. Decisions on regulation, completeness, and efficiency continue to be based both on economic theory and on cultural perceptions and priorities.

The financial innovation and economic disruption that prompted change in housing policy and finance in the 1970s and 1980s did not produce a uniform international response. Among the nations examined here, there is evidence of a 'universal shift away from subsidies to housing suppliers, in favor of subsidies to lower-income households on the demand side of housing markets' (Kemp, 1990). But otherwise the experience with these nations' reallocation of risks and rights has been very diverse. The US has reduced intermediation risks while allowing households' life-cycle risks to rise, especially for those with lower incomes. Britain has allowed entry risk to rise for the poorer households who cannot afford private-sector rents and lack the wealth for a downpayment. Germany has reduced its engagement in social housing, but other sectors – especially the private for-profit and non-profit and the cooperatives – have leaped into the breach. Still, affordable housing is a problem for the very poor. France, with its large social rental base, has made efforts to spread housing subsidies evenly among all the poor; this has kept tenure risks down, but entry and re-entry risks are at all-time highs. Meanwhile, the housing performance of the private sector in the US and UK, the most thoroughly marketized economies, has been mediocre in producing affordable lower-income housing units.

However, certain general themes emerge amidst these diverse reactions to globalization:

- Government remains an important actor in the housing market; its subsidies and guarantees define the terrain of securitization and hence the limits of the market.
- Government has shifted away from directly or indirectly building up the supply of housing, and toward supporting housing demand.
- Risk has been shifted away from financial institutions toward households and governments.
- Government expenditures and subsidies for housing have, on average, shifted away from lower-income households and toward upper-income households.
- The implicit or explicit social contracts for housing that guided policy after World War II have been discarded.

We have emphasized that the social contracts for housing during the Golden Age, which functioned as macroeconomic stimuli, met social needs, and raised living standards, had two key supports: a benign international macroeconomic environment with a strong dollar; domestic political commitments to meet minimal social and human needs. The first support fell in the early 1970s, as Bretton Woods came apart; and the second support has been under sustained attack since then, with the result that state commitment to housing and other social needs has eroded. Undoubtedly, putting together renewed social contracts for housing will require changes in the international macroeconomic environment as well as shifts in political forces at the domestic level.

Arguably, of the countries reviewed here, the United States is in the strongest position to reverse course without being fatally hurt by capital flight and plummeting currency values. But far from showing international leadership in restoring the right to shelter, the US has led the advanced nations' attack on the welfare state and on social housing. The US Housing Act of 1949, with its call to 'remedy the serious housing shortage, ... and realiz[e] as soon as feasible the goal of a decent home and a suitable living environment for every American family', is a distant memory. Homeownership rates have remained robust only because lender competition and government guarantees have permitted home-loan applicants to acquire homes with lower downpayments (and more tenure risk). Meanwhile, the rental stock is declining in both number and quality, and the lack of affordable housing for the poor has reached crisis proportions. Schwartz, Ferlauto and Hoffman (1988) estimated a decade ago that 2 million new housing units were needed annually to meet housing demand. Housing unit growth has been far less; meanwhile, waiting lists for housing vouchers have lengthened in virtually every locality (with mean waiting times for vouchers that are years, not months, long). According to an April 1998 report, 5.3 million households have 'worst case' housing needs.[13] Between 1993 and 1995, the number of rental units affordable to very low income households actually shrank by 900 000. Meanwhile, Congress has denied the Clinton Administration requests for new rental assistance since 1995 (US Department of Housing and Urban Development, 1998). And while deregulation and securitization led to greater housing finance access for some middle and high income families, these shifts have been associated with a reallocation of government guarantees and subsidies that have, taken together, increased financial risk for low income families and often led to the ultimate consequence of tenure risk – homelessness.

The US may simply be further ahead of the other nations reviewed here in shifting directions on housing policy in response to a political realignment that has exploited, and not healed, a social divide that yawns ever wider along class, racial, and gender lines. To call this tragic is understatement indeed. For if the United States will not stand up in the face of the pressures exerted by financial globalization, if it cannot broker a more orderly international financial environment and restore a domestic social contract, which other nation can?

NOTES

1. See Hays (1995). The shifting emphasis from supply-side to demand-side programs is evident in the number of housing units aided over time. In 1960 HUD financed 425 000 public housing units and had no other active programs. By 1980, the number of public housing units stood at almost 1.2 million. Other HUD programs in 1980 reduced mortgage prices for 596 000 housing units and provided subsidies for 1 153 000 rental units. By 1994, public housing provision had climbed only slightly, to 1.4 million units, while the Section 8 rental subsidy program had almost tripled to more than 3 million housing units (Burchell and Listokin, 1995: 599).
2. Katz (1989) reviews the recent history of the American welfare state. The largest housing subsidy, the mortgage interest deduction, has a regressive effect. Follain, Ling and McGill (1993) review estimates of federal expenditures for this deduction in 1989; these range from $39 billion to $110 billion. Citizens for Tax Justice estimate 1996 federal tax expenditures for this subsidy at $351 billion.
3. Masnick (1991) has documented the consistent declines in the number of lower-cost ($400 or less in 1989 dollars) rental units in the US between 1974 and 1987. By contrast, expensive rental units ($500 or more) increased by 38% between 1974 and 1980, and by 126% between 1980 and 1987.
4. The term 'Eurocurrency' refers generically to any currency held outside its country of issue. A Eurodollar is then a dollar held outside the US.
5. This terminology suggests the housing-economics term 'tenure status', pertaining to whether a household owns or rents its homestead. Here we follow the broader definition suggested by Wilson (1979: 11), who argues that tenure status 'defines the legal position of households in residential markets with respect to their rights and obligations as participants'.
6. The popularity of this mortgage insurance combination was not due solely to its floating interest rate. Insurance policy commissions could be front-loaded; so premiums in the first two years of a 25-year policy might consist entirely of commission payments. Of the £17 billion premium income paid to life insurance companies in 1993, commissions comprised £2 billion (Hutton, 1995: 206).
7. Between April 1988 and February 1990, UK interest rates climbed from 9.5% to 15.4% (Malpass, 1993: 91). Callen and Lomax (1990: 507) found that UK mortgage rates tracked the 3-month LIBOR more closely in the 1980s than it previously had.

8. Mortgage securitization by commercial banks was facilitated in February 1989 when the Bank of England ruled securitized loans were off-balance sheet items: thus securitization could be used to improve capital/asset ratios and comply with Basle standards.
9. As an aid to distressed owners, Britain has an income-based shelter support policy which pays a portion of the interest on mortgages held by borrowers who become unemployed. However, this policy only mitigates the widespread increase in tenure risk for UK homeowners
10. This massive post-war effort to adequately house the French population was *de facto*, not *de jure*; only in 1989 was a right to housing passed into law (Schaefer, 1993: 172–6).
11. A mortgage interest deduction was adopted only in 1983, with terms less generous than in the US and UK – only 25% of mortgage interest can be used as a tax deduction, and for just 5 years (Wood, 1990).
12. The largest residential lender in France is a public agency, the CDC, which finances public housing loans with low-cost deposits collected by savings banks in tax-free passbook accounts.
13. This term refers to renter households without housing assistance whose incomes are less than 50% of the local median and who pay more than 50% of their income for rent (or who live in severely substandard housing).

REFERENCES

Balchin, P. (1995) *Housing Policy in Europe*, London: Routledge.

Ball, M. (1990) *Under One Roof*. New York: St. Martin's Press.

Ball, M. and Martens, M. (1990) 'German Universal Banking and the Mortgage Market,' in M. Ball, *Under One Roof*, New York: St. Martin's Press.

Boleat, M. (1985) *National Housing Finance Systems: A Comparative Study*, Kent: Croom Helm.

Bradt, K.W. (1991) 'Securitization in Europe,' in *Asset Securitization: Theory and Practice in Europe*, edited by C. Stone, A. Zissu, and J. Lederman, London: Euromoney Books. pp. 1–24.

Burchell, R.W. and Listokin, D. (1995) 'Influences on United States Housing Policy,' *Housing Policy Debate*, **6**(3), 559–618.

Callen, T.S. and Lomax, J.W. (1990) 'The Development of the Building Societies Sector in the 1980s,' *Bank of England Quarterly Bulletin*, November, 503–10.

Cerny, P.G. (1994) 'The Dynamics of Financial Globalization: Technology, Market Structure, and Policy Response,' *Policy Sciences*, **27**, 319–42.

Davidson, P. (1982) *International Money and the Real World*, New York: Wiley.

Diamond, D.B. and Lea, M.J. (1992a) 'Housing Finance in Developed Countries: An International Comparison of Efficiency,' *Journal of Housing Research* (special issue), **3**(1), 1–271.

Diamond, D.B. and Lea, M.J. (1992b) 'The Decline of Special Circuits in Developed Country Housing Finance,' *Housing Policy Debate*, **3**(3), 747–77.

Dymski, G. and Isenberg, D. (1997) 'Social Efficiency and the "Market Revolution" in US Housing Finance,' in *Evolving Roles of Government in Japan and the United States*, edited by Shinya Imura, Takashi Nakahama and Hiroshi Shibuya. Tokyo: Nihon Keizai Hyoron Sha (in Japanese).

Dymski, G. and Veitch, J. (1992) 'It's Not a Wonderful Life: Housing Affordability in Los Angeles,' mimeo, University of California, Riverside.

Epstein, G. and Gintis, H. (1994) *Macroeconomic Policy after the Conservative Era*, New York: Cambridge University Press.

Feldman, M. and Florida, R. (1990) 'Economic Restructuring and the Changing Role of the State in US Housing,' in *Government and Housing: Developments in Seven*

Countries, edited by W. van Vliet and J. van Weesep, Volume 36 of *Urban Affairs Annual Reviews*, Newbury Park: Sage Publications, pp. 31–46.

Follain, J.R., Ling, D.C. and McGill, G.A. (1993) 'The Preferential Income Tax Treatment of Owner-Occupied Housing: Who Really Benefits?' *Housing Policy Debate*, **4**(1), 1–23.

Fukao, M. and Hanazaki, M. (1987) 'Internationalization of Financial Markets and the Allocation of Capital,' *OECD Economic Studies*, **8**, 36–92.

Glyn, A., Hughes, A., Lipietz, A. and Singh, A. (1990) 'The Rise and Fall of the Golden Age,' in S. Marglin and J.B. Schor (eds), *The Golden Age of Capitalism*, Oxford: Oxford University Press.

Guttmann, R. (1994) *How Credit-Money Shapes the Economy*, Armonk, NY: M.E. Sharpe.

Gyourko, J. (1990) 'Controlling and Assisting Privately Rented Housing,' *Urban Studies*, **27**(6), 785–93.

Harloe, M. (1995) *The People's Home? Social Rented Housing in Europe and America*, Cambridge: Blackwell.

Hays, R.A. (1995) *The Federal Government and Urban Housing: Ideology and Change in Public Policy*, 2nd edition. Albany: State University of New York Press.

Hutton, W. (1995) *The State We're In*, London: Vintage.

Katz, M.B. (1989) *The Undeserving Poor: From the War on Poverty to the War on Welfare*, New York: Pantheon.

Kemp, P. (1990) 'Income-Related Assistance with Housing Costs: A Cross-National Comparison,' *Urban Studies*, **27**(6), 795–808.

Kleinman, M. (1996) *Housing, Welfare and the State in Europe*, Cheltenham: Edward Elgar.

Kregel, J.A. (1993) 'Banks Supervision: The Real Hurdle to European Monetary Union,' *Journal of Economic Issues*, **27**(2), 667–76.

Leather, P. and Murie, A. (1986) 'The Decline in Public Expenditure,' in P. Malpass (ed.), *The Housing Crisis*, London: Routledge.

Maclennan, D. (1995) 'Housing to 2001: Can Britain Do Better?' *Housing Policy Debate*, **6**(3), 655–94.

Malpass, P. (1986) 'From Complacency to Crisis,' in P. Malpass (ed.), *The Housing Crisis*, London: Routledge.

Malpass, P. (1993) 'Housing Tenure and Affordability: The British Disease,' in G. Hallett (ed.), *The New Housing Shortage*. London: Routledge.

Masnick, G.S. (1991) 'A Critique of Key Assumptions in the Current Housing Affordability Debate: What the Data Tell Us', Notes distributed at the Fannie Mae Colloquiam on Domestic Housing Policy, University of Southern California, January 18.

Mussa, M. and Goldstein M. (1993) 'The Integration of World Capital Markets,' in *Changing Capital Markets: Implications for Monetary Policy*, Conference Proceedings. Kansas City: Federal Reserve Bank of Kansas City, pp. 245–313.

Newman, S. and Schnare, A. (1988) *Integrating Housing and Welfare Assistance*, Working paper, MIT Center for Real Estate Development, Cambridge, MA.

O'Brien, R. (1992) *Global Financial Integration: The End of Geography*, London: Pinter Publishers.

Pearsall, J. (1984) 'France,' in *Housing in Europe*, edited by M. Wynn. Kent: Croom Helm, pp. 9–53.

Prak, N.L. and Priemus, H. (1985) *Post-War Public Housing in Trouble*, Delft: Delft University Press.

Schaefer, J.-P. (1993) 'Housing Affordability in France,' in *The New Housing Shortage: Housing Affordability in Europe and the USA*, edited by G. Hallett, London: Routledge, pp. 151–78.

Schwartz, D.C., Ferlauto, R. and Hoffman, D. (1988) *A New Housing Policy for America*. Philadelphia: Temple University Press.

Stone, CA. and Zissu, A. (1992) *'Le Prêt Immobilier Cautionne*: An Innovative Substitute for the French mortgage,' *Journal of Housing Research*, **3**(2), 401–21.

Tomann, H. (1990) 'The Housing Market, Housing Finance and Housing Policy in West Germany: Prospects for the 1990s,' *Urban Studies*, **27**(6), 919–30.

United States Department of Housing and Urban Development (1998) *Rental Housing Assistance – The Crisis Continues: The 1997 Report to Congress on Worst Case Housing Needs*, Office of Policy Development and Research, April.

Wachter, S. (1990) 'The Limits of the Housing Finance System,' *Journal of Housing Research*, **1**(1), 163–85.

Whitehead, C.M.E. (1993) 'Privatizing Housing: An Assessment of UK Experience,' *Housing Policy Debate*, **4**(1), 101–40.

Wilson, F.D. (1979) *Residential Consumption, Economic Opportunity, and Race*, New York: Academic Press.

Wood, G.A. (1990) 'The Tax Treatment of Housing: Economic Issues and Reform Measures,' *Urban Studies*, **27**(6), 809–30.

9. A general framework for the analysis of currencies and commodities

Warren Mosler and Mathew Forstater

Keynes lashed out against neoclassical theory for treating capitalism as a barter or 'real-exchange' economy, and offered his 'monetary theory of production' as an alternative to the traditional approach based on the 'Classical dichotomy'. This aspect of Keynes's work has been developed by two traditions, the Post Keynesian and the Circulation Approaches (Deleplace and Nell, 1996). Post Keynesians have elaborated, among other topics, the relation of money (and money contracts), uncertainty, and historical time (Davidson), asset pricing and financial instability (Minsky), and endogenous money and credit creation (Moore, Wray). While Post Keynesians have generally emphasized money as a stock of wealth, circuit theory (Graziani, Parguez, Schmitt) has highlighted the importance of a rigorous analysis of the circulation of money for understanding the operation of capitalist economies, including the principle of effective demand.

Both Post Keynesian and Circulation Approaches accept the widely held view that modern money is not commodity money but rather token (or fiat) money (Moore, 1988; Graziani, 1988). Accordingly, they criticize conventional theory for continuing to utilize a framework that treats modern money as though it were still a commodity money. This chapter begins with two comments on this fundamental point. First, while modern money does not derive its value from its status as a commodity, once a token is declared necessary for the payment of taxes it can be analyzed within the same framework as any other commodity. Second, absent from most Post Keynesian and Circuit analyses is the institutional process by which a token obtains its value (purchasing power). Many analyses 'add in' government spending and taxation, and the central bank, after an initial investigation of the operation of a private money-using economy, implying that the currency currently in use, along with its value, preceded the State (Lavoie, 1992, pp. 151–69).

Analyses of the circuit that begin with banks financing firms' production (or households' purchases) and end with firms (or households) paying back their loans leave unanswered the question of why anyone would initially sell real goods or services for the unit of account. The 'common-sense' reply, 'because they can use the funds to buy other goods and services' is not a satisfying one, for the further 'infinite regress' question remains the same: 'why do those sellers want the unit of account?' What is missing is the process by which the unit of account is endowed with value.

This chapter takes the position that the question remains unanswered because it cannot be (adequately) answered unless the State is incorporated from the very beginning of the analysis. 'Money is a Creature of the State' (Lerner), and thus a 'monetary' analysis cannot be conducted prior to the introduction of the State. Interestingly, the Chartalist view of a tax-driven currency can be found in the writings of Keynes (not to mention Adam Smith!), the Post Keynesians, and the Circulation theorists, yet it is almost always presented as an aside, with the implications remaining unexplored (see Wray, 1999, on Smith, Keynes, and Post Keynesians such as Minsky; for the Circulationists, see Graziani, 1988).

In the Chartalist view, the State, desirous of moving various goods and services from the private sector to the public domain, first levies a tax. The State currency unit is defined as that which is acceptable for the payment of taxes. The imperative to pay taxes thus becomes the force driving the monetary circuit. This chapter seeks to refine the concept of the monetary circuit using a multidimensional model designed to reveal and illuminate the workings of a tax-driven currency. It will also be shown that this same model lends itself to the analysis of any commodity. In an adaptation of Moore's (1988) terminology, the model includes 'horizontal' and 'vertical' components of the monetary circuit. Following outline and discussion of the model, it will be utilized to dispel the myth that deficits imply future taxation, as well as to briefly analyze the 1997 Asian Financial Crisis.

THE VERTICAL COMPONENT

We begin with the vertical component of the model, as presented in Figure 9.1:

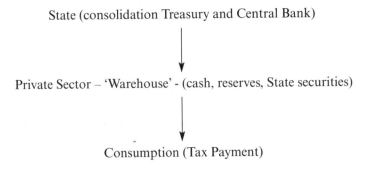

State (consolidation Treasury and Central Bank)

Private Sector – 'Warehouse' - (cash, reserves, State securities)

Consumption (Tax Payment)

Figure 9.1 Currency analysis: the vertical component

The tax liability lies at the bottom of the vertical, exogenous, component of the currency. At the top is the State (here presented as a consolidated Treasury and Central Bank), which is effectively the sole issuer of units of its currency, as it controls the issue of currency units by any of its designated agents. The middle is occupied by the private sector. It exchanges goods and services for the currency units of the state, pays taxes, and accumulates what is left over (State deficit spending) in the form of cash in circulation, reserves (clearing balances at the State's Central Bank), or Treasury securities ('deposits' offered by the CB). For comparative purposes later in the chapter, this accumulation will be considered 'warehoused'. The currency units used for the payment of taxes, or any other currency units transferred to the State, for this analysis, is considered to be consumed (destroyed) in the process. As the State can issue paper currency units or accounting information at the CB at will, tax payments need not be considered a reflux back to the state for the process to continue. In fact, the assumption of such reflux would imply a function of that process that this analysis emphasizes does not exist.

This completes the basic vertical component. Agents are said to participate in vertical activity if they obtain the unit of account from the State, pay taxes to the State, or intermediate the process. Central bank policy determines the relative distribution of the accumulated currency units of the private sector between cash, reserves (clearing balances), and Treasury securities. State (deficit) spending determines the magnitude of those accumulated financial assets.

THE HORIZONTAL COMPONENT

The horizontal component concerns the broad category of credit. In contrast with the vertical component, gross expansion of the horizontal component is endogenous, and nets to 0. The majority of circuit analysis begins and ends with the horizontal component. Even when the State is introduced, it too is assumed to behave horizontally. State taxing and borrowing are treated identically to private sector selling and borrowing. Although this treatment of the State may not be technically incorrect, the use of the vertical component adds a characterization of State activity previously ignored.

Any commodity has at least a vertical component. Horizontal activity represents leveraged activity of a vertical component. For analytical purposes, a unit of a currency is a commodity with no cost of production, no substitution, no inherent storage costs or transaction costs, and no product differentiation. Corn can be used to specifically demonstrate how a currency lends itself to the same analysis as commodities (Figure 9.2a).

With corn, the farmer can be considered at the top of the vertical component, and consumption at the bottom. The private sector remains in the middle, and

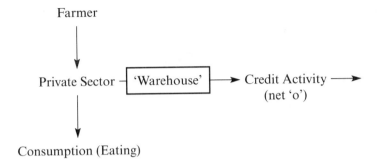

Figure 9.2a   General commodity analysis

transfers non-corn (generally units of a currency) up to the farmer who sends down the corn in exchange. If the private sector purchases more corn than it immediately consumes, the difference is warehoused (accumulated). If we were to use the same language with corn as we do with currency, we would say that when the farmer exchanges more corn to the private sector than the private sector consumes, the farmer is engaging in the deficit spending of corn.

The corn futures market is a leveraging of physical corn. There is a short position for every long position. Likewise, the creation of bank loans and their corresponding deposits is a leveraging of the currency, and every short position, or borrower, has a long position, or depositor, on the other side of the ledger. The futures market also happens to be a market that leverages the currency, as corn, for example, is exchanged for units of the currency. Thus the horizontal component for currency analysis can be indicated by introducing credit into the picture (see Figure 9.2b).

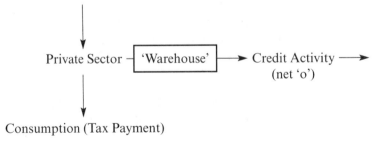

Figure 9.2b   Currency analysis: vertical and horizontal components

This model is consistent with the Post Keynesian notion that reserve imbalances can be reconciled only by the central bank. In this model, the horizontal activity always nets to 0. Reserves are clearing balances that can only come from vertical activity. Furthermore, in the US system, the Fed controls the mix in the 'warehouse' and can, for example, by purchasing securities on the open market, decrease securities held by the private sector and increase reserves of the private sector (clearing balances). Because of deposit insurance, in effect the Fed guarantees that inter-bank checks will clear when presented at the Fed. This means that if the banking system doesn't have sufficient reserves as required by the Fed, at least one bank will be showing an overdraft at its account at the Fed. Such an overdraft is, of course, a loan from the Fed, and an example of vertical activity. So, in the US system, required reserves come from the Fed in one form or another on demand, and the Fed sets the terms of exchange – interest rate and collateral – for the transaction.

EXOGENOUS PRICING

The State is effectively the sole issuer of its currency. As Lerner and Colander put it, 'if anything is a natural monopoly, the money supply is' (1980, p. 84). This means that the State is the price setter for its currency when it issues and exchanges it for goods and services. It is also the price setter of the interest (own) rate for its currency (Keynes, 1936, Chapter 17). The latter is accomplished by managing the clearing balances and securities offered for sale. The corn farmer, however, is generally not the single supplier of corn, and therefore is not a price setter. In addition, as there is no central warehouse, or its equivalent, the 'own rate' for corn is 0% or negative, reflecting only a cost of storage and a cost of short selling.

The model allows for two primary paths in the vertical component of a currency. The first is State spending, mainly by the Treasury. The second is State lending, mainly by the Central Bank, as part of the process by which bank deposit money is accepted by the State for the payment of taxes. When deposit money is used for the payment of taxes, banks are acting as intermediaries between the State and the private sector. This happens whenever a bank draft (check) is used for payment of taxes. The banking system is simultaneously obligated to accept funds from the State on terms dictated by the State to cover clearing balances debited when such checks clear.

Initial demand for the currency – that which is necessary to pay taxes – originates with those with tax liabilities. When analyzing an economy, knowledge of the type of tax liabilities in force is fundamental to understanding its operation. For example, an asset tax, such as a property tax, will yield different results than a transaction tax, such as a sales tax, value added tax, or income tax.

UTILIZING THE MODEL: BASIC CIRCUIT ANALYSIS

We now proceed with an example of how this model can be integrated into an analysis of the monetary circuit. In this example, we begin with the following assumptions:

(1) The State has levied an equal head tax on all individuals.
(2) The State hires only labor.
(3) There is no desire to save net financial assets (no deficit spending and no corresponding involuntary unemployment; see Mosler, 1997–8).
(4) The State does not hire all the available labor (there is a private sector).
(5) Producers qualify for bank credit.
(6) Consumers have no access to credit.

The monetary circuit begins with the vertical component, when the State declares that which it will accept for payment of taxes. The head tax is payable only in units of that currency. This causes taxpayers to offer goods and services in return for units of the currency. The State is now able to use its currency to purchase goods and services. This process results in the monetization of transactions in the State's currency. Taxpayers are continuously offering goods and services for sale, and soon other private sector agents, who desire that which is offered for sale, seek the means of obtaining units of the currency demanded by the sellers. The forces at work in the vertical component are sufficient to cause sellers of goods and services to denominate their offers in units of the State's currency. This results in an exchange of the unit of account from the State to the private sector, and from the private sector to the State, as the State spends and the taxes are paid.

Credit (horizontal activity) arises when a buyer desires to make a purchase by borrowing that which the seller demands. The buyer could borrow directly from the seller. This would result in the transfer of the items sold in exchange for a promissory note of the buyer, denominated in the State's currency, accepted by the seller. This note can be considered a form of money, depending on one's definition of money. The note presumably has value, or the seller would not have accepted it. But clearly any value is subject to change, as the buyer's financial condition may vary. There is also no reason such a note could not be negotiable, and circulate in the economy, as each new holder of the note attempts to use it to purchase from other sellers. Reflux could occur either when the original issuer of the note obtains it back via a sale of goods or services, or when the original issuer of the note retires it by exchanging it for State currency.

Notice that while the note was circulating, it was not an acceptable means of tax payment. The note was, however, an example of the leveraging of the State currency. It was endogenous horizontal activity. The holder of the note had a 'long' position and the issuer a 'short' position. The net was always 0. Furthermore, the note was denominated in units of the State's currency. Horizontal activity is always denominated in units of a vertical component.

The same transaction could have been intermediated by a bank. Perhaps the seller did not want to accept the note of the buyer, but would accept a bank deposit. The buyer could then go to a bank and request a loan. If approved, the result would be that the bank would hold the buyer's note, and grant the seller a deposit in the bank. Banking thus assumes the credit risk of the buyer (presumably expressed in the interest rate charged). Banks undertaking this type of business activity are similar to insurance institutions, managing risk through analysis and diversity. Again, this is horizontal activity.

Bank deposits are the accounting records of loans. There is gross expansion of financial assets, but the net is always 0. For every deposit there is a loan from which it originated. Do note, however, that as bank deposits are acceptable for tax payment, they may function as part of the vertical component. Again, the banks acting in this capacity are, in the case of deposits being used for tax payment, intermediating vertical activity.

Taxpayers not wishing state employment, or who don't qualify for State employment, will seek other, alternative means of obtaining currency. Directly or indirectly the needed funds must, given the above assumptions, ultimately come from someone employed by the State. In the simplest case, individuals offer goods and services to those employed by the State in return for some of the currency originally earned from the State.

Non-taxpayers, too, are apt to become monetized, as when they see goods and services for sale they, too, desire units of the State currency of denomination. They may, for example, sell their labor to those employed by the State, and then, with the currency units thus obtained, make purchases from tax payers not employed by the State.

At some point, an entrepreneur may attempt to organize production, with the objective of making a profit, which can then be used to make personal purchases. This may begin by borrowing from a bank to pay the wage bill, and end with the recovery of expenditures and profit through sales of final output. The example of this paragraph is representative of existing circuit analysis. But now we can go further, as even the most complex of the interactions of firms, consumers, taxpayers, and the State are readily examined in the context of our model.

This example assumed a head tax. It could have assumed a transaction tax, such as an income tax. Note, however, that an income tax on income earned by the private sector from State employment will not drive the model. Working for the State, one would simply get a net payment of currency units for which there would be no further use. What would be required is an imputed income tax on transactions within the private sector. These transactions – private sector employment – would then generate a net private sector tax liability that would require sales of goods and services to the State. Note that this would have to include an imputed tax, otherwise the private sector would (continue to) trade in some other medium of exchange.

It is also clear that transactions taxes have the effect of discouraging those transactions subject to the tax. Thus the model lends itself to the analysis of the differences between various asset taxes and transactions taxes.

FISCAL BALANCE

From inception, the State must spend or otherwise provide that which is necessary to pay taxes. And, for all practical purposes, the private sector will be willing to obtain more currency units from the State in exchange for real goods and services than the minimum required for its current tax liability. The extra currency units accumulated are called net private sector savings of financial assets denominated in the unit of account, elsewhere termed H(nfa) (Mosler, 1997–8).

This is analogous to the private sector buying more corn from the farmer than just the exact amount of current consumption. If the State (or farmer) does not offer to provide the amount desired by the taxpayer (or consumer), there is, by definition, a shortage. Horizontal activity cannot provide for any net accumulation. A collective desire in the private sector can only be resolved in the vertical component. As Moore (1988) argues, only the central bank can resolve a reserve imbalance. In a similar vein, Keynes demonstrated that, except in the unlikely case of an 'accident', actual and desired net savings will only be equal at full employment 'by design', i.e., the State running a budget deficit (Keynes, 1936, p. 28).

This is not to say that horizontal activity cannot effect a change in the desire to net save. For example, a rise in the price of corn on the futures exchange due to a shortage could certainly reduce the desire to net save corn. The corn market may stabilize at a higher price. Such stability occurs when the actual net savings of corn equals the desired net savings of corn. Likewise, a reduction in State deficit spending could result in a deflation that stabilized when prices fell enough for private sector agents to lower their collective desire to net save, and make purchases either through spending net savings or incurring new debt.

The horizontal component is a leveraging of a vertical component. This implies price sensitivity to supply and demand changes that may originate in the vertical component. Changes in fiscal balance are analogous to changes in the expected harvest or mine output. Changes in taxation are analogous to changes in consumption demand. Fiscal balance occurs only when the State runs a fiscal policy that allows actual to equal desired H(nfa) (Mosler, 1997–8). With most other commodities, the market is allowed to maintain this balance. Price changes are continuous as inventories rise and fall for the various commodities.

The State currency, however, is a case of a single supplier. So we must look to other examples of single suppliers for the more accurate analogy as to the processes that equate actual and desired net savings. An example can be a water monopolist with an unlimited supply and no marginal cost of production. In this case it would be in an area where there is no other available supply, and a sufficiently captive population.

Micro theory recognizes that this single supplier of the needed water would set a price for water and then let the population purchase as much as it desired at that price. A higher price would perhaps lower sales, and a lower price may increase sales, depending on the elasticity of demand. Some of the change in sales would be due to changes in water held in storage facilities, and some due to discretionary consumption, such as bathing. The amount sold and used for drinking, for example, might be less elastic than that sold for washing cars. But in any case, the single supplier of the water would not likely choose an alternative strategy of selling a fixed quantity of water and letting the market decide the price. If it did, it would be a very difficult situation to manage. Depending on elasticity, fixing the quantity a bit too high could cause a large drop in price, and fixing the quantity a bit too low could cause a sharp spike in prices. And, as weather and demand changed, volatility could be high, particularly if desired gallons held in storage facilities were subject to changing hopes and fears. In fact, even if the water monopolist set out to budget the number of gallons it wished to sell, and let the market decide price, it would likely soon change policy. A skyrocketing price would likely result in an increase in the quantity offered for sale, and a falling price might result in a decline in the amount brought to market. So in any case the monopolist would likely end up behaving as a price setter. Only if and when the single supplier status is lost is the position of price setter eroded.

In the case of the State as single supplier of its currency of issue, the State is in the position of price setter of its currency. It can unilaterally set the terms of exchange that it will offer to those seeking its currency. Ironically, no State currently seems to recognize this. To the contrary, States act as if they were in competition with other buyers when conducting purchases with their own currency. They believe and act as if they must raise revenue through taxing or borrowing to fund spending. They have chosen the option of setting the quantity of their currency they wish to spend via a budgeting process, and then exchanging that currency at market prices for desired goods and services. Like the water monopolist, spending too much will drive up prices (reduce the value of the currency) and spending too little triggers a deflation (increase the value of the currency). In addition, there is no long-term 'right amount' as the (world-wide) desire to net save that currency may be constantly changing. Hence a fluctuating NAIRU, removing most practical value from the concept.

The other practical option for the State, as single supplier of its currency, if it wishes to maintain a market economy, is to administer a buffer stock. Gold has traditionally served this role. The State would set the price at which it would buy or sell gold, and then conduct monetary and fiscal policy such that the buffer stock remained credible. Graham (1937) long ago proposed that commodities other than gold might serve a similar function. In 'Full Employment and Price Stability' the option to use labor as the State's buffer stock was presented (Mosler, 1997–8). Clearly, when administering a buffer stock, purchases made at the designated price are not inflationary. They do prevent deflation below that level. Nor are sales from the buffer stock deflationary. Rather, they serve to inhibit inflation.

DEFICIT SPENDING AND FUTURE TAXATION

It has been continuously argued and widely accepted that State deficit spending represents future taxation. Our model, however, clearly demonstrates that this is not the case. For example, if farmers sell more corn than the population will consume that period, they can be said to be deficit spending corn which will sit in the warehouse. Does that imply either that consumption must go up some day, or that future production will be curtailed? Not necessarily. It may be argued that the future value of corn will fall some day, but that would depend on the desired inventory in the future. In fact, corn traders carefully watch the inventories. They have some conception of the 'right' size, consistent with stable prices. That 'right' amount will naturally fluctuate with population size, availability of substitutes, etc. In the case of the single supplier, like the water monopolist who sets price and lets the market buy all it wants, sales in excess of current consumption again do not necessarily mean either future increases in consumption or lower future output. Nor do they necessarily mean a fall in future water prices.

The same is true for the State as issuer of its currency. The State does not force anyone to exchange goods and services for its currency. The exchange is with willing sellers who desire the currency. Deficit spending occurs only if the private sector is desirous of accumulating units of the currency in order to net save. Hyperinflation is the condition in which the private sector no longer desires the currency unit (as reflected in the price level).

THE ASIAN CRISIS OF 1997

The Asian crisis of 1997 can be analyzed in the general commodity framework presented here. What happened can be described as a dollar squeeze. In the face of declining $US federal budget deficits, horizontal expansion in Asia continued through the first half of 1997. Agents borrowed $US and either spent them directly on projects or used their $US to purchase local currency to run their businesses. That meant they were short the $US and long their local currency, which was generally invested in local enterprise. Often it was the local central bank that encouraged this type of risk taking by setting the domestic interest rate higher than the $US rate and simultaneously maintaining a pegged exchange rate. While the local businessmen were borrowing $US and exchanging them for local currency, the central bank was more than willing to accommodate them, and accumulate $US reserves. However, when the private sector turned to being net sellers of the local currency to pay their $US obligations the central banks were reluctant to lose their $US reserves to support the local currency and instead let it float downward. At the lower foreign exchange rates the local businesses were unable to meet their $US obligations and a liquidity crisis, which is still not resolved, followed.

Continuing with our commodity framework, it was similar to being short corn while the warehouse stocks were declining. Now, with depressed local currencies, many of these countries are running sizeable $US trade surpluses. That means someone else is running $US deficits, as the horizontal component between nations always nets to 0. As long as the US fiscal balance remains as it is, there is little that can be done to alleviate the world-wide $US squeeze, except a decrease in the net desire to save $US denominated assets. Falling prices may decrease the net desire to save, inducing the additional spending, but it is not common for this to happen. In fact, it is hard to find a sector of the US economy that can continue to increase its indebtedness sufficiently to extend US GDP growth. The two large growth areas were the expansion of sub-prime and Asian credit, both of which are slowing dramatically. Furthermore, it seems all nations are pushing (fiscal) deficit reduction at the same time, taking away the possibility of export-led expansions.

We have yet to see any mention of US fiscal policy as a cause for concern and a contributing culprit in the Asian crisis. No one seems to recognize the importance of deficits in the same way they recognize the importance of the size of the stocks of other commodities. That may be why markets don't react in anticipation of the inevitable short squeeze, as none of the market participants are aware of the connection. Therefore, only after the shortage is acute does the market finally react, as shorts have no choice but to cover their positions by selling other assets to obtain needed $US. So it hits hard and fast. Note that the Japanese economy expanded rapidly enough in the late 1980s to drive the budget into surplus. Soon after, the stock market and real estate market crashed as agents were forced to sell these assets to obtain needed yen. Eight years later the stock market is still more than 60% off its highs and real estate continues to drop at double digit rates annually, in spite of years of near 0% interest rates.

A yen short squeeze can only be resolved in the vertical component. And long-term budget targets conflict with that necessity.

CONCLUSION

This chapter outlines an alternative way of viewing the monetary circuit that takes into consideration the central role of the State from the beginning of the analysis. Vertical and horizontal components of the monetary circuit were introduced and their relation analyzed. It was shown that this framework is applicable not only to currency, but to any commodity, and that deficit spending, as herein defined, is a practical necessity for all currencies and commodities. From inception, one simply cannot consume more than has been produced, and a private sector desire to save any currency or commodity requires deficit spending. Having no national debt in local currency is equivalent to having no inventories of corn, water, or any other commodities. While currency does not obtain its value by virtue of its status as a commodity, once endowed with value a tax-driven currency can be analyzed like any other commodity. In addition to debunking the myth that deficits imply future taxation, it was also shown that such a framework is highly applicable to the current Asian financial crisis.

REFERENCES

Deleplace, G. and Nell, E.J. (eds) (1996) *Money in Motion: The Post Keynesian and Circulation Approaches*, London: Macmillan.

Graham, B. (1937) *Storage and Stability*, New York: McGraw Hill.

Graziani, A. (1988) 'Le financement de l'économie dans la pensée de J.M. Keynes,' *Cahiers d'Economie Politique*, 14–15.

Keynes, J.M. (1936) *The General Theory of Employment, Interest, and Money*, New York: Harvest Harcourt Brace.

Lavoie, M. (1992) *Foundations of Post-Keynesian Economic Analysis*, Aldershot: Edward Elgar.

Lerner, A.P. and Colander, D.C. (1980) *MAP: A Market Anti-inflation Plan*, New York: Harcourt Brace Jovanovich.

Moore, B. (1988) *Horizontalists and Verticalists*, Cambridge: Cambridge University Press.

Mosler, W. (1997–8) 'Full Employment and Price Stability', *Journal of Post Keynesian Economics*, **20** (2), 167–82.

Wray, L.R. (1999) *Understanding Modern Money: The Key to Full Employment and Price Stability*, Aldershot: Edward Elgar.

10. Price stability and full employment as complements in a new Europe: a market-based price stabilization policy for the new ECB

Jan Kregel

SUMMARY OF THE ARGUMENT

New Europe, Old Monetary Policy

A new Europe will be born on 1 January 1999. But it will not be based on a New Monetary Policy. Instead it will preserve policies employed in a Europe divided for use in a Europe united by a single currency. These policies have not been successful in the past because they fail to understand the basic differences between a commodity money system and a system of State-mandated fiat money.

Can We Learn from the Gold Standard?

We argue that the new European Central Bank should instead return to the principles of market-driven price stabilization policies that were presumed to operate under the Gold Standard. But gold no longer plays any role in modern economies. Adjustments must thus be made to take into account the fact that fiat money systems differ from commodity-based systems in terms of the automatic or homeostatic mechanisms at work to stabilize prices.

Preserving the Complementarity of Stabilization and Employment Policy

In a commodity money system price stability and income stability are complements. Despite the fact that modern monetary systems are fiat money systems, central banks continue to operate monetary policy on the presumption of a price stabilization mechanism that could only operate under a commodity money that no longer exists. As a result price stability and income stability have become substitutes, leading to the unnecessary and economically wasteful trade-off between full employment and inflation.

Recognizing Differences between a Gold and a Labour-standard System

The present chapter argues that central banks are capable of making full employment and price stability complements by recognising the market price stabilization mechanisms at work in what Keynes called 'Representative money' systems, or Knapp called systems of 'State money'. This theory suggests an alternative policy for price stabilization that is compatible with full employment. This theory follows Nobel Prize winner John Hicks (1985) in recognising that modern monetary systems are on a de facto labour standard.

Preserving Market Price Stabilization Mechanisms in a Fiat Money System

Instead of stabilizing the price of goods in terms of gold, the appropriate strategy for the central bank is to stabilize the price of goods in terms of labour. Since the central bank cannot directly influence the value of money, which in a State money system is determined by the government, it should pursue the stabilization of money wages. Just as the price of gold was fixed under the gold standard, the central bank should fix the money price of basic labour, by offering to employ all workers willing and able to work at a given wage. The jobs that are offered could be designed to provide public goods, or could involve training and education to increase labour productivity. This would remove unemployment benefit and other programmes of labour support from the government budget. Just as under the gold standard mechanism, a rise in the purchasing power of gold increased demand for gold and led to higher employment and output in the gold mining sector, a rise in the producing power of labour above the basic wage would create an incentive for private employers to bid workers away from basic employment. On the other hand, when producing power falls below the wage due to a cyclical decline, the offer of basic employment will place a floor on overall demand that supports private sector production, and act as an automatic stabilizer.

THE PROBLEM OF PRICE STABILITY AND UNEMPLOYMENT

The problem of ensuring price stability is not a new one. For the last three generations concern has been directed towards rising prices. However, as the Bank for International Settlements pointed out in its *Annual Report* for 1996 (BIS,

June, 1997) price stability means avoiding both rising and falling prices. History also suggests that those who believe that prices will rise continuously will usually be mistaken, since extended periods of falling prices have been as common as extended periods of rising prices. Currently, prices are falling in China and in Japan. According to two recent expert studies, one in the US, and one in Germany, if price changes were measured more accurately, none of the world's major economies would be experiencing inflationary conditions.

The new European Central Bank has the responsibility of maintaining price stability. The institution emerges from a historical experience that has been preoccupied with reducing the rate of inflation. It will bring with it the intellectual heritage of the German central bank, born of two post-war hyperinflations. It will also function in an academic framework in which it has been generally accepted that the disturbances caused by inflation to the efficient operation of the price mechanism have been a major cause of low growth and high unemployment levels. According to this theory, agents have difficulty discerning the difference between changes in relative prices due to inflation and changes caused by real factors. This may lead to a misallocation of resources if a general increase in prices is mistaken for a change in relative prices.

Recently falling inflation rates have done little to improve growth and employment conditions. Attention has thus been shifted to the inefficiencies caused by impediments to the operation of the competitive price mechanism in the labour market itself. Yet, the 1980s and 1990s have been periods in which labour markets have undergone a process of deregulation and have become increasingly flexible. The experience in terms of employment levels has been extremely varied. While the UK has experienced employment gains, other European countries have seen unemployment surpass 1930s depression levels. Many consider the positive result achieved in the UK to have been due not only to the elimination of labour market restrictions, but also to the fact that the UK was forcefully encouraged to exit from the Exchange Rate Mechanism of the European Monetary System. The UK thus benefited from being able to reduce interest rates in conditions of improved foreign competitiveness accompanied by a substantial stimulus from a government budget deficit. Somewhat paradoxically, although the UK is one of the few countries to meet the fiscal convergence conditions without budgetary subterfuge, it has decided not to enter EMU because its economic performance is too vigorous compared to the rest of Europe.

Some would argue that since labour costs are a primary component of production costs a policy of price stability must also include wage stability. The levels of unemployment that are currently being experienced in Europe are simply those required to keep wages stable. This is the idea behind the 'natural rate' approach, which simply defines equilibrium in the labour market, and thus full employment, as the level of employment associated with price stability. Any attempt to increase employment would create excess demand and cause wages to rise, and eventually lead to rising prices. A policy of price stability will then of necessity produce a natural rate of unemployment. Actions to reduce unemployment must then concentrate on improving the operation of the labour market, so as to produce wage stability at higher employment levels, or to increase productivity so as to allow wage increases to be offset by increasing production per employee.

It is interesting that despite continued efforts to increase flexibility and competition in labour markets, and extremely high rates of productivity growth, it would appear that the 'natural' level of unemployment in Europe has been increasing rather than decreasing. Price stabilization policies have thus been associated with rising levels of natural unemployed workers. It would also appear that in many countries nominal wage increases have been lagging behind the increasing productivity of labour, so that real wages have not been increasing but have been declining. This should have led to an increase in the employment of labour in substitution for capital. Investment and capital accumulation certainly have fallen in most European countries along with the lower real wages, but this has not produced an increase in the employment of labour.

THE MECHANISMS FOR COMBINING PRICE STABILITY AND HIGH EMPLOYMENT

Historically, periods of increasing government intervention and control of the market mechanism have been provoked by rising unemployment rates. Equally, the independence of central bank policy to pursue price stability has been conditioned by the ability to combine price stability with acceptable levels of employment. Once unemployment passes the political acceptable level, governments intervene and central banks find their independence constrained, no matter what the legal guarantees. This suggests that it would be extremely shortsighted for the European Central Bank to consider its operations independently of their impact on the level of employment. A truly successful central bank policy produces price stability without having to accept high or increasing levels of unemployment.

The conventional approach to price stabilization policies is linked to changes in the purchasing power of a commodity money such as gold. The central idea is that there is a homeostatic (i.e. self-equilibrating) market arbitrage mechanism that ensures price stability when the monetary system is based on the use of a commodity as money. This self-adjusting process is the result of a fixed relation between the unit of account and a quantity (measured in weight) of gold. It is usually achieved by setting the ratio at which the government mint would convert the commodity, gold bullion, into coined money denominated in units of account. The amount of gold bullion circulating as coin was determined by the demand for gold bullion in commercial uses, and the conditions under which additional supplies could be produced by mining. If the prices of goods rose, the purchasing power of the unit of account represented by the coined gold would fall relative to the commercial value of gold bullion. Gold coin would be withdrawn from circulation, as goods were produced and sold for gold, and the gold melted down into bullion for commercial use.

This is a triangular arbitrage the profitability of which can be eliminated by changing one of the three exchange ratios: the mint ratio, the unit of account–goods ratio (goods prices) or the gold bullion–goods ratio. Since the mint ratio is fixed, and gold bullion cannot exchange directly for goods, the adjustment must come in goods prices. The arbitrage mechanism puts downward pressure on goods prices as goods are sold for gold, and reduces the circulation of gold coin as gold is melted into bullion and disappears onto the gilt ceilings of the castles of kings and archbishops.

On the other hand, if prices fell the purchasing power of gold coin would rise. It would become profitable to sell coin in exchange for goods to provision labour to work in the gold mines to produce more bullion to be minted into coin. This would increase demand for goods and for labour, support goods prices and increase the gold circulation until mining bullion was no longer profitable.

Thus, the system automatically reacts to an increase or decrease in goods prices by pursuing arbitrage opportunities that produce pressure on prices in the opposite direction. It naturally self-regulates the price level and produces price stability. At the same time, it operates to increase the demand for labour when prices are falling, and decrease it when prices are rising. It thus also provides self-regulation of demand for labour.

It is often believed that a gold-based monetary system produces price stability because the quantity of gold available to circulate as currency is given exogenously. But it is easy to see that this is not the case. In general, price stability under a gold-based system required an endogenously determined money supply. Indeed, prices were unstable when the supply of money was not elastic and the homeostatic self-equilibrating arbitrage mechanism was prevented from operating. It should also be clear that the arbitrage produced self-stabilization because the mint ratio was not a 'price' subject to the forces of supply and demand, but was administratively fixed.[1]

This principle can be seen more clearly in the operation of the better known international gold standard adjustment mechanism. In an open system, a rise in the domestic price level relative to international prices causes a fall in the domestic purchasing power of gold relative to its purchasing power abroad. An arbitrage opportunity would be created in which gold is sold against goods in the country where its purchasing power was high, and bought in exchange for goods in the country where its purchasing power was low. This would increase the supply of imported goods in the high price country, causing a trade deficit represented by gold exports. Gold would thus naturally move until its purchasing power was equal wherever it was used to buy goods. This represents the stable price level (some adjustments would have to be made for differential rates of productivity growth).

It is irrelevant whether it was the decline in the domestic supply of gold or the increase in cheap imports that caused the decline in activity and prices, the result was to produce an equilibrium in which the purchasing power of gold was uniform across countries and country price levels tended to be uniform in proportion to the differing mint ratios. Again, note that price stability required variation in the domestic circulation of gold. Indeed, the whole point of Hume's famous essay was to demonstrate the folly of trying to fix the quantity of gold circulating in a country by limiting its export; it would just be arbitraged away by the operation of the free market. Price stability could thus be guaranteed by fixing the mint ratio of gold in terms of the domestic unit of account, and then allowing the free competitive price mechanism to operate.

FROM COMMODITY MONEY TO FIAT MONEY

The introduction of paper money in the form of bank notes, and then of deposits, caused a great deal of difficulty to economists who had grown used to analysing commodity money systems. The basic question was how bank notes might disturb the operation of the homeostatic arbitrage mechanism. The 'currency' school was founded on the idea that paper money could be viewed simply as a one-for-one substitute for gold (or could be made to behave as such); the automatic mechanism thus remained intact. This, of course, required that banks simply operate as safekeep depositories for gold. Today we would call this a 100% obligatory reserve system. Thus, under a gold-based paper currency system, the government determined the gold content of the paper money denominated in standard unit of account and the notes simply served as substitutes for coin. This was accomplished by the Treasury or Central Bank replacing the mint, and offering to convert the unit of account into its fixed weight in gold. The 1844 Bank Act was an attempt to legislate this principle.

There is also an automatic process at work here to keep prices stable. If goods prices rise, the purchasing power of the unit of account over goods falls, but its purchasing power over the given weight of commodity gold remains constant while the purchasing power of gold over goods rises. Thus there is a triangular arbitrage that involves selling goods short for unit of account, converting into gold and using the gold to buy goods. This leads to a run on the currency, an increased supply of goods, a decline in the gold supply at the central bank and an increase in the gold circulation. The main conclusion of the currency school is that this process would stop once the entire gold supply of the bank is in active circulation and the notes have all been redeemed and are sitting in the vault of the bank. Indeed, the system should operate just as a commodity-based gold coin system. The automatic mechanism can only be disturbed, and thus rising prices could result, if the currency issue should be greater than the gold supply in the bank.

This would occur under a fractional reserve banking system. In this case the automatic adjustment mechanism may reach a point where the desired sales of the paper currency exhaust the gold in the bank. At this point the paper currency becomes inconvertible, and the central bank suspends its offer to buy and sell the currency for a fixed amount of gold because it can no longer honour its offer to buy currency. This is the equivalent of suspension of the mint ratio. The remaining currency will then circulate at a discounted weight in gold. Although suspensions were frequent in history, the idea behind the gold standard was that this could not happen if the 'mint ratio' were inviolable. Clearly, under fiduciary systems the conversion ratio of notes into gold is not inviolable. In these conditions the automatic mechanism by which private market arbitrage produces price stability will be disrupted. Let us see how.

There are two ways for the central bank to avoid running out of gold. The first, to reduce the gold content of the unit of account to eliminate the arbitrage, simply confirms the rise in the price level. It thus clearly defeats the stabilizing operation of arbitrage and institutionalizes the rise in goods prices. The second is to increase the demand for the paper currency. This could only be done by increasing the discount rate. The interest differential from holding currency relative to gold would have to be sufficient to offset the differential purchasing power between notes and gold. This is presumably one of the sources of the idea that the rate of interest has to adjust to offset any loss in the purchasing power of the currency. In this way the monetary authority can preserve the fixed gold content of the currency by ensuring that the currency is willingly held by changing the return on currency relative to gold. If goods prices in terms of paper have risen by $x\%$, then paper will only be held if the rate of interest covers its $x\%$ loss in purchasing power. This prevents inconvertibility, but again it does so by blocking the automatic adjustment process. Prices will remain higher, and the paper money supply will increase by the interest payments.

Thus, a clear sign that price stability was not being achieved in a fiat money system was an increase in the supply of paper money. This led to the idea that since stable prices were associated with stability of the quantities of means of payment, it would be possible to achieve price stability by holding the quantity of money constant. But this inference is clearly unwarranted, for, as seen above, the automatic adjustment mechanisms inherent in a commodity money gold-based system depend on variability in quantities and on one fixed relationship: the mint ratio defining the bullion content of the unit of account in coin or paper currency.

UNDERSTANDING STATE FIAT MONEY SYSTEMS

In a modern economy, gold has long ago disappeared, and notes are no longer held on the fiduciary promise to repay gold. Instead, notes issued by government have taken the place of gold and commercial bank deposits have taken the place of notes. Now, the only promise to repay bank deposits is in terms of a different kind of money, the money issued by the government. And government money is not repaid at all. Thus, the basis of the triangular arbitrage that provided price stability in a gold-based system is no longer present because money is no longer produced by labour and money has no independent commercial use.[2] Do these changes from commodity to fiat or representative money make any difference to the policy used to ensure price stability? Central bankers certainly do not think so, as they continue to use control of the quantity of central bank money as the means to the goal of stability without noticing that this was not what ensured stability under the gold standard, and that the market mechanisms that once operated under the gold standard are no longer present.

Economists have been less certain. It was a problem that was first faced in the 1920s when many countries abandoned their gold-based systems. Economists such as Keynes and Cassell tried to devise a set of monetary policy rules that would behave as if it were subject to the automaticity of the gold standard in the absence of a fixed gold content of notes. The answer that they came up with was what Keynes called a 'managed money' system. Cassell invented the idea of purchasing power parity as the equivalent of the constant purchasing power of gold across countries. If the national currency could buy the same basket of real goods in any country at existing exchange rates, then there was no possibility for arbitrage. If domestic monetary policy were operated so as to stabilize the prices of a basket of (traded) goods, and if all countries did so, then exchange rates would remain stable, as they had been under the gold standard. Thus, active monetary policy was required to replicate the results of international and domestic arbitrage by imposing purchasing power parity, but how was monetary policy to replace the gold standard arbitrage mechanism? There were two possible extremes. One was to retain commodity backing for the currency, the other was to move to a pure fiat money system.

One proposal was to replace gold with some other commodity. Instead of setting a fixed weight of gold, the central bank could fix the value of government money in terms of a basket composed of commodities of constant composition. This proposal was first made in the 1930s by the expert of security analysis, Benjamin Graham (Graham, 1937). This would not be a price stabilization scheme as such, for the prices of the individual goods in the basket would be free to adjust to market conditions, rather it would impose the rule that the weighted increases and decreases would cancel out, leaving the price of the basket unchanged. The price mechanism would thus provide incentives to increase the supply of scarce goods, and decrease the prices of goods in surplus among those included in the basket. There would also be a triangular arbitrage in which a rise in the price of all the commodities in the basket would make it profitable to sell them short in their individual markets and use the proceeds to purchase the basket from the monetary authority, using the component to meet delivery on the short sales. The higher spot prices would also encourage additional production as backwardation prevailed in futures markets increasing demand for future production. Alternatively, if prices were falling, commodities would be bought in the market for resale to the central bank, supporting prices as well as producers' incomes. Such schemes were also proposed on an international level to replace the gold standard system.

However, as the post-war managed money system evolved, gold was slowly eliminated and the dollar became the centre of the international system. There were no further attempts to create a system that would replicate the automatic adjustment mechanism of the gold standard, while the idea that monetary policy could produce price stability by keeping creation of money stable continued to gain adherents. Government money came to replace gold as the basis of the system. But, without an alternative use for government money, and without fixing the 'government money' content of private deposit money, there was no arbitrage mechanism to link the monetary and real sectors in a way that would provide complementarity between price and employment stability. Indeed, without the gold backing in a fixed ratio to the circulating paper currency, the entire current approach to monetary policy lacks theoretical foundation, since in the absence of a commodity such as gold backing it, there is no explanation of why money should be held at all. Its only use is in making transactions.

In the modern monetary system private banks issue deposit liabilities that can be converted into government money on sight. This is the rough equivalent to the convertibility of notes to a fixed quantity of gold, except gold has now been replaced by the stock of government money in the form of notes and reserves forming the monetary 'base'. Note that it is not the government that sets the ratio of deposits to government money (except as a limit under obligatory reserve systems), it is the private commercial banks who do this. In effect they serve as market makers for their own debt, guaranteeing that it will have a unit price with government money. Rather than a fixed ratio, there will be an elastic relation between the two that is determined either by legal or prudential reserve requirements that are necessary to preserve the unit price, and the decisions of the public concerning their holdings of public and private money. Now it is not a falling purchasing power of commercial bank deposits that leads individuals to shift from deposits to government money, but rather a change in the credit risk of the issuing banks as represented by the difficulty in keeping the unit price of liabilities stable. Unlike a shift from paper money to gold due to an increase in goods prices, a shift in the relative advantages of government and commercial bank money will occur because of questions of the credit worthiness of the commercial bank, but will have no direct impact on production or prices in the goods market. Rather, the commercial banks will have to increase interest rates in order to attract more government money in deposits or through inter-bank borrowing or from the central bank.

The central bank does not have the same worry concerning the price of government money, since it is defined by government expenditure policy. The rate of interest would then be set by the requirements of private banks in meeting their commitment to unit pricing on their deposit liabilities. As long as this link holds, there is no differential impact on the two types of money from a rise in goods prices. There is thus no triangular arbitrage. Rather, the arbitrage is to short money (borrow) and buy goods as long as the rate of inflation is above the rate of interest. This is a self-reinforcing, or momentum arbitrage, for it increases the demand for goods and thus causes higher prices. It can be brought to a halt by removing the source of the arbitrage, but in difference from the gold standard it does not act directly on the sale and production of goods, but rather on the portfolio composition of households and financial institutions. If the rate of interest is raised above the rate of inflation, money will be preferred to buying spot goods for future sale. A spread arbitrage mechanism then operates along the financial asset spectrum. By raising short rates, it leads investors to increase their demand for short funds. This reduces the demand for longer-term funds, and drives up longer rates, and so on out the maturity spectrum. Then the arbitrage jumps to the real asset spectrum and influences the purchase of real investments and finally, through time preference changes the allocation of present versus future consumption, reducing spending and increasing saving. The fall in demand then leads to falling prices. This mechanism is to be found in a series of theories starting with Wicksell's proposal that monetary stability would require equivalence of the money interest rate with real interest rates. This is the condition that would be compatible with a constant quantity of money.

However, as Hayek, Sraffa, Keynes, Lindahl and a host of others have pointed out, as an indicator for monetary stability, the comparison of the money and real rate is ambiguous and theoretically flawed. Further, it is now a generally accepted empirical fact that investment tends to be relatively interest inelastic, as are savings. There may thus be major breaks in the chain before the monetary impact reaches final demand. And even at this point, there is no guarantee that there will be a direct impact on prices if markets are non-perfectly competitive.

This is the current state of monetary policy for a system which is presumed to behave as if it were a gold-based system, but with central bank money substituted for gold. Since it is presumed that a constant, exogenous gold supply, rather than the automatic arbitrage mechanism, was the source of price stability, monetary policy is used to keep the supply of money stable, either through quantitative controls, or by means of manipulation of interest rates. However, this produces a completely different form of arbitrage, which is much less likely to produce price stability. At best, it can only produce price stability by producing cyclical fluctuations in the demand for goods and the demand for labour. It thus requires that inventories of goods should be held to be ready to meet demand fluctuations without excessive price movements, and that excess supplies of unemployed labour be held to keep wages constant.

AN ALTERNATIVE APPROACH TO PRICE AND EMPLOYMENT STABILITY

However, there is an alternative school of thought that argues that the disappearance of gold has changed the homeostatic properties of the monetary system in important ways. Indeed, there are some who argue, with the benefit of substantial historical support, that the explanation of the operation of the gold-based commodity money standard is purely theoretical and indeed never occurred in history. The Chartalist approach suggests an alternative explanation for the existence of money. In a modern nation state, money is held because the government creates credits on its citizens by imposing tax bills which can only be discharged by rendering the government money that is created when the government purchases goods and services from the private sector. These debts in the form of tax due bills can only be discharged on terms determined by government when it determines its fiscal policy. Thus, every eligible taxpayer in the system has a short position in government money that is annually renewed in an amount represented by the annual tax liability. To cover this short position citizens must acquire government money. This can only be done by providing services to the government in exchange for credits denominated in government money. Thus, in any given tax year each individual must either borrow money from the government or sell goods and services to the government, in an amount sufficient to extinguish its tax liability. The demand for government money is thus explained by the need to discharge tax liabilities. The supply of private sector goods and services to the government, which is identically government expenditure, thus has a floor that is determined by the size of the tax bill levied on the public.

Given that the government sets the terms for discharging the tax liability, it can choose to set either the prices of the goods that it buys, or it can buy at market prices the quantities that it requires. In most cases, the government determines its spending and lets the market determine the prices at which it sells. The real value of the government's tax dollar, or tax Euro, is thus determined by the private sector. If the government wants to increase the real value of the tax Euro it can only do so by using its budget to drive down prices. That is, by reducing expenditures relative to taxes so that there are excess supplies in the market, or what is the same thing, there is an excess demand for currency to pay tax bills. Thus, the government acts to set private activity at the level that produces the desired real value of the tax Euro. This is a rough equivalent of the mechanism reviewed above in which the central bank attempts to operate on the overall level of saving and investment to influence market demand and thus create the desired level of market prices.

Alternatively, the government has the ability to fix the prices at which it is willing to receive real goods in exchange for tax Euros. This would determine the real value to the tax Euro directly, and would leave the private sector level of activity free to adjust to reach the level required to satisfy the imposed tax liabilities. In this case the government accepts any balance or imbalance between taxes and receipts that is produced by the activities of the private sector.

It is interesting that in the former case, in which the government acts to keep productive potential below the maximum desired by the private sector, it is considered as a reduction of the interference of government in the operation of the private economy, while the latter, in which the private sector is given free reign to produce as much of whatever it desires, it is considered to be unacceptable interference in the operation of the free market mechanism.

This is perhaps the point to note that this view does not in any way preclude the existence of private exchange and production, nor even of a private money. Private money may circulate as a substitute for government money, or government money may be the base for additional creation of means of payment. This additional means of private money would have the same elastic relation as deposits discussed above with reference to a gold-based fiduciary system, unless it has a 100% reserve backing. But, if households only sell services in an amount sufficient to pay their tax bills, net outstanding government money should be zero. Where does the government money that serves as the basis for private monetary creation come from?

First note that while there is nothing to impede a government from taxing to pay for all its expenditures, it is impossible for it to tax more than it spends, i.e. to run a surplus (unless it has run a deficit in the past). If the government were to try to run a surplus this would mean that individuals would want to sell to the government to earn money to pay their taxes, but the government is not buying and thus not supplying the money to meet their liabilities. The result must either be tax delinquency or forced government lending. Alternatively, this situation could be described as one in which there are individuals who are willing and able to sell output, or their labour, at the going prices, but there is no buyer. Also note that in conditions of budget balance, there would be no net currency outstanding, or the currency outstanding would be determined by the leads and lags between government purchase of goods and services and the payment schedule for taxes. The inability to sell output or labour to pay taxes would then appear as being caused by a lack of money creation. This has been a lament throughout the ages – lack of demand due to a shortage of money. But, the reason is not the lack of money, *per se*, it is the lack of the budget deficit required to increase the basis for net money creation.

For there to be an accumulation of government money there will have to be an accumulated deficit. Thus, the government money that serves as the basis for the creation of private money will be the result of government budget policy. There is thus a clear linkage between fiscal and monetary policy. This is not new, Chicago economists such as Henry Simons have long recognized this linkage and used it in particular during the depression to formulate recovery policy in the form of reflation of the economy.

Now, consider a case in which households choose to sell more goods and services than they need to pay their tax bills. The government is thus in deficit, and there is net creation of government money. However, if the private bank demand for reserves plus the public's demand for currency exceeds the difference between government spending and taxes, there will be an excess supply of government money held by banks as reserves and they will try to make the best of it by lending. But, the excess supply of government money available for reserve balances may drive the interest rate towards zero interest rate. To prevent this from happening the central bank would have to take government money onto its balance sheet, by selling its own, or the government's, debt to the private banks or to the public. Here the interest rate is used to ensure portfolio balance, for as Dennis Robertson was fond of saying, 'All the money that is anywhere must be somewhere.' In the present context this means that the difference between the government money created by government spending and what it reclaims in taxes represents the public's desire to net save in the form of government money, and this saving must find a place in the portfolios of the banks and the public. If this occurs at a zero rate of interest the central bank may want to increase its own holdings to drive the rate up. The proportion of the deficit that is financed by the issue of bonds held in the portfolio of the public is thus a question of portfolio balance, and has no clear impact on the price level of goods. The price level of goods will be determined by the policy followed by the government in determining what it is prepared to accept for a unit of account. If it follows a policy of setting prices rather than quantities it creates the possibility for the private sector to arbitrage against the prices set by the government. If private sector prices rise it can shift its sale of goods and services to the government away from areas of higher prices and towards those of lower prices.

This approach sounds very similar to the idea behind the substitution of a commodity basket for gold, only the government is not operating as both a buyer and a seller of the goods. It is only a buyer, and thus price fixer, over the quantity of goods that it buys[3] – private sector prices might diverge from these. Thus, it creates a downward pressure on prices when they are rising and a support for prices when they are falling.

The justification of substituting a multi-commodity unit for gold was because of the greater production elasticity of commodities relative to gold (cf. Hart, Kaldor and Tinbergen, 1964) and the fact that a range of commodities would have a broader and more direct impact of the general level of prices and incomes. If we follow this logic, the government could have the greatest impact on price stability if it operated by fixing both buying and selling prices in those goods which bore the greatest proportion to overall production. The major proportion of government expenditures is made up of labour. This suggests that the setting of government wages has a major impact on prices; it should also affect private sector wages. But, we are used to thinking of the government setting quantities, and then adapting its wages to market conditions. The alternative position would be for the government to set the price at which is was willing to purchase labour and then let the private sector determine how much labour it wanted to sell in order to acquire tax money. It is really unnecessary for the government to act as both buyer and seller, as under the gold standard. All it has to do is act as residual buyer in the labour market to ensure the stability of the real value of the tax Euro.

This stability would be preserved by an arbitrage mechanism in which the private sector would be a net seller or supplier of labour (i.e. lay off workers) when profitability was in decline. This would put a floor under wages. On the other hand, when the private sector was expanding, and private sector wages were rising, additional labour could be attracted by offering wages above the government wage. This would increase labour supply to the private sector and put a break on private sector wages. It also means that the public sector deficit will be placing a floor under incomes as private sector activity falls, and vice versa. This is a mechanism that is very similar to that which was the basis of the initial arbitrage under the gold-backed currency. Only in that system, the residual sector was the gold mining sector that expanded employment and sustained income levels as prices fell, and vice versa.

Thus, in a fiat money system in which the value of money is determined by the government, the homeostatic mechanism that ensured stability under the gold standard has to be replaced. The gold mines no longer play the role of employer of last resort. Since government money has replaced gold, it falls to the government to take on the role of price stability by acting as the gold mine, by acting as the employer of last resort. Indeed, the government is well placed to do this, for it is now commonly accepted that the use of gold as the backing for the currency was a waste of economic resources. The government need not put labour to work producing gold, it can act to provide public goods that would not be provided by the natural operation of the private sector.

THE ALTERNATIVE APPLIED TO THE NEW EUROPE

What does this imply for the operation of the new European Central Bank? Let us now engage in a hypotheticality. In light of the above, how would the EMU have to operate to confront the threat of social disruption caused by the continuous rise in European unemployment, and yet maintain the commitment of the ECB to stability of the Euro? Or, to put the point differently, how could we make full employment in the EU compatible with price stability? Let us define some terms. Full employment means the absence of involuntary unemployment in Keynes's original sense of the term. That is, that everyone willing and able to work at the current wage should be able to find employment.[4] Price stability cannot mean a constant value for some index of prices – indeed recent studies in the US and Germany suggest that the Austrians were right to warn against the use of aggregates of this sort. A better definition of stability is that associated with a 'fair and orderly' market, employed to judge the operation of specialists on the NYSE. It is a measure of the minimum trade by trade variation in prices, and the size of trade that causes prices to move by the minimum acceptable variation. The idea is that by reading the tape a trader should be able to consider this as good information concerning the state of the market, so that if he were to trade on that information he could execute an order of standard size at a price which was not more that one-tick away from the last reported trade without his order influencing price (although a trade at larger sizes might do this). This is a definition of price stability which attempts to preserve the information function of prices (there are other functions – to calculate real wages, or interest rates, or the purchasing power of money in general, all of which are subject to the same deficiencies cited above). This allows prices to change over time, without those changes producing information inefficiencies.

Now, let us assume that the European Central Bank should accept as its basic task the stabilization of the tax Euro, by acting to institute a homeostatic mechanism for a fiat money system that is similar to that reputed to have operated under the gold standard. This means that its actions must be compatible with what we have defined as the government using its ability to set prices to determine the value of the currency.

This it could do if, following the idea of the gold standard, it were to adopt a policy of fixing the price of basic labour. This would require the central bank to offer to hire all workers who were willing and able to work, but could not find employment in the private sector, at a basic wage. This would replace the current minimum wage. Such a policy would not only create an arbitrage mechanism that provides wage stability and an automatic stabilizer to private sector demand, it would directly solve the problem of unemployment.[5] As mentioned above, this approach to stabilizing the value of the tax Euro depends on the level of private activity and of the overall government deficit being free to adjust. From this point of view, the problem of the deficit targets is not that they will restrain the expansion of the government money supply and produce excessively tight monetary conditions. Given that GDP growth has seldom been higher than 2.5% for the major European countries, a 3% limit should not represent a constraint on growth. Rather, they limit the ability of the private sector to respond to economic conditions. For example, it may be the case that the wage bill for all workers offering to work at the basic wage may cause the deficit to exceed the pact's limits. In this sense, the growth and stability pact may be destabilizing because it prevents the ECB from operating a market-based stabilization policy and does not allow the full expression of public saving and investment decisions.

Such policy would not mean that the central bank gives up control over interest rates, rather it means that if it wants to control interest rates it has to allow the deficit to fluctuate. It would also require a certain reallocation of staff from running regressions on the relation of money growth to prices, to management of the public employment and training schemes to be offered to workers who choose to accept the basic stabilization wage.

In simple terms, the scheme[6] would require the following characteristics:

(a) The ECB should fix a basic wage at which it is willing to provide employment for all those who accept the offer.
(b) It should provide for money creation sufficient to meet the wage bill of the stabilisation pool of labour. Just as most central banks operate 'exchange equalisation accounts', the ECB already has the power to issue its own liabilities to facilitate its open market repo operations to influence interest rates and the money supply. These could be used to satisfy its balance sheet requirements.
(c) Create a public employment and training programme which is flexible in terms of adjusting to changes in the size of the stabilization pool. The formal administrative operation could be contracted out on a national basis, in a way similar to the way the US job corps programme was run by private sector contractors.
(d) Act to adjust the basic wage if the size of the pool falls too low or too high. These changes would be accompanied by supporting changes in fiscal policy.

(e)   The ECB continues to determine the short-term policy interest rate by offering to buy or sell government debt when the rate rises above or falls below the desired rate.

NOTES

1. To facilitate subsequent discussion, it is important to note that this arrangement does not require any stock of gold to be held by the mint. All the gold bullion required to be converted to coin is supplied by the buyer of coin, and all the coin to be converted to gold is supplied by the buyer of bullion. The mint need hold no net stocks of either bullion or coin.
2. In the *General Theory* Keynes identified these characteristics as a low or negligible elasticity of production and substitution.
3. It is a seller in the sense that it provides government services against the tax liabilities.
4. Keynes's original definition was related to the operation of prices in the labour market (if real consumption wages fell, then it would be expected that demand for labour would rise, but if labour supply was also greater, going opposite the supposed negative relation between labour supply and real wages, then unemployment need not fall. Thus, if both demand and supply increase, the fall in the real wage does not bring the market any closer to equilibrium).
5. In a much more transparent and efficient way than by defining full employment as that rate of unemployment that produces price stability.
6. More detailed descriptions of how the scheme might operate are found in Mosler (1997–8) and Wray (1998).

REFERENCES

Bank for International Settlements (BIS) (1997) *Annual Report for 1996*, Basle, June.
Graham, B. (1937) *Storage and Stability*, New York: McGraw-Hill.
Hart, A.G., Kaldor, N. and Tinbergen, J. (1964) 'The Case for an International Commodity Reserve Currency', Geneva, UNCTAD, March–June.
Hicks, J. (1985) 'Keynes and the World Economy,' in F. Vicarelli (ed.), *Keynes's Relevance Today*, London: Macmillan.
Keynes, J.M. (1936) *The General Theory of Employment, Interest and Money*, London: Macmillan.
Mosler, W. (1997–8) 'Full Employment and Price Stability', *Journal of Post Keynesian Economics,* Winter, 167–82.
Wray, L.R. (1998) *Understanding Modern Money*, Cheltenham: Edward Elgar.

11. Competition and employment

Nina Shapiro

While Keynes conducted his analysis under the assumption of perfect competition, the Keynesians have made market imperfection the central feature of theirs. Price rigidities are the reason for unemployment in both the new and 'old' (ISLM) Keynesian models, with the agency and transaction costs of the new Keynesian analysis explaining the sticky wages and prices of the old Keynesian one. Markets 'fail' when their trade is impeded, and while their perfection might not be possible – the 'asymmetric' information of agents block it – it is nonetheless desirable. Perfect competition is the market structure of the 'classical' system, just as imperfect competition is the 'microeconomic world' of the Keynesian one (Tobin, 1993).

The optimality of perfect competition is considered below, where the results of the traditional analysis are questioned, and shown to be the product of a special conception – the tâtonnement of the Walrasian system. It is when competition is the Walrasian tâtonnement, and only when it is the tâtonnement, that its results have the optimality highlighted in economics.

COMPETITION

The competition of economics is beneficent. It adjusts the supply of goods to the demand for them, and their prices to their costs, shifting resources into their most valuable uses, and normalizing their rewards. The imbalances of markets are corrected, and their prices aligned, through their competition, and when the competition of markets is perfect, so are their adjustments. Their equilibrations are 'instantaneous', and equilibria 'Pareto optimal'.

But the competition that equilibrates the markets of economics is a peculiar kind. It is a 'bloodless' affair, a competition without winners and losers, rivalry or strife. All competitors have the same chance of success, and all succeed to the same extent. There are no competitive prizes or surprises, 'extraordinary' gains or losses, for the competition occurs under the perfect knowledge conditions of the Walrasian tâtonnement.

The tâtonnement is the Walrasian market mechanism, the price adjustment process of the Walrasian system. It 'mimics' the price changes of the market, adjusting prices in accordance with its laws, and in abstraction from the impediments of their operation in the 'short run': the imperfect knowledge of traders, and wrong investments that constrain their actions.

In the tâtonnement there are no disappointed expectations or 'noisy' price changes. Sellers know the prices of all goods and services – not just the prices of their own or their competitors' – and none are supplied or demanded without knowledge of the prices of all others. Since all goods and services are traded together, at the same time and place, the prices of all can be known before the trade of any is decided, and while the prices that trades are based on change, and prices can change a lot in the tâtonnement, no transaction is effected until the equilibrium prices are decided. Trade is conditional upon the realization of those prices.[1]

The price changes of the tâtonnement are notional. They are not changes in the prices at which goods and services are traded, or changes in the prices at which they are supplied and demanded. Goods and services are supplied and demanded at equilibrium prices only – they cannot be offered for sale or ordered for purchase at any other prices – and the supplies and demands of the tâtonnement are not the sale and purchase offers of traders but the sale and purchase plans. They are planned supplies and demands.

It is the plans of traders that change with the tâtonnement's prices, not their trade or terms of trade, and that change of plan is all that happens during its price adjustments.[2] No production is undertaken, finance contracted, or asset purchased, on the basis of the tâtonnement's prices, and since no exchange or production occurs in the tâtonnement, no investment or sale can be mistaken. Capital losses are impossible and price changes entirely benign.[3]

But while trades can be conditional, and commodities auctioned, the price changes of no markets are 'notional'. The price changes of all vary the revenue of their sellers and subject them to losses, and when those effects of price changes are recognized, the competition of markets does not look so beneficent. The outcome of their price changes will be Keynesian rather than Walrasian, and this will be the case regardless of the speed of their price adjustments. Indeed, the more flexible their prices, the more Keynesian will be their results.

Assume a competitive economy with all the conditions of the Walrasian one except those of its tâtonnement, and consider what happens in that economy when the demand for products drops.

If the fall in demand is unexpected – and it will not be a 'shock' if it is not – prices will fall unexpectedly, and since that change in prices is not 'notional', it will disappoint the expectations of firms. Firms will have supplied their markets on the basis of yesterday's prices, the ones ruling prior to the demand shock, and while they will be able to sell all they want at the going market prices (they are perfectly competitive enterprises), the prices their products are going for – the ones clearing their markets – will not be the prices expected at the time they chose their profit-maximizing output. Their output will be too high for existing prices, and profits lower than they were before the fall in prices. Products will be sold for less than their supply prices, and with prices requiring output reductions, production will be cut, setting off the cumulative employment and income declines of the Keynesian multiplier.

Perfectly competitive firms are 'quantity constrained' also, demand constricts the output of those firms too, for their production must be adjusted to their prices – profits cannot be maximized otherwise – and prices depend on demand. The higher the product demand, the higher will be the product price, and the higher the price, the higher will be the profit maximizing output of the product – the one the firm 'will want' to supply at its 'given' price. That output rises and falls with demand for the product, and is as dependent on aggregate demand as the output of the monopolistic enterprise, with changes in aggregate demand reflected, in both cases, in changes in demand for the firm's product (the 'horizontal' firm demand curve of perfect competition moves up and down with the aggregate demand, while the 'sloped' one of imperfect competition shifts out and in).

If the labor markets of the economy are as competitive as the product ones, the fall in demand will depress their prices also. Wages will decrease with the growth of unemployment, as the competition of the unemployed pulls down the pay of the employed, and while that fall in wages may restore the profit margins of firms, it will not restore their profits. The profits of firms depend on their sales as well as their profit margins, and the deflation will not improve these. It will not bring the demand for products back up.

Deflation increases the real cost of debt as much as it increases the real value of cash, and when debts cannot be 'recontracted' in the light of price changes, deflation has the debt effects of Fisher as well as the wealth ones of Pigou. It shifts the revenue of firms to their creditors, squeezing their profits and bankrupting their operations. The financially weak firms fail, and the investment funds and confidence of the others are reduced, and while households may benefit from the increase in the worth of their cash holdings, their expenditure is deficit financed too (Caskey and Fazzari, 1987). Their discretionary income will fall with the fall in prices, and if liquidity preference holds up the nominal interest rate, or if it does not fall as much as the fall in prices – and it cannot fall below zero – the cost of credit will rise also. The deflation will increase the real interest rate as well as the real burden of debt, depressing expenditure for that reason too, and its real interest and debt effects can offset its real balance ones. Indeed, they will most likely swamp them (Caskey and Fazzari, 1992).[4]

Outside the 'tâtonnement' deflation is injurious, and when deflation depresses demand rather than increasing it – and the most that can be hoped for is that it does not reduce it – the competition of the labor market is 'ruinous'. It not only reduces the value of labor, it destroys the market for it, for the fall in wages would decrease rather than increase the demand for labor. Wages and employment would fall together, with the fall in each reducing the level of the other, and that cumulative decline in wages and employment would continue until there were no jobs left for workers to fight over, or wages left to deflate.[5] Instead of 'neutralizing' the monetary changes of the economy, the competition of its labor markets would volatize its prices (Keynes, 1936), and the economy would have neither the full employment equilibrium of the Walrasian system, nor the involuntary unemployment one of the Keynesian. It would not equilibrate.

The money 'illusion' of workers is rational – they know their competition can be ruinous. Their employment problems would be greater if their wages were more 'flexible', and the institutions that restrict their competition – trade unions, labor contracts, efficiency wages and other like practices – stabilize the economy. Perfect competition is not optimal.

MARKET IMPERFECTION

While the imperfections of labor markets hold up prices, the imperfections of product markets hold up investment. They stabilize the revenue from production, reducing the uncertainties that make investment volatile, and liquidity 'preferable'.

Competitive industries have variable prices. Their prices change with both the demand for and supply of their products, and while the product demand may not change much, the product supply can vary a lot. It changes with the flux of the industry participants, varying with the industry entry and exit and changing as precipitously as them, and when industries are perfectly competitive, with their products homogeneous and producible by anyone, the industry output is so variable that its level is indeterminate (Richardson, 1990). Any number of firms could produce the industry's product, and any number could produce it at any given time, and without knowing the number which will supply the product, the determination of its price is impossible.

The prices of perfectly competitive industries are unpredictable – they cannot be foreseen, 'perfectly' or otherwise. Firms cannot know the prices they will receive for their products, and they cannot know the prices they will get for them in the short run as well as the ones they will realize in the long run. Even short period expectations can be mistaken, for when the industry entry is 'costless', and knowledge of industry conditions 'perfect', the number of firms in the industry tommorrow need not be the same as the number in it today or yesterday.[6]

The profits of a perfectly competitive industry will be as uncertain as its prices. They will fluctuate with the fluctuation of its prices, and while the profits and losses of an industry may cancel out in the long run, this will not help the firms bankrupted by the losses.[7] These will not recover the funds invested in their products, and with the variance of profits high, and distribution over time unknown, product-specific investment is unlikely (Pindyck, 1991). Neither plant and equipment nor product development investments will be rational – the 'downside' risk on both is too high – and there will be little, if any, investment in production.[8]

The markets of firms have to be stabilized for their investment to be profitable, and the entry barriers of their markets stabilize them. Product differentiation protects the sales of firms, as does special knowledge and skill in the production or development of their products. Those imperfections of their competition 'make' their markets, liquidifying the investment in them, and in the absence of the imperfections that protect product markets, long-period expectations could not be positive.

The imperfections of product markets are critical to investment, its level would be much lower without them. And those imperfections not only increase investment, they also stabilize it, for they secure its value, 'calming the nerves' of those who undertake it.[9] Investment is less subject to precipitous changes when market imperfections protect it.

Monopolistic firms do not have the financial fragility of perfectly competitive ones. Their markets are established, and credit good, they can borrow on their assets and draw on their reserves. Their profits are more certain, and assets more secure, than those of their perfectly competitive counterparts, and since they have the liquidity needed to weather revenue shortfalls, and the security for a long-run view, they can invest for the long term. Their investment can be based on market and technological developments, and neither short-run demand changes nor changes 'in the news' need curtail it.[10]

With the revenue of firms more certain under imperfect competition, so will be the income of their employees. Their jobs will be more secure, and with their income less variable, they will be able to spend a greater amount of it. The necessity of providing for the future will be less, and insofar as the saving out of income rises with the risk of job loss and fear of that loss, the saving out of any given level (and distribution) of income will be lower under imperfect competition than perfect competition.

The lower saving propensity of imperfect competition will boost consumer spending, and while the expenditure of workers depends on their income as well as their saving propensity, real wages are not necessarily lower under imperfect competition. They can be as high as they are under perfect competition, and this is not only because the higher productivity of monopolistic enterprises can offset their mark-ups, or because their workers can share in their rents, but also because perfectly competitive firms have profit margins too.

The profits of perfectly competitive firms are normal only when their industries are in long-run equilibrium, and their industries are not normally in that equilibrium. Their prices can be higher or lower than their average costs, and profit margins greater than the profit margins of monopolistic enterprises. The differences in the size of their profit margins and those of monopolistic firms, and whether or not the profit margins of the monopolistic ones will be larger, depend on the pricing practices of the monopolistic enterprises.

If the product pricing of the monopolistic firms is geared to the future, and it would not be 'rational' if it were not, the prices of their products will not 'maximize' profit. Instead of short-run profit considerations determining prices, long-run growth ones will decide them. An 'entry-preempting' or market-penetrating price will be set (Shapiro, 1995), and with long-run conditions deciding prices, the ups and downs of the business cycle will not upset them. Prices will be held constant in the face of those changes, and the increase in the profit share in the upswing of the cycle will be less than it would be under the marginal cost prices of perfectly competitive enterprises.

The prices of perfect competition are 'flexible' in both directions, they rise when demand increases as well as fall when it decreases. Their increase can choke off an expansion, cutting the real wage and marginal propensity to consume, and the average level of those prices over the cycle may entail a lower real wage than the one that would be realized under the 'rigid' prices of imperfect competition. Real wages may be higher when competition is imperfect, and the higher investment of imperfect competition need not come at the expense of consumption. Both can be greater.

While the imperfections of markets have their costs, so does their competition. Their competition cannot be perfected without increasing their instability, and the employment effects of their competition are quite different than the ones highlighted in economics. Indeed, they are the exact opposite.

NOTES

1. The equilibrium trade condition of the tâtonnement is needed for its realization of the Walrasian equilibrium, for if trade occurred in the tâtonnement, trader endowments would change, making the outcome of its price adjustments dependent on the course of those changes. The equilibrium it was 'groping' for would be 'path dependent,' and non-Walrasian ('quantity constrained') equilibria likely. For an extended discussion see Fisher (1987).
2. This is emphasized in Clower's criticisms of the Walrasian theory. See, in particular, Clower and Howitt (1997).
3. The conditions of the tâtonnement preclude consumption as well as exchange and production, and that suspension of consumption is particularly problematic in that the tâtonnement is far from 'timeless'. It takes a lot of time, and in some cases an 'infinite' amount of time, for its price adjustments to be completed (Hahn, 1987).
4. The real interest effects of deflation are highlighted in Delong and Summers (1986) and Hahn and Solow (1995).

5. If wages fall faster than prices, employment will fall not only because of the deflation, but also because of the decline in real wages.
6. Insofar as rational expectations entail knowledge of the equilibrium prices, they are incompatible with the conditions of perfect competition.
7. The profits will be unpredictable even if their average value is known, for the time path of their distribution is not given with their mean (Dixit, 1992).
8. For the investment problems of perfect competition, and their implications for the optimality of its results, see Richardson (1990).
9. The stabilizing effects of monopoly are noted in Keynes's discussion of the volatility of investment (1936, p.163).
10. The greater stability of investment under imperfect competition is emphasized in Eichner's work (1976 and 1991).

REFERENCES

Caskey, J.P. and Fazzari, S.M. (1992) 'Debt, Price Flexibility, and Aggregate Stability', *Revue D'Economie Politique*, **102**, 520–43.

Caskey, J.P. and Fazzari, S.M. (1987) 'Aggregate Demand Contractions with Nominal Debt Commitments: Is Wage Flexibility Stabilizing?' *Economic Inquiry*, **25**, 583–97.

Clower, R. and Howitt, P. (1997) 'Foundations of Economics', in d'Autume and J. Carelier, *Is Economics Becoming a Hard Science?*, Cheltenham: Edward Elgar.

Delong, J.B. and Summers, L.H. (1986) 'Is Increased Price Flexibility Stabilizing?' *American Economic Review*, **76**, 1031–1044.

Dixit, A. (1992) 'Investment and Hysteresis', *Journal of Economic Perspectives*, **6**, 107–32.

Eichner, A.S. (1976) *The Megacorp and Oligopoly*, Cambridge: Cambridge University Press.

Eichner, A.S. (1991) *The Macrodynamics of Advanced Market Economies*, Armonk: M.E. Sharpe, Inc.

Fisher, F. (1987) 'Adjustment Processes and Stability', in J. Eatwell, M. Milgate and P. Newman, *The New Palgrave*, 1, pp.26–28, London: Macmillan Press.

Hahn, F. (1987) 'Auctioneer', in J. Eatwell, M. Milgate and P. Newman, *The New Palgrave*, 1, pp.136–38, London: Macmillan.

Hahn, F. and Solow, R. (1995) *A Critical Essay on Modern Macroeconomic Theory*, Cambridge, MA: MIT Press.

Keynes, J.M. (1936) *The General Theory of Employment, Interest, and Money*, New York: Harcourt, Brace and Co.

Pindyck, R.S. (1991) 'Irreversibility, Uncertainty, and Investment', *Journal of Economic Literature* **29**, 1110–48.

Richardon, G.B. (1990) *Information and Investment*, Oxford: Oxford University Press.

Shapiro, N. (1995) 'Markets and Mark-Ups: Keynesian Views', in S. Dow and J. Hillard, *Keynes, Knowledge, and Uncertainty*, Aldershot: Edward Elgar.

Tobin, J. (1993) 'Price Flexibility and Output Stability: an Old Keynesian View', *The Journal of Economic Perspectives*, **7**, 45–66.

12. Another look at wage and price flexibility as the solution to unemployment[1]

David Dequech

The most central question of macroeconomic theory in the last five decades concerns whether money-wage and price flexibility leads to full employment. Many important arguments against money-wage and price flexibility have been presented by different authors over the years. Based on some ideas developed in previous papers, I try to contribute to this discussion, by organizing it and providing a more rigorous foundation for some of these arguments, as well as presenting new ones. Additionally, I consider the institutions of market structure and argue against oversimplifying the comparison between different market forms in terms of their impacts on employment.

The chapter begins by putting the debate in a historical context, marked by the rise and fall of the neoclassical synthesis. It then reviews and organizes several usual arguments against the idea that money-wage and price flexibility ensure full employment. The next step is to expand and reinforce these arguments, initially dealing with expectations and confidence and, finally, dealing with the relation between the institutions of market structure, uncertainty and employment.

1 A HISTORICAL PERSPECTIVE

Keynes upset the idea that market forces, left by themselves, would lead the economy to full employment. This led to an attempt to absorb his ideas into neoclassical thought, in a process that culminated with the neoclassical synthesis.

The first important step in the direction of the neoclassicization of Keynes's revolution was taken by Hicks in 1937. A debate followed about the shape and position of the IS and LM curves. Because of the possibility of an interest-inelastic IS curve and of a liquidity trap, the apparatus created by Hicks had to be complemented with something else to demonstrate the tendency towards full-employment equilibrium. Thus, the way towards the neoclassical synthesis proceeded by incorporating into the IS–LM model the neoclassical-Keynesian treatment of the labour market.

Given a situation of unemployment, even if a reduction in money-wages fails to *directly* bring the labour market to equilibrium at the level of full employment, this result was supposed, by the proponents of the neoclassical synthesis, to be *indirectly* reached through the operation of wealth effects from the fall in prices associated with the fall in money-wages. Even within the context of neoclassical-Keynesian thought, the Keynes effect may be insufficient to lead to full employment. Thus, a second wealth effect had to be conceived of, one by which consumption is increased. This is exactly what the so-called real balance or Pigou effect supposedly assures.

The dominance of the neoclassical synthesis broke down in the early 1970s, due to the dissatisfaction of many mainstream economists with (a) the synthesis' theoretical lack of 'microfoundations' and (b) its empirical failure in dealing with the phenomenon of stagflation. This led to the emergence of New Classical Economics, first with Money Business Cycles (MBC) theory and later with Real Business Cycles (RBC) theory. In reaction against this, New Keynesian Economics appeared.

What is the position of these schools regarding the relation between money-wage and price flexibility and unemployment? New classicals have contested the very existence of involuntary unemployment. The reduction in the level of employment during recessions is seen as due to an optimal response of workers to perceived or actual variations in the real reward for labour. Unemployment thus results from an intertemporal substitution of leisure for labour. New Keynesians do not defend a unique position. According to Greenwald and Stiglitz (1993: 25–26, 36), many of them still stick to the view that, at least theoretically, an economy in which money-wages and prices were flexible would eventually reach full employment equilibrium. The mechanisms responsible for this are not discussed in detail but implicitly it is the real balance effect that does the job. For this strand of New Keynesianism, the important task is to explain the nominal rigidities which are believed to hinder the attainment of full employment. However, another strand of New Keynesian Economics, of which Greenwald and Stiglitz themselves are exponents, holds that increased money-wage and price flexibility might exacerbate the problem of unemployment. The deleterious effects of such flexibility on macroeconomic performance are also pointed out by 'old' neoclassical Keynesians such as Hahn and Solow (1986, 1995).

2   REVIEWING AND ORGANIZING SOME ARGUMENTS AGAINST WAGE AND PRICE FLEXIBILITY

Whatever its practical meaning, the real balance effect, as well as any effect based on money-wage and price flexibility, may be criticized in theoretical terms. The argument is seriously flawed. Several problems with it have already been pointed out by other authors. These problems are so many that an effort is required to adequately organize the discussion.

According to Keynes (1936: 259–60), the effect of money-wage and price reduction on employment depends on what happens to aggregate demand relative to aggregate supply. Keynes and others who reason in these terms are implicitly assuming that producers project the current situation and particularly current demand into the future when they decide about production and employment. I shall deal more properly with this assumption in section 3. I initially discuss issues related to contrasting the effects of money-wage and price flexibility on aggregate supply and *ex-post* aggregate demand.

Employment is determined by what happens in the goods market. For Keynes, the labour demand function is not the marginal product of labour curve (see Davidson, 1967), contrary to a widespread view, even among some interpreters close to the Post Keynesian side, such as McCombie (1987–8: 207) and Vercelli (1991: 177; 197–8). Keynes (1936: 5, 17) accepted that under pure competition the marginal product of labour and the real wage are equal, because he assumed profit-maximization (Davidson, 1983: 562). He also accepted an inverse relation between the real wage and the level of employment, but only because he assumed diminishing returns to labour in the short period (Keynes, 1936: 17–18; also Davidson, 1967: 508; Minsky, 1975: 40–41). Keynes thus inverted the causality in this relation as seen by neoclassical economists.

The impact of a reduction in money-wages on employment depends on what happens with supply and demand in the goods market. Even if the impact on the supply side were favourable, because of a fall in costs, demand could be negatively affected.

I shall not consider here the stimulus that a reduction in money-wages may give to employment through its effect on exports. Even if there were no reasons to suspect that this stimulus may be modest (see Davidson, 1994, Chapter 16), the effect of lower money-wages on exports cannot provide a solution for unemployment in the world as a whole. It can only provide a way of exporting unemployment from one country to another.

I therefore concentrate on domestic demand. I begin by examining investment and move on to consumption. In both cases, I start with the assumption that the money supply is exogenous, and then relax it to incorporate endogenous money. The case of an exogenous money supply is interesting because this assumption may facilitate the contrast of ideas inspired by Keynes with those of much of mainstream economic theory. Keynes did not completely incorporate an endogenous money supply in *The General Theory*, possibly for tactical reasons (Harcourt, 1987: 246).[2] It can be argued that even with an exogenous money supply the case against money-wage and price flexibility is very strong. In contrast, some authors (e.g. Palley, 1996) seem to occasionally overemphasize the importance of endogenous money in their rebuttal of pro-wage-cutting arguments.

After discussing the impact of money-wage and price flexibility on domestic demand, I refer to a more fundamental argument against such flexibility.

2.1 Investment

(a) Exogenous money   Wage and price flexibility may generate an expectations effect through which investment is reduced. A fall in money-wages may lead to expectations of further reductions and to the postponement of investment plans until money-wages are even lower (Keynes, 1936: 263; Dutt, 1986–7: 285; Asimakopulos, 1991: 125). For Smithin (1988: 145), this is the most persuasive argument against money-wage cuts. In addition, due to the influence of wages on costs and prices, there may appear an expectation of a lower stream of revenues to be obtained from goods produced with the additional equipment (Davidson, 1994: 186).

(b) Endogenous money   A fall in money-wages may cause a reduction in prices and this implies an increase in the firms' debt load (Keynes, 1936: 264, 268). There is a redistribution of wealth from investors to their creditors. This is the investment side of the Fisher debt effect. The increase in the firms' debt load may discourage them from investing (Minsky, 1975: 139) and/or may reduce the banks' willingness to finance new investment projects (Palley, 1996: 46). The increase in the real debt burden may lead debtors (not only firms, but also the general public) to default, and this, in turn, would lead banks to reduce the supply of credit money. The situation is worsened if there is insolvency and bankruptcies (Kalecki, 1944), including bank failures. This would reduce investment even further.

2.2 Consumption

(a) Exogenous money   The previous discussion immediately implies the possibility of consumption being negatively affected by the multiplier effect of investment reduction.

Additionally, in the case of consumption there may operate an expectations effect too: consumption may be postponed if there is an expectation of further reductions in the price of consumption goods. This has been incorporated into mainstream textbooks.

Another thing to point out is that wages are not only a component of cost but also a component of demand (Minsky, 1986: 123). A fall in the money-wage rate, if not offset by an increase in the volume of employment, implies a fall in the money-wage bill and may affect consumption. If any fall in consumption out of wages is not offset by an increase in consumption out of profits (Chick, 1983: 153–4), aggregate consumption decreases.

Related to the previous point is the possibility of a redistribution of income from wage recipients to profit recipients, which depends on how prices fall compared to wages. Depending on the difference in the marginal propensities to consume out of wages and out of profits, consumption may fall.

A similar problem may occur due to the redistribution of income from flexible money income recipients to fixed money income recipients (rentiers). Again, the effect on consumption depends on the different marginal propensities to consume (Keynes, 1936: 262).

(b) Endogenous money   The existence of inside debt implies another possible effect of declining money-wages and prices on consumption, via the redistribution of income, from inside debtors to inside creditors. This is the consumption side of the Fisher debt effect.

Indeed, an endogenous money supply may invalidate not only the Keynes effect (Keynes, 1936: 266; Davidson, 1994: 196n), but also the real balance effect (Elliott, 1992: 150; Lavoie, 1992: 247–8), for in this case the money supply falls with wages and prices. Nominal wealth may not increase at all.

2.3   A More Fundamental Problem: the Viability of the Monetary System

Davidson (1978: 231–2; 1980: 536–7) asserts that an uncertain world requires contracts, and contracts, as the basis of a viable monetary system, require money-wage stability, given the influence of money-wages on supply prices. With money-wage and price flexibility, the very possibility of organizing capitalist production is jeopardized (see also Weintraub, 1982: 448).

3   EXPANDING AND REINFORCING THE ARGUMENTS: EXPECTATIONS AND CONFIDENCE

It is now time to examine more closely how employment is determined. In particular, expectations and confidence must be considered more fully.[3] The expectations of the firms' decision-makers regarding the goods market are crucial for the determination of employment. These expectations refer to costs and revenues. Each firm can build its own supply and expected demand function, in the costs-revenue and employment plane. The firms' functions can then be aggregated to yield the aggregate supply and aggregate expected demand functions (Chick, 1983: 63–4).

The presence of uncertainty in these decisions led me to introduce the notion of a state of short-term expectations, in which both expectations and confidence are important (Dequech, 1999b). Let me begin with expectations. Keynes assumed, in Chapter 5 of *The General Theory*, that expectations were formed by projecting the current situation into the future, as long as producers did not see any reason to think differently. This should be seen as a convention. As should become clearer after I discuss confidence, this is but one possible pattern of expectations.

What about confidence? If one assumes, as Keynes often did, that short-term expectations are fulfilled, even if by accident, one is assuming away the problem of how disappointment may lead people to lose confidence in the convention and abandon it. Nevertheless, even in this case confidence has to be considered.

A distinction between decision-makers and economic theoreticians is necessary at this point. Even if expectations are assumed to be fulfilled, decision-makers should not be portrayed as knowing this *ex ante*. Thus, once uncertainty is admitted, if the theoretician assumes that production decisions are based on expectations which are formed in a projective way, he/she is assuming, even if implicitly, that producers have enough confidence in these expectations to allow the latter to guide their behaviour. This is in principle independent of whether expectations are assumed to be fulfilled or not. If they are fulfilled, the confidence in the way they were formed may be reinforced (but even then something else may change which leads producers to abandon the convention).

The presence of uncertainty also means that liquidity considerations are important for production, not only investment, decisions. Firms may produce less and prefer more liquidity than they would if producers had more spontaneous optimism and confidence (and banks may refuse to lend them finance for working capital).

I can now turn again to the issue of money-wage and price flexibility, and in particular to what happens to employment if there is a fall in money-wages and prices. I shall leave for the next section an analysis that contrasts different market structures.

At this point, after having emphasized expectations and confidence, the first, and perhaps more general, argument I can present against the real balance effect and any other effect which is believed to always bring the economy to full employment equilibrium (or to any equilibrium, for that matter) is the following. If time, expectations and confidence are incorporated into the analysis, any supposed adjustment process must occur in time, and thus *expectations and confidence* should be shown to be formed in accordance with such a result. In particular, it would be necessary to make explicit how expectations and confidence are formed and to drop many *ceteris paribus* assumptions that characterize the neoclassical method in order to allow the factors that influence expectations and confidence to play their role. In other words, we must generalize Keynes's (1937: 109) argument against Leontief that 'it is for those who make a highly special assumption to justify it, rather than for those who dispense with it, to prove a general negative' (see also Possas, 1987: 68).

Another general argument against money-wage and price flexibility is that this flexibility would imply breaking with institutions which have contributed to reducing uncertainty. Without such institutions, the degree of perceived uncertainty tends to increase and, for a given degree of uncertainty aversion, confidence tends to be reduced. With less confidence, decision-makers of several types will attribute a larger liquidity premium to money and other liquid assets, especially for precautionary reasons. This affects the goods market negatively, through what may be called a *confidence effect*. The interest rate may even rise, contrary to the Keynes effect (see Keynes, 1936: 263; Weintraub, 1982: 448; and Elliott, 1992: 148).

Although an increase in uncertainty and a decrease in confidence are sometimes mentioned in the literature on wage and price flexibility, these points need to be theoretically and consistently founded, and this is what I have tried to do. Uncertainty needs to be properly conceived of as gradable. Moreover, expectations must be distinguished from confidence, and confidence must be distinguished from animal spirits. Just treating animal spirits as the sole, exogenous determinant of investment is not adequate to explain why money-wage and price flexibility may have a deleterious effect on employment.

Let me examine these and other issues more closely. In what follows, I begin with the simplifying assumption that *producers* still form their expectations of *demand* by projecting the current situation into the future and have such confidence in these expectations as to allow them to guide production decisions. Later on, I relax this assumption and show that its removal makes it even more difficult for one to believe that wage and price flexibility is the solution to unemployment.

3.1 Conventional Projective Short-term Expectations of Demand

If producers still behave on the basis of projecting the current demand into the future, the effect of a money-wage cut on their expectations of demand will take place in a future production period and will depend on what happens to current demand.

3.1.1 Investment

(a) Exogenous money Investment decisions are also usually made with the assumption that at least some factors affecting cost and demand will remain stable over the lifetime of capital goods. Breaking with the conventions of stable wages and prices tends to have on investment the confidence effect described above. Even if the investors' expectations about the profitability (revenues and costs) of a project are not affected by money-wage and price flexibility, the confidence with which such expectations are held tends to be lower, because the degree of uncertainty is higher. A decrease in confidence may have a negative effect on investment (Dequech, 1998).

If investors were following the convention of projecting the current situation into the future, as Keynes argues that they often do, they may lose their confidence in this convention and abandon it, in case money-wage and price flexibility is increased. Even if their expectations are still conventional, their behaviour may stop being conventional as their confidence in the convention breaks down.

Other investors may abandon the convention (or whatever pattern of expectations they have been following) by becoming more pessimistic about the future. This is the case, already considered in the literature mentioned above, in which lower money-wages and prices lead investors to expect a lower stream of revenues to be obtained from the goods produced with the additional capital goods. For these investors, too, liquid assets become relatively more attractive.

(b) Endogenous money If the money supply is at least in part endogenous, *another type of confidence effect* may occur. We have to consider the liquidity preference of the banks' decision-makers, who have to make an asset choice too. By increasing uncertainty, money-wage and price flexibility tends to lead bankers too to lose confidence in their expectations of returns from loans and to attribute a greater liquidity premium to money and other liquid assets (bankers too might have been following the convention of projecting the current situation into the future). *Ceteris paribus*, this reduces the availability of funds to those firms that are still willing to invest.

Other bankers may become more pessimistic, especially if there is an increase in defaults and bankruptcies. This is the case already dealt with in the literature. For those bankers who had been following a convention, this would be another way of breaking with it.

3.1.2 Consumption

(a) Exogenous money Consumption too may fall due to an increase in uncertainty and a consequent decrease in confidence. Both profit and wage

recipients may become more uncertain about what is going to happen to their income in the future, and try to save more (I write 'try' because of the paradox of thrift).

(b) Endogenous money   The increase in the real debt burden, discussed above, also affects wage-earners (Minsky, 1975: 54), as well as profit-receivers in their capacity as consumers. As happens with firms, the ensuing problems of reduced creditworthiness, insolvency, etc., may reduce both the consumers' willingness to go into debt and the credit available to them.

At this point it is useful to comment on the distinction between *lower* and *falling* wages and prices, which can be related to the difference between comparative statics and dynamics. Hahn and Solow (1986) emphasize this distinction and argue that, although lower wages and prices could be the solution for macroeconomic problems, a reduction in wages and prices has to take place in real-time dynamics, and this is troublesome. The above discussion can be used to show that even lower wages and prices (as opposed to falling wages and prices or wages and prices which are expected to be falling) may not have a positive impact on employment, because of their distributive effects. Nevertheless, I agree with Hahn and Solow that what they call real-time dynamics is extremely important. It is in it that expectations and confidence play their major role.

3.2   A Breakdown in the Short-term Convention

In the previous section, an expectations effect and a confidence effect were allowed to involve bankers, consumers and, in their capacity as investors, entrepreneurs. This affected producers' expectations only indirectly, via its effects on current demand, and, by hypothesis, did not affect the producers' confidence in projective expectations. Now it is time to allow room for a direct change in the expectations and particularly in the confidence of entrepreneurs in their capacity as producers.

Even before current demand is affected, a cut in money-wages and other producers' prices may alter a producer's state of short-term expectations. Alternatively, this may happen after the first production period following the money-wage and price cut; projecting the most recent results may lead to mistakes and this may make producers review their procedure of forming expectations. Either way, producers may change their expectations, abandoning the belief that future demand will be like current demand. Another possibility is that they continue forming expectations projectively, but with less confidence than before the money-wage and price cut.

Once we accept that production decisions also involve uncertainty, we can imagine that producers may also consider their confidence in expectations when deciding what to do. I referred in Dequech (1998) to a subjective rate of discount applied to expectations of returns from assets. Similarly, I suggest here that producers, if they are aware of the uncertainty involved in production decisions, may apply a discount factor over their expectations of demand. This discount factor is a combined result of uncertainty perception and uncertainty aversion.

Suppose producers decide about production by conceiving of the firm's supply and expected demand curve. Even if they do not form more pessimistic expectations of demand and continue to project current demand into the future, the expected demand curve may shift downwards. This would happen if producers have less confidence in their expectations than before, because of an increase in perceived uncertainty. They would apply a larger discount factor to their expectations such that the discounted expected demand would be lower for each level of employment. This is a very plausible result of money-wage and price cutting. The aggregate expected demand curve will also shift down, tending to reduce aggregate employment.

Producers may also apply a discount factor, more specifically a multiple greater than unity, to their cost expectations. If producers continue to enter into contracts to purchase and hire inputs and to obtain finance, this implies some control over nominal costs and confidence in cost expectations. Their expectations of demand have to be properly discounted so that producers consider their ability to honour these contractual commitments. Particularly important here is the fact that with lower money-wages and prices nominal proceeds tend to be reduced – even if once and for all (the question is whether the producers know if this is a once-and-for-all cut or not and if they know the exact percentage by which their nominal demand is going to be changed).

If money-wage and price flexibility leads people away from contracts, there is more uncertainty regarding costs as well. Producers then have less confidence in their cost expectations and may apply a larger multiple to these expectations, which would shift their supply curve upwards. More seriously, without contracts the very possibility of organizing capitalist production is jeopardized. This leads me to the next topic.

3.3   The Viability of the Monetary System Once More

Davidson has long emphasized the importance of contracts for the organization of production in an uncertain world, as well as the importance of stable money-wages for stable prices and consequently for contracts. His point is that firms might not be willing to produce anything if they do not have any significant control over monetary flows. Davidson (1978: 385) argues that some institutions provide a basis for 'a *conventionality* of belief in the stability of the system' (emphasis added). In particular, contracts and especially the money-wage contract are crucial for the 'conventionality of belief' in price stability (see also Dequech, 1999a).

An adequate foundation for this argument can be provided by defending a notion of uncertainty according to which: (1) uncertainty does not imply complete ignorance; (2) there may exist institutions which provide an ontological basis for some kind of knowledge even in an environment liable to unpredictable structural change; (3) uncertainty is gradable.

4   EXPANDING AND REINFORCING THE ARGUMENTS: INSTITUTIONS, MARKET STRUCTURE AND UNCERTAINTY

4.1   The Forms of Competition

It has long been argued by mainstream economists that unemployment is either voluntary or due to the presence of monopolistic elements typical of imperfect competition and/or unionized labour (in the latter case it could also be considered voluntary, if labour prices itself out of employment). An attempt to provide a solid foundation for arguments against the view that wage and price flexibility could assure full employment has to deal with the institutions that characterize the form of competition. For this purpose, and regarding the goods market in particular, one can conceive a form of competition in which prices are flexible, especially in response to an excess of supply over demand. The presence of many atomistic firms or, more precisely, free entry, would be an ideal feature in this exercise. However, if uncertainty is admitted into the picture, then competition cannot be considered as perfect in the usual sense, which requires perfect knowledge on the part of producers, not to mention consumers (Chick, 1992; Elliott, 1992). Perhaps pure competition, in Chamberlain's sense, is a better denomination (Sardoni, 1992: 380; Dutt, 1992: 136). The firm faces uncertainty at least as to the market price. This is the notion of free competition compatible with Keynes's *General Theory*.

A point neglected by other authors is the need to reconcile the assumption of such a purely competitive market form with the discussion of the sources of uncertainty. The possibility of innovation is a major source of uncertainty in economic decisions (Dequech, 1997). However, this possibility cannot be used as a source of uncertainty if one assumes some form of pure competition, because innovation implies a new product or some cost advantage. Nevertheless, uncertainty under pure competition can still be related to the possibility of other types of structural changes, for example, of a political, social or cultural nature.

The assumption of pure competition should be handled with special care, and for adequate purposes. It is crucially important to distinguish between two types of discussion. Keynes and some of his followers, particularly some Post Keynesians, can be seen as arguing that even if pure competition existed or could be established, flexible wages and prices may not ensure full employment.[4] The assumption can be made for this purpose even if its unrealisticness is fully admitted. Even such an unrealistic assumption can be useful for policy discussions, since it can serve to contradict policy proposals to make wages and prices more flexible. Most of the discussion in sections 2 and 3 above can be directed to this track.

A second, different discussion concerns whether pure competition exists or can exist. The idea here can be to show that, regardless of whether flexible wages and prices ensure full employment, a purely competitive economy cannot exist or at least not for long. In capitalism, a market structure characterized by the exclusive presence of many small, equal firms tends to be endogenously destroyed. This can provide a second type of argument, which I also endorse, against flexible-wage-and-price policies.

To begin with, even if pure competition could be established, uncertainty would still exist. This uncertainty, even being of a restricted type (by definition, as seen above), threatens the long-term survival of anything similar to pure competition. The point is that uncertainty itself provides an incentive for firms to secure market power as a means to control the future (see Peterson, 1987: 1597–8, who looks at the modern corporation from this perspective).

Moreover, competition should be understood in a dynamic way, as in Marx's discussion of relative surplus and in Schumpeter (1943, Chapter 7), who acknowledges his debt to Marx in this regard. Competition implies a built-in mechanism of change: the search for extraordinary profits, for monopoly, even if only temporary. This leads firms to innovate. 'This process of creative destruction is the essential fact about capitalism' (Schumpeter, 1943: 83). Any policy proposal to 'purify' competition is doomed to fail, as there is an inherent tendency to differentiation among firms. The possibility of innovation should not be assumed away when discussing this type of policy proposal more fully. In reality, competition can never be pure in this sense (not to mention the difficulty or even the impossibility of reconciling such a form of competition with the advantages of a larger firm size, such as economies of scale, pointed out by Sraffa in his classic 1926 article, and better access to credit).

4.2 A Dynamic View of Market Structures and Macroeconomic Performance

A traditional view exists according to which the price rigidity characteristic of oligopolistic and monopolistic market structures implies lower production and employment and higher prices than in more competitive structures. In his discussion of monopolistic practices, Schumpeter (1943, Chapter 8) addressed the issue of price rigidity and the argument that it is responsible for a lower volume of employment than in 'perfect' competition. This argument, he says, is 'vitiated by a *ceteris paribus* clause that is inadmissible in dealing with our process of creative destruction. From the fact, so far as it is a fact, that at more flexible prices greater quantities could *ceteris paribus* be sold, it does not follow that either the output of the commodities in question, or total output and hence employment would actually be greater'.

In his specific discussion of price rigidity, Schumpeter's main point is that perfect and universal price flexibility could further destabilize the system (also Shapiro, 1997 and Hodgson, 1988: 187–91). This point has basically to do with the expectations and confidence effects mentioned above. The expectational parameters should not be included in the *ceteris paribus* clause. However, Schumpeter's contribution to a critique of the traditional view goes far beyond this point and is, alas, neglected in macroeconomic discussions of wage and price flexibility.

First, the traditional view overemphasizes price competition, but this is just one among many forms of competition (Schumpeter, 1943: 84–5). Oligopolistic market structures cannot be said to be less competitive than ones in which barriers to entry are lower. Indeed, the very gradability of competitiveness is questionable (Possas, 1989: 169). I will therefore write only of market structures which are more *price*-competitive than others.

Perhaps more important is Schumpeter's methodological stance. Practices such as price rigidity must be considered from a long-run perspective. When this perspective is combined with a dynamic conception of competition, we can realize that 'the impact of new things – new technologies for instance – on the existing structure of an industry considerably reduces the long-run scope and importance of practices that aim, through restricting output, at conserving established positions and at maximizing the profits accruing from them. We must now recognize the further fact that restrictive practices of this kind, as far as they are effective, acquire a new significance in the perennial gale of creative destruction'. Monopolistic practices may protect rather than impede long-run expansion (Schumpeter, 1943: 87–88, 105–6).

Of particular importance here is the fact that firms in less price-competitive market structures are often in a better position to introduce successful innovations. This is particularly true of big business, although size is not an absolute determinant (Schumpeter, 1943: 100–101, 106). Whether oligopolistic structures do have this effect or not may be a controversial question (see Freeman and Soete, 1997, for a balance of the literature on this), but it has to be considered. The introduction of new goods and new methods of production may be of great importance in creating new profit opportunities (and preventing a stationary state; see also Davidson, 1978: 92).

A possible positive influence on innovations should not lead us to hastily conclude that a monopolistic and oligopolistic economy will necessarily have a higher level of production and employment than a more price-competitive one. This discussion is more complex than it may seem. I would like to mention at least three complicating factors.

First, there is the fact that monopolistic and oligopolistic market structures are characterized by a lower degree of capacity utilization.[5] Although planned excess capacity is part of those monopolistic practices which Schumpeter rightly interprets in a broader context, it implies a stronger accelerator effect of investment over the cycle, which tends to amplify fluctuations of production and employment. On the other hand, although this accelerator effect may be less intense in more price-competitive structures, the entry and exit of firms volatilizes the level of production and employment.

Second, and perhaps more complicated, *the same process* that led to the emergence of large corporations brought into life what may be called modern financial markets. As Keynes argues, this facilitates the financing of investment but it may also exacerbate the degree of instability of capitalism. Davis (1994a: 168–9) goes so far as to argue, in his reading of Keynes, that the separation between ownership and control has 'decidedly negative effects on the level of investment expenditure'. Whatever the validity of this as an interpretation of Keynes's view, the conclusion seems unwarranted without a consideration of the possible positive effects of big business, pointed out above and which Keynes tended to neglect or was not interested in discussing.

Third, there is the problem of technological unemployment. Innovations open new profit opportunities, but they may also increase productivity and render old products or production methods obsolete, destroying more jobs than they create. Employment can grow significantly less than production.

5   CONCLUDING REMARKS

The theoretical framework developed in previous papers and adopted here provides a more solid foundation for existing arguments against wage and price flexibility and suggests new ones. Both expectations and confidence may be negatively affected by such a flexibility. Moreover, the institutions of market structure have to be properly dealt with. If pure competition is discussed, the purposes of doing so need to be well understood. In addition, the discussion has to be compatible with the view on the sources of uncertainty. Finally, a dynamic view of competition must be adopted, which makes it more complicated to compare different market structures in terms of their impact on employment.

NOTES

1. This chapter is a slightly modified version of Chapter 10 of my PhD dissertation, recently submitted at the University of Cambridge. I would like to thank my supervisors, Geoff Harcourt and Paul Davidson, for their advice and support. The responsibility for remaining mistakes is solely mine. Financial support from CNPq (Brazil) is also gratefully acknowledged.
2. Dow (1997) challenges the conventional wisdom that Keynes (1936) assumed an exogenous money supply. Some writers (e.g. Cottrell, 1994: 159) seem to associate the assumption of an exogenous money supply with Keynes's (1936, Chapter 17) identification of a negligible elasticity of production as an essential property of money. However, the inelasticity of production does not mean that the quantity of money cannot be increased (exogenously or endogenously). It merely means that labour cannot be employed to produce money. This property of money is of crucial importance for Keynes's theory; the exogeneity of money is not.
3. For a detailed discussion of the main determinants of expectations and confidence, see Dequech (1999c).
4. As Harcourt (1987: 244) argues, in *The General Theory* Keynes took the degree of competition as given and his acceptance (1936: 5) of the 'first postulate' (real wage equal to marginal product of labour) was qualified for the case of imperfect competition. Also conditional was his acceptance (1936: 283) of the equality between price and marginal cost (Chick, 1992: 151).
5. Uncertainty is a major reason for this. Excess capacity works as a reserve that guarantees flexibility against unexpected circumstances (Steindl, 1952: 9). This is similar to the precautionary demand for liquidity, with the difference that in the present case the reserve has to be physical, due to the time required to build capital equipment.

REFERENCES

Asimakopulos, A. (1991), *Keynes's General Theory and Accumulation*, Cambridge, Cambridge University Press.

Chick, V. (1983), *Macroeconomics After Keynes*, Cambridge, MA, MIT Press.

Chick, V. (1992), 'The small firm under uncertainty: a puzzle of the *General Theory*', in Gerrard, B. and Hillard, J. (1992), pp. 149–64.

Cottrell, A. (1994), 'Keynes's vision and tactics', in Davis, J. (1994), pp. 153–65.

Davidson, P. (1967), 'A Keynesian View of Patinkin's Theory of Employment', *Economic Journal*, 77. Reprinted in Davidson, P. (1990), pp. 501–24.

Davidson, P. (1978), *Money and the Real World*, London, Macmillan, 2nd edition. First edition, 1972.

Davidson, P. (1980), 'The Dual-faceted Nature of the Keynesian Revolution: Money and Money-wages in Unemployment and Production Flow Prices', *Journal of Post Keynesian Economics*, **II**, No. 3, Spring. Reprinted in Davidson, P. (1990), pp 530–42.

Davidson, P. (1983), 'The Marginal Product Curve Is Not The Demand Curve for Labor and Lucas's Labor Supply Function Is Not the Supply Curve for Labor in the Real World', *Journal of Post Keynesian Economics*, **6**, No. 1, Fall. Reprinted in Davidson, P. (1990), pp. 555–66.

Davidson, P. (1990), *Money and Employment – The Collected Writings of Paul Davidson, Volume I*, New York, New York University Press.

Davidson, P. (1994), *Post Keynesian Macroeconomic Theory*, Aldershot, Edward Elgar.

Davis, J. (1994a), 'The locus of Keynes's philosophical thinking in *The General Theory*: the concept of convention', *Perspectives on the History of Economic Thought*, **X**, pp. 157–78.

Davis, J. (ed.) (1994b), *The State of Interpretation of Keynes*, Boston, Kluwer.

Dequech, D. (1997), 'Uncertainty in a strong sense: meaning and sources', *Economic Issues*, **2**(2), September, pp. 21–43.

Dequech, D. (1998), 'Asset choice, liquidity preference and rationality under uncertainty', *Journal of Economic Issues*, (forthcoming).

Dequech, D. (1999a), 'On some arguments for the rationality of conventional behaviour under uncertainty: concepts, applicability and criticisms', in Sardoni, C. (1999), *Keynes, Post Keynesianism and Political Economy*, London, Routledge, forthcoming.

Dequech, D. (1999b), 'Uncertainty, conventions and short-term expectations', *Revista de Economia Política*, forthcoming.

Dequech, D. (1999c), 'Expectations and confidence under uncertainty', *Journal of Post Keynesian Economics*, forthcoming.

Dow, S. (1997), 'Endogenous Money', in Harcourt, G.C. and Riach, P. (1997), pp. 61–78.

Dutt, A. (1986–87), 'Wage rigidity and unemployment: the simple diagrammatics of two views', *Journal of Post Keynesian Economics*, **IX**, No. 2, Winter, pp. 279–90.

Dutt, A. (1992), 'Keynes, market forms and competition', in Gerrard, B. and Hillard, J. (1992), pp. 129–48.

Elliott, J. (1992), 'Keynes's critique of wage cutting as antidepressionary strategy', *Research in the History of Economic Thought and Methodology*, **9**, 129–69.

Freeman, C. and Soete, L. (1997), *The Economics of Industrial Innovation*, London, Pinter, 3rd edition.

Gerrard, B. and Hillard, J. (eds) (1992), *The Philosophy and Economics of J. M. Keynes*, Aldershot, Edward Elgar.

Greenwald, B. and Stiglitz, J. (1993), 'New and Old Keynesians', *Journal of Economic Perspectives*, **7**, no.1, Winter, pp. 23–44.

Hahn, F. and Solow, R. (1986), 'Is wage flexibility a good thing?', in Beckerman, W. (ed.) (1986), *Wage Rigidity and Unemployment*, Baltimore, Johns Hopkins University Press, pp. 1–19.

Hahn, F. and Solow, R. (1995), *A Critical Essay on Modern Macroeconomic Theory*, Oxford, Blackwell.

Harcourt, G.C. (1987), 'The legacy of Keynes: theoretical methods and unfinished business', in Reese, D. (ed.) (1987), *The Legacy of Keynes*, San Francisco, Harper and Row. Reprinted in Harcourt, G.C. (1992), pp. 235–49.

Harcourt, G.C. (1992), *On Political Economists and Modern Political Economy*, London, Routledge, edited by Claudio Sardoni.

Harcourt, G.C. and Riach, P.A. (eds) (1997), *A 'Second Edition' of The General Theory*, Vol. 1, London, Routledge.

Hicks, J. (1937), 'Mr Keynes and the "classics": a Suggested Interpretation', *Econometrica*, **5**, April, pp. 147–59.

Hodgson, G. (1988), *Economics and Institutions*, Philadelphia, University of Philadelphia Press.

Kalecki, M. (1944), 'Professor Pigou on "The Classical Stationary State": A Comment', *Economic Journal*, **54**, April, pp. 131–2.

Keynes, J.M. (1936), *The General Theory of Employment, Interest and Money*, London, Macmillan. 1964 edition, Harvest/HBJ.

Keynes, J.M. (1937), 'The General Theory of Employment', *Quarterly Journal of Economics*, **51**, February. Reprinted in Keynes, J.M. (1973), pp. 109–23.

Keynes, J.M. (1973), *The Collected Writings of John Maynard Keynes*, Vol. XIV, London, Macmillan.

Lavoie, M. (1992), *Foundations of Post-Keynesian Economic Analysis*, Aldershot: Edward Elgar.

Lucas Jr., R. and Sargent, T. (1979), 'After Keynesian Macroeconomics', *Federal Reserve Bank of Minneapolis Quarterly Review*, **3**, No. 2. Reprinted in Lucas Jr., R. and Sargent, T. (eds) (1981), *Rational Expectations and Econometric Practice*, London, Allen & Unwin, pp. 295–319.

McCombie, J. (1987–88), 'Keynes and the nature of involuntary unemployment', *Journal of Post Keynesian Economics*, **X**, No. 2, Winter, pp. 202–15.

Minsky, H. (1975), *John Maynard Keynes*, New York, Columbia University Press.

Minsky, H. (1986), *Stabilizing an Unstable Economy*, New Haven, Yale University Press.

Palley, T. (1996), *Post Keynesian Economics*, London, Macmillan.

Peterson, W. (1987), 'Macroeconomic Theory and Policy in an Institutionalist Perspective', *Journal of Economic Issues*, **XXI**, no. 4, December, pp. 1587–1621.

Possas, M. (1987), *A dinâmica da economia capitalista*, São Paulo, Brasiliense.

Possas, M. (1989), *Dinâmica e Concorrência Capitalista*, São Paulo, HUCITEC/UNICAMP.

Sardoni, C. (1992), 'Market forms and effective demand: Keynesian results with perfect competition', *Review of Political Economy*, **4**, No. 4, pp. 377–95.

Schumpeter, J.A. (1943), *Capitalism, Socialism and Democracy*, New York, Harper, 3rd edition, 1950.

Shapiro, N. (1997), 'Imperfect competition and Keynes', in Harcourt, G.C. and Riach, P. (1997), pp. 83–92.

Smithin, J. (1988), 'On flexible wage policy', *Economies et Societés*, **22**, No. 3, pp. 135–53.

Steindl, J. (1952), *Maturity and Stagnation in American Capitalism*, Oxford, Blackwell.

Vercelli, A. (1991), *Methodological Foundations of Macroeconomics: Keynes and Lucas*, Cambridge, Cambridge University Press.

Weintraub, S. (1982), 'Hicks on IS-LM: more explanation?', *Journal of Post Keynesian Economics*, **IV**, No. 3, Spring, pp. 445–52.

13.   Employment policies in an open semi-industrialized economy: reflections on the Mexican economy

Julio López and Guadalupe Mántey[1]

1   BACKGROUND

After more than a decade of restructuring and opening of the economy to foreign markets and competition, unemployment in Mexico today is greater than it was before the economic adjustment and modernization process launched in 1983. Although the open unemployment rate has been kept rather low (the urban rate was 3.8 percent of the Economically Active Population (EAP) in 1980, 7.1 percent in 1986, and about 3.3 percent in 1997), underemployment has been steadily rising and is very high.[2]

Rising underemployment has been caused by a dismal growth performance (output per head fell by about 7 percent between 1982 and 1997). By the same token, faster growth is required in order to raise the demand for labor.

Is it possible to achieve strong economic and employment growth, capable of decreasing underemployment? It can be shown that Mexico has today a considerable growth potential that can be put to use in the short run. The misuse of production capacity is the indicator that most synthetically underscores this potential.

Although fragmentary and debatable on methodological grounds, available information suggests that a large percentage of capital equipment today is kept idle. For example, the Survey of Entrepreneurial Opinion, undertaken by the Bank of Mexico in the manufacturing sector, shows that executives estimate a figure of about 26 percent idle capacity for 1997, when the rate of growth of GDP hovered around 7 percent on a yearly basis. No figures exist for the economy as a whole, but one of the authors has estimated that idle capacity in 1996 was around 25 percent (López, 1998).[3]

It is true that not all idle capital equipment could be put to use immediately. But even so, it can be reasonably posited that some – and perhaps rather large – short-run elasticity of output exists in Mexico. In the following pages we make some suggestions regarding an economic policy to stimulate capacity utilization and labor demand.

2   A SHORT-TERM EMPLOYMENT STRATEGY

2.1   A Simple, Short-run Macroeconomic Model

It is useful first to specify a simple model (López, 1998). Employment L is a positive function of Y, effective output. Effective output is equal to Y^d, the level of the output determined by effective demand. The sustainable output Y^s is equal to the lesser of two values: Y^k, the output for full use of capital, and Y^x, the output of external equilibrium.

$$L = L\,(Y) \tag{13.1}$$

with $L_1 > 0^4$

$$Y = Y^d \tag{13.2}$$

$$Y^s = min\ (Y^k,\, Y^x) \tag{13.3}$$

Y^d, the output determined by effective demand is obtained by the equation:

$$Y = Y\,(X,\, A,\, I^p,\, \omega,\, g,\, s,\, \tau,\, m) \tag{13.4}$$

where X is exports, A is the autonomous part of consumption, I^p is private investment, and ω, g, s, τ and m are the share of wages, government expenditure, capitalists' savings (we assume workers do not save), taxes, and imports, in GDP, respectively.
    With:

$$Y_1,\, Y_2,\, Y_3,\, Y_4,\, Y_5 > 0;\ Y_6,\, Y_7,\, Y_8 < 0$$

Y^x, the level of output at external equilibrium, can be expressed as follows:[5]

$$Y^x \le M^{*e}(1/m^*) + Z^{*s} \tag{13.5}$$

$$Y^x \le X^*(1/m^*) + Z^{*s} \tag{13.6}$$

M^{*e} are the imports that can be financed with current exports, X^*. Z^{*s} is the 'sustainable' deficit in the trade balance in the medium and long run (which is largely based on conventions, international financial markets' conditions, etc. and thus can fluctuate widely even in the short run).

Exports depend on world demand, Y^*, on the competitiveness of internal goods, which is established by the real rate of exchange θ, on the supply conditions of domestic firms, δ, and on a vector of other, non-modeled variables ($\bullet$). We can also assume that the share of imports in the GDP, m^*, depends on the same determinants (excluding world demand).

$$X^* = X^*(Y^*, \theta, \delta, \bullet) \tag{13.7}$$

with $X_1^*, X_2^*, X_3^* > 0$

$$m^* = m^*(\theta, \delta, \bullet) \tag{13.8}$$

with $m_1^*, m_2^* < 0$

$$\theta = E(p^x/p) \tag{13.9}$$

E is the nominal rate of exchange (units of domestic currency per dollar), p^x is the index of international prices, and p is the index of national prices.

The trade balance is:

$$Z^* \equiv X^* - M^* = Z^*(Y^*, \theta, \delta, Y, \bullet) \tag{13.10}$$

with (by assumption)

$$Z_1^*, Z_2^*, Z_3^* > 0, Z_4^* < 0$$

We now examine the processes determining internal prices p, profit margins μ, and real wages W^R. With respect to prices, two types of sectors are distinguished. On the one hand we consider the sector that competes directly with the external producers, in the internal or external markets, namely the 'open' sector. In this sector, the price is given and is equal to the world price in domestic currency p^*E. In the 'closed sector' – i.e. that sector where foreign competition is absent – we simply posit that firms fix their prices by adding a mark-up to their unit prime costs, such that:

$$p = p(W, E, \mu, \pi, \bullet) \tag{13.11}$$

with $p_1, p_2, p_3 > 0, p_4 < 0$

That is, internal prices in the closed sector depend on money wages W, the nominal exchange rate E, the unit profit margin μ, labor productivity π, and a vector of other variables •. We assume also unit profit margins depend on the supply conditions of firms δ (more on this later):

$$\mu = \mu(\delta, \bullet) \qquad (13.12)$$

with $\mu_1 < 0$.

Finally, we assume the real wage rate W^R to be inversely related to the real exchange rate, when the latter rises due to a depreciation. This is because a depreciation capable of bringing about a rise in the real exchange rate requires money wages to rise by less than the nominal rate of exchange.

$$W^R = W^R (\theta, \bullet) \qquad (13.13)$$

with $W^R_1 < 0$.

We define now the distributive equilibrium as the point where workers are satisfied with the real wage being earned, and where capitalists are content with the profit margin obtained (Carlin and Soskice, 1990). The distributive equilibrium determines a situation in which the inflation rate is constant, since entrepreneurs are satisfied with their margin, and workers with their real wage. *Ceteris paribus*, the distributive equilibrium will depend exclusively on the real rate of exchange.

2.2   Alternative Short-run Employment Policies

Expansionary fiscal and monetary policies were advocated by the father-founders of the theory of effective demand, (Keynes 1929, 1936; Kalecki 1944; see also Carvalho 1997 and Kregel 1994–5). Expansionary policies were also successfully implemented in the European economies in the immediate postwar period.

However, in Mexico's present circumstances, where domestic markets are open and capital movements are not controlled, *a requirement of any employment strategy is that growth of domestic production must go hand in hand with an expansion of exports, a decline of the import coefficient, or a combination of both*. This is indispensable because the external balance must be kept in check. Thus purely domestic-induced expansionary policies are impractical.

Theoretically a sufficiently drastic depreciation of the peso would make any locally made output competitive if nominal wages are kept constant. However, currency depreciation normally brings about inflation because wages will tend to rise. Furthermore, if real wages fall, a depreciation causes a fall in domestic demand, which may impair its benefits on the external balance. We shall analyze these phenomena with the aid of the graph at Figure 13.1 (inspired by Carlin and Soskice, 1990). There, we establish four relationships in the $\theta - Y$

plane. The first one refers to the GDP of external equilibrium, denoted by Y^x, which has a positive slope in the $\theta - Y$ plane (above the Y^x line the trade balance has a surplus, and below a deficit). Secondly, we draw the level of output with full use of capital, Y^k, as a straight line parallel to the vertical axis. We assume that the level of output at the starting point, determined by the level of demand during that period, Y_0, is below the level of the output at full use of capital, i.e. there is idle capacity.

Third, we then draw the distributive balance F as a straight-line horizontal to the $\theta - Y$ plane. *Ceteris paribus*, the distributive equilibrium depends exclusively on the real rate of exchange. Above the F_0 line there would be no distributive equilibrium: the real rate of exchange would be too high, so that real wages or profit margins would tend to be below their equilibrium level. If workers try to defend their real wage, and capitalists their margin, then there would be inflation.

Lastly, aggregate demand, which we denote by $Y^{d,d}$ (the second supra-index d indicating that demand is associated with a depreciation) is drawn as a straight line with a negative slope in the $\theta - Y$ plane. The reason is, first, that depreciation brings about a fall in the share of wages in income, and accordingly consumption per worker will also shrink. Furthermore, depreciation increases both the debt ratio of domestic firms – particularly when they are indebted in foreign currency – and the supply price of imported capital goods, weakening private investment in fixed capital. Thus, investment, as well as its domestic multiplier, is reduced. Some evidence shows that these negative effects on internal demand are normally not offset by the improvement in the trade balance brought about by the depreciation.[6]

Now, as shown by the graph, Figure 13.1, a depreciation that would raise the real rate of exchange from θ_0 to θ_1, by reducing total demand would also reduce effective output from Y_0 to Y_1.[7]

If we discard depreciation, how then could an increase in the output of external equilibrium, be achieved? We will argue that improving the supply conditions of domestic firms, with a selective expansionary credit policy, could be a good alternative. We shall consider first the microeconomic effects of this policy, with the help of Figures 13.2a and 13.2b.

In these graphs the two types of sectors mentioned above are distinguished. In the open sector (Figure 13.2a), the price is given. To simplify we shall also assume that the demand curve is perfectly elastic at the given price. In the closed sector (Figure 13.2b), on the other hand, producers enjoy a monopoly situation and face a downward-sloped demand curve, which shifts leftward or rightward when internal demand falls or rises.

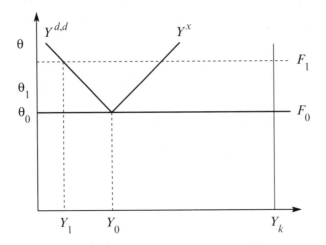

Figure 13.1   Relationship between real wages, domestic demand and the external balance

In both graphs, short-term aggregate production (for given productive capacities) is on the horizontal axis, and the cost and price of a unit of output (also in the short term) are on the vertical axis.

The aggregate supply curves in both cases have positive slopes because of the risks involved in production. Indeed, it seems sensible to assume that low-cost producers have a curve of constant unit direct costs in the short term, as they have ample spare capacities. While these two assumptions by themselves would result in a horizontal supply curve, higher production entails higher risks (i.e. Keynes's 'borrower's risk' (1936), Kalecki's 'principle of increasing risk' (1937, CWMK Vol. I), or Greenwald and Stiglitz' higher 'bankruptcy costs' (1993).) Thus, *for a given state of expectations*, higher supply may require a higher price.

Finally, each sector's supply has an upper limit Q^*, which is reached when its productive capacities are fully utilized. At that point the supply curve becomes parallel to the vertical axis. In both graphs, by assumption production is lower than potential output (i.e. producers are unable, or unwilling, to utilize all their productive capacity).

The graphs depict the likely effects of a selective expansionary credit policy for the open and closed sectors of the economy. In both cases, we assume that due to a greater access to cheaper and steadier credit, the supply curve shifts to the right, to Q_c. As a result of the increased supply, the open sector is able to expand output – which means that exports grow, the import coefficient declines,

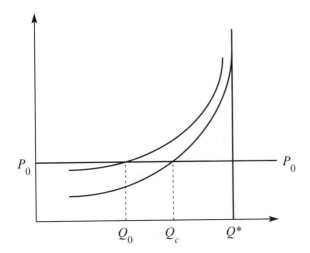

Figure 13.2a   Macroeconomic effects of a selective expansionary credit policy in domestic firms (open sector)

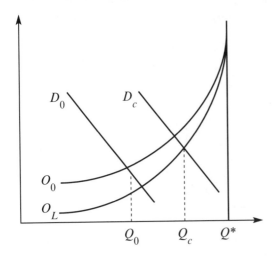

Figure 13.2b   Macroeconomic effects of a selective expansionary credit policy in domestic firms (closed sector)

or a combination of both occurs. In Figure 13.2b we assume that the rightward shift of the supply curve in the open sector, and the increased availability of credit, contribute to a rightward shift of the demand curve to D_c.

In both cases, output would increase to Q_c. Capacity utilization would accordingly be raised, and employment would be higher.

We can see the macroeconomic effects of the selective expansionary credit policy in Figure 13.3. This is similar to Figure 13.1, although here we represent aggregate demand associated with lower internal prices, which we shall denote as $Y^{d,s}$ (the supra-index s alludes to the fact that domestic prices fall due to improved supply conditions of firms) as a straight line with a positive slope in the $\theta - Y$ plane. In other words, the real rate of exchange rises because increased access to cheaper and steadier credit improves the supply conditions of firms, which lower their profit margins and internal prices, p. Thus, a rise in θ achieved by improving the supply conditions of national producers, will have positive effects on both external and internal demand. The investment multiplier will increase because real wages rise and profit margins as well as prices decline. The latter will cause an upward shift of the distributive equilibrium line, from F_0 to F_1. Thanks to the fall in prices and the ensuing rise in the real rate of exchange, demand will rise from Y_0 to Y_1^d.

There is more, however. If credit facilities were given under priorities based upon an industrial policy aiming to lower import coefficients, for any given level of the real exchange rate and effective output, the output of external equilibrium will be higher. In other words, the Y^x curve shifts also rightwards, from Y^{x0} to Y^{x1}.

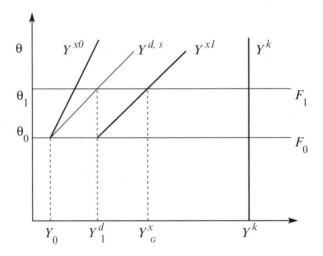

Figure 13.3   Macroeconomic effects of a selective expansionary credit policy in domestic firms (aggregate demand)

If the improvement in the supply conditions of firms has little expansionary effect on domestic demand, and its effect upon exports and substitution of imports is high, then the $Y^{d,s}$ curve would lie to the left of the Y^{x1} curve (as in Figure 13.3). In that case, expansionary fiscal and monetary policies could be implemented (to bring output to Y_G^x). In the opposite case, policies to reduce domestic demand would be necessary.

2.3   Monetary Issues in the Model

Before going deeper into our strategy, it will be useful to have a clear understanding of the theoretical foundations on which it rests with regard to the effects of financial variables on the real economy. These issues are of the utmost importance for a country compelled to grow open to a deregulated international financial environment.

2.3.1   Monetary policy goals and price level determinants
As mentioned above, we assume prices in the closed sector are determined by a margin over costs (Kalecki, 1954). Unlike other models, however, we also assume that this mark-up is flexible depending upon variables such as the state of confidence and liquidity preference (Kregel, 1987), investment decisions and finance availability (Kaldor, 1957), productive factors' struggle for a larger share in income (Taylor, 1983; Alberro and Ibarra, 1987) etc.

This approach rejects the view that prices are primarily determined by fiscal deficits, either directly by causing excess demands, or through their effects on high-powered money and therefrom on price expectations. Contrariwise, it acknowledges that prices are strongly dependent upon exchange rate behavior, on account of its direct impact upon costs, its influence on confidence, and the role it plays in capital asset values and the return demanded on them by investors. It also recognizes that prices depend on the cost and availability of credit. Figures 13.4 and 13.5 show the validity of these hypotheses in the Mexican case. They reveal that the exchange rate practically determines the inflation path, and that credit expansion is inversely related to the rate of inflation – as one would anticipate for an economy that behaves under imperfect competition.

We assume that the monetary authority is mainly concerned with preserving healthy financial institutions, and stimulating adequate levels of employment (Akhtar, 1995; Minsky, 1986), though these objectives should not jeopardize other important goals such as achieving price stability, as well as a competitive real exchange rate.

2.3.2   Deregulated international financial markets and monetary policy in the open economy
One of the most characterizing features of our present global economy is the rapid growth of international finance, particularly if compared with the slow

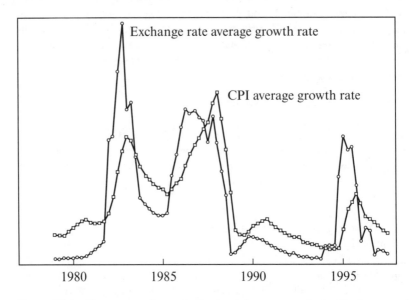

Figure 13.4   Monetary policy and price level determinants in the Mexican case (1)

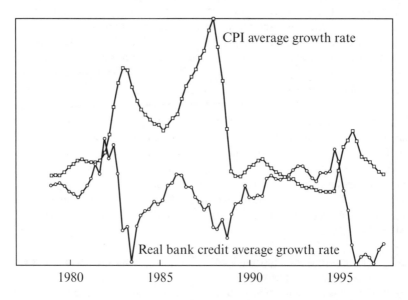

Figure 13.5   Monetary policy and price level determinants in the Mexican case (2)

growth of income and employment (Grabel, 1993; Dillon, 1997). This disequilibrium translates into huge and violent speculative capital flows that run from country to country in search of short-term returns that temporarily preserve their value.

Excess international finance has allowed deficits in current account that do not automatically adjust (BIS, 1990; Davidson, 1993). In fact, euromarkets have enabled countries to evade adjusting their exchange rate, relying instead on monetary and fiscal stabilization strategies.

Restrictive monetary policies have fulfilled the double task of keeping inflation low, while securing external funds to finance the current account imbalance. Thus in Mexico, during the last two decades, monetary policy has been tightened when international financial markets are booming; at the same time, current account deficits have been tolerated. Granger causality tests indicate that the current account is caused by the capital account, and not the other way around (Mántey, 1997).

International capital flows are driven by short-term interest rates when exchange rates are expected to be stable. Real interest rate differentials are pervasive (Meller, 1988; Felix, 1993), and exchange rates seem to be more responsive to these differentials than to trade deficits or purchasing power parities.

The so-called Dutch disease in many countries, that is, the appreciation of the exchange rate by an inflow of capital that causes deficit in the current account (Cambiaso, 1993), is only the result of the ongoing imbalance between the real and financial spheres of the global economy.

Any open economy, but particularly a developing one, is compelled to implement monetary policies that prevent capital outflows, since these are nowadays more disruptive than trade deficits. But capital inflows may be also troublesome, insofar as these tend to overvalue the domestic currency and worsen competitiveness. Overall equilibrium in the balance of payments, combined with price stability and a competitive real exchange rate, therefore, may require some degree of control over short-term capital flows, such as the one currently in force in Chile (Stiglitz, 1998; Ffrench-Davis, 1998).

2.3.3 Sensible monetary and fiscal policy for the liberalized developing economy

While we may assume profit margins and domestic prices will decline in response to a selective expansionary monetary policy, this response may be insufficient and delayed. Thus the real exchange rate may not rise fast and strongly enough to keep the trade balance in check when output and employment recover. Thus monetary policy will have to engage in providing the external funds that finance the current account deficit, while simultaneously sustaining the exchange rate to abate inflation. The same goals will be shared by fiscal policy.

It is well known that investors look for quality when uncertainty on private financial assets arises, and accordingly they demand government securities to avoid risks. On the other hand, monetary authorities usually influence short-term interest rates by buying or selling government securities. The placement of government debt, therefore, can be used as a lever to raise international funds.

In order to use this tool as a policy variable, however, governments ought to fulfill certain conditions imposed by foreign investors, such as a balanced budget, an adequate level of foreign reserves, convertibility of the domestic currency, and other economic policies amiable to foreign investments. If these requisites are met, the country will receive substantial flows of foreign capital, though short term in the main.

This 'noise-led' growth strategy (Grabel, 1993) has three evident flaws: it causes current account imbalances, leads to domestic financial fragility, and is vulnerable to international financial markets' instability. Nonetheless, in the short run, developing countries must rely on external resources in order to raise employment with a minimum of interference in relation to financial openness.

Furthermore, it is our belief that the disadvantages mentioned above are not insurmountable. Indeed, the tendency to current account imbalances can be reasonably dealt with in the medium term with appropriate domestic economic

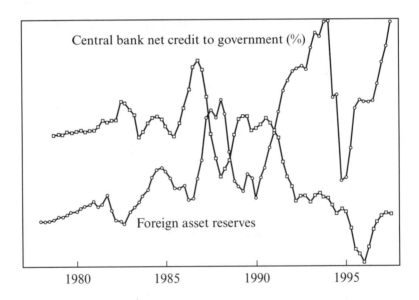

Figure 13.6   Monetary policy and price level determinants in the Mexican case (3); variables adjusted for range and scale

policies, mainly by means of credit guidelines that direct finance towards productive activities, according to a well-designed short- and long-term industrial policy. Domestic financial fragility can be confronted with adequate supervision of the financial sector, and especially with stable growth which brings about the profits necessary to validate private debts. Finally, vulnerability to international financial markets' instability can be partially, although never completely, coped with by implementing some degree of control over capital movements.

International financial markets reward the economy whose government enforces fiscal discipline in the budget, provided the country possesses foreign reserves in an amount sufficient to provide due service to standing obligations. This last condition can be procured by the government itself by means of a protectionist policy towards the autonomous central bank. In Mexico, the central government has been depositing with the monetary authority, a significant part of the proceeds from the placements of securities, in order to sustain an adequate level of foreign reserves. Figure 13.6 shows that from the beginning of the 1990s, net credit from the central bank to the government has been negative, and it has been negatively associated to variations in foreign assets reserves.

3   A FINANCIAL STRATEGY FOR FULL EMPLOYMENT IN A SEMI-INDUSTRIALIZED OPEN ECONOMY

Our proposal to increase the rate of employment while keeping prices stable, and allowing free trade, is based on a purposeful intervention in domestic credit markets.

We start from the premise that current unemployment in Mexico, is accounted for by a deficiency of effective demand, which is to a large extent the result of the rationing and high price of credit. In spite of the recovery after the crisis, and the two years of fast growth (in 1996 and 1997), credit from commercial banks, in real terms, has declined to the level it had fifteen years ago. The banking system has not yet overcome the problem of non-performing loans arisen as a result of credit deregulation in the 1980s, notwithstanding that public resources channeled to its bail out amount to more than twice the market value of total government negotiable securities outstanding. To some extent, the continuous decay of banking assets is the result of an uneven recovery of economic activity, which keeps corporate earnings in consumption goods industries and non-tradables sectors low, as a reflection of high domestic unemployment and depressed wage rates.

High real interest rates to secure foreign investments and stabilize the exchange rate, and wide spreads, as a result of oligopolistic competition in banking, increase the burden of accumulated debts. In fact, the banking system has fallen in a vicious circle, for debtors are unable to fulfill their obligations due to lack of effective demand, and bankers are unable to provide the credit required to stimulate demand (González, 1997).

The clue, however, is not just to restore institutional credit mechanisms, but to do it in such a way that the additional purchasing power be channeled towards production from the depressed activities, and from strategic branches of the economy, without exerting additional pressure on the current account of the balance of payments.

We believe this can be achieved by means of a twofold credit scheme that would provide discriminating credit facilities among firms and individuals on the basis of foreign currency availability.

3.1   The Two-tier Credit System

According to our strategy, there would be two types of credit facilities. The first would be somewhat similar to a traditional commercial banking system, where credit expansion is regulated by reserve requirements, and selective credit policies are imposed. The bank money generated through this mechanism would be fully convertible into foreign currencies, and could be used to carry out international transactions.

The second mechanism would resemble a cooperative system, in which firms and individuals would lend each other services and commodities with their values expressed in monetary units. It would work like a revolving fund. This system would provide only short-term credit to restore the circular flow of income within the national borders. Due to the latter, it could not be converted into foreign currencies, nor could it be used to carry out international transfers. Initially, this facility would be extended freely by the institutions in charge of its administration, who would provide clearing and settlement services on commission. As idle capacities vanish, or inflation accelerates, however, some restrictions should be enforced.

For convenience, the two systems would be operated by the same financial intermediaries. The cooperative system would work as an ordinary credit card system, with certain limitations on its acceptance as a means of payment. A fraction of wages could be paid with deposits to workers' credit accounts. Tax obligations could be fully discharged against taxpayers' credit accounts (Mosler, 1998). Public services and selected goods and services could be purchased with the credit card. The items selected would reflect credit policy objectives. As a first approach, we suggest eligible commodities be those with the lowest import content, and inputs indispensable for expansion of exports, or substitute of imports.

The two systems would coexist as a means to stabilize growth despite volatility in international financial markets. In face of an external credit crunch, or a sudden capital outflow, the former facility would be constrained by demanding larger reserve requirements to banks; and the second facility would be enlarged, allowing the banks to transfer funds to the deregulated scheme. This switch would also be beneficial to diminish the pressure on the balance of payments.

Since the expansion of the cooperative scheme does not pose a great threat on foreign reserves, the monetary authority could safely fulfill the role of lender of last resort, in very much the way it was conceived by Bagehot during the age of the gold standard. When external capital inflows slacken, the central bank would provide enlarged liquidity to support the cooperative scheme, thereby preventing a sharp decrease in income and employment. The effects of the ebb flows of foreign capital on domestic interest rates would be ameliorated, and the steady growth of income would preclude a rise in non-performing loans in the convertible credit system.

3.2 Industrial Policy through Credit Guidelines, Firms' Targets and Incentives

The two-tier credit scheme could be used to direct capital investment towards given short- and long-term objectives, while stabilizing output in the short run.

In order to direct finance to the most efficient uses from the social point of view, a regime of selective credit regulations and firms' compromises could be set up, in very much the way it was implemented in Japan in the aftermath of the Second World War (Torres, 1995). The traditional (convertible) credit system would be suitable for this purpose. The criteria for credit allocation banks should observe would reflect the industrial policy objectives defined by the government, who would also determine the targets firms should achieve in order to be benefited with convertible credit facilities. The availability of these facilities, as well as its price, would be used as incentives to guide private sector choices about expenditures, production, techniques etc., towards socially established goals. As already mentioned, we suggest credit priorities for firms to be settled on the basis of their potential earning and saving of foreign currency.

NOTES

1. The authors are professors at the National Autonomous University of Mexico.
2. In a recent detailed study, Jusidman (1995) estimated that the share of informal employment in total employment was about 40 percent in 1993.
3. These figures for idle capacity do not take into account that many firms, perhaps the majority, do not work the number of shifts that technically are possible.

4. X_j refers to the partial derivative of the variable X with respect to the variable that occupies the j place among the arguments of the corresponding function.
5. Variables followed by an asterisk * are in dollars.
6. The Krugman and Taylor paper (1978), where these problems are formally analyzed, is still very much worth reading. See also Taylor (1988) and, on the Mexican experience, see for example J. López (1991) and Castro *et al.* (1997).
7. The government could implement expansionary macro policies to increase demand and employment. But in any event a wage–price spiral would develop after a depreciation.

REFERENCES

Akhtar, M.A. (1995), 'Monetary policy goals and central bank independence', *Banca Nazionale del Lavoro Quarterly Review*, No. 195, December, pp. 423–39.
Alberro, J.L. and Ibarra, D. (1987), 'Programas heterodoxos de estabilización', *Estudios Económicos*, special number, October, pp. 3–13.
Bank for International Settlements (1990), *International Capital Flows, Exchange Rate Determination and Persistent Current Account Imbalances*, BIS, Basle, June.
Cambiaso, J. (1993), 'Síntomas del mal holandés por la vía de la cuenta de capital', *Monetaria,* enero-marzo. **XVI**, No. 1, pp. 1–26.
Carlin, W. and Soskice, D. (1990), *Macroeconomics and the Wage Bargain*, Oxford University Press.
Carvalho, F. (1997), 'Economic policies for monetary economies. Keynes's economic policy proposals for an unemployment-free economy', *Revista de Economia Política*, **17** No. 4 (68), Oct.–Dec., pp. 31–51.
Castro, C., Loría, E. and Mendoza, M.A. (1997), 'EUDOXIO: Modelo macroeconométrico de la economía mexicana', Fac. Economía, UNAM, Mexico.
Davidson, P. (1993), 'Reforming the world's money', *Journal of Post-Keynesian Economics*, **15**, No. 2, Winter, pp. 153–79.
Dillon, J. (1997), *Turning the Tide: Confronting the Money Traders*, Ecumenical Coalition for Economic Justice, Toronto.
Felix, D. (1993), 'Suggestions for international collaboration to reduce destabilizing effects of international capital mobility on LDC's', Washington University in St. Louis Department of Economics Working Paper Series, No. 13, February.
Ffrench-Davis, R. (1998), 'Policy Implications of the Tequila Effect', *Challenge*, March–April, pp. 15–43.
González, C. (1997*), Determinantes de la Cartera Vencida en México: Un Análisis de Cointegración y Modelo de Corrección de Errores*, M.A. Thesis, Maestría en Ciencias Económicas, UNAM, Mexico.
Grabel, I. (1993), 'Crossing borders: a case for cooperation in international financial markets', in G. Epstein, J. Grahams and J. Nembhard (eds.) *Creating a New World Economy: Forces of Change and Plans for Action*, Temple University Press.
Greenwald, B. and Stiglitz, J. (1993), 'Financial market imperfections and business cycles', *Quarterly Journal of Economics*, February, pp. 77–114.
Jusidman, C. (1995), 'Tendencias de la estructura económica y el sector informal en México', Secretaría del Trabajo y Previsión Social, México.
Kaldor, N. (1957), 'A model of economic growth', *The Economic Journal,* December, pp. 591–624.
Kalecki, M. (1944), 'Three ways to full employment', in *Collected Works of Michal Kalecki*, Vol. I, edited by J. Osiatynsky, Oxford University Press, 1990.

Kalecki, M. (1937), 'The principle of increasing risk', in 'Essays in the theory of economic fluctuations'. In *Collected Works of Michal Kalecki*, Vol. I, edited by J. Osiatynsky, Oxford University Press, 1990.

Kalecki, M. (1954), 'Theory of economic dynamics', included in *Collected Works of Michal Kalecki*, Vol. II, edited by J. Osiatynsky, Oxford University Press, 1991.

Keynes, J.M. (1936), *'The General Theory of Employment, Interest and Money'*, Harcourt, Brace: New York.

Keynes, J.M. (1929) 'A programme of expansion', in *Essays in Persuation*, W.W. Norton & Company: New York, 1963.

Kregel, J. (1987), 'Rational spirits and the Post-Keynesian macrotheory of microeconomics', *The Economist*, **135**, No. 4, pp. 520–43.

Kregel, J. (1994–95), 'The viablity of economic policy and the priorities of economic policy', *Journal of Post-Keynesian Economics*, **17** No. 2, pp. 261–77.

Krugman, P. and Taylor, L. (1978), 'Contractionary effects of devaluation', *Journal of International Economics*, November, pp. 445–6.

López, J. (1991) 'Contractive adjustment in Mexico', *Banca Nazionale del Lavoro Quarterly Review*, September, pp. 293–318.

López, J. (1998), 'La macroeconomía de México. El pasado reciente y el futuro posible'. Ed. Porrúa, México.

Mántey de A.G. (1997), 'La política monetaria de México en el entorno financiero internacional desregulado: una propuesta alternativa', mimeo, Universidad Nacional Autónoma de México.

Meller, P. (1988), 'Neo-estructuralismo, neo-monetarismo y procesos de ajuste en América Latina', *Colección Estudios CIEPLAN*, No. 23, March, pp. 3–13.

Minsky, H.P. (1986), 'Global consequences of financial deregulation', Washington University Working Paper Series, No. 96, September.

Mosler, W. (1998), 'Full employment and price stability', *Journal of Post-Keynesian Economics*, **20**, No. 2, Winter, pp. 167–182.

Stiglitz, J. (1998), 'More instruments and broader goals: Moving toward the post-Washington consensus', WIDER Annual Lecture, 7 January, Helsinki, WIDER.

Taylor, L. (1983), *Structuralist Macroeconomics: Applicable Models for the Third World*, Basic Books Inc: New York.

Taylor, L. (1988), *Varieties of Stabilization Experiences*, Clarendon Press: Oxford.

Torres, D. (1995), *Aspectos Relevantes de la Economía Japonesa de Posguerra*, M.A. Thesis, Maestría en Ciencias Económicas, UNAM, México.

14. Thwarting systems and institutional dynamics: or how to stabilize an unstable economy

Eric Nasica

INTRODUCTION

Starting in the middle of the 1950s, and for the next forty years, Hyman Minsky developed an original business cycle theory based on an endogenous and financial conception of economic fluctuations, and more specifically, on the 'financial instability hypothesis'.[1] The complexity and the richness of Minsky's analysis, associated with an almost total lack of formalization on his part, has not made the understanding of his approach any easier. It somewhat also explains the comparative disregard with which his theory of fluctuations has been considered until recently.

In the last ten years, various economists have begun to consider this problem worth tackling and have attempted to provide a modeled version of the financial instability hypothesis. With this aim in view, they have been using analytical methods derived from mathematical work on nonlinear and chaotic dynamical systems.[2] The results obtained have been very stimulating. In their models, nonlinearities combined with relations depicting financial arrangements are not assumed in an *ad hoc* fashion. Actually, nonlinearities allow a good description of the behaviors Minsky analyses in his theory of investment. More than anything else, these models quite faithfully account for one of the essential aspects contained in Minsky's approach, namely that the economy is subject to 'financial dynamics', insofar as it evolves along a succession of phases of comparative stability and instability. The idea being that, contrary to what is asserted by new classical economists, this succession of phases is induced by endogenous processes and financial phenomena.

However, a closer examination of Minsky's analysis leads one to consider these nonlinear models with a critical eye or at least to suggest a substantial enrichment of their assumptions. Indeed, these models neglect another essential aspect of the financial instability hypothesis, an aspect I propose to call 'institutional dynamics'. The latter characterizes the influence of institutional mechanisms and of the interventions of public authorities on the dynamics of market economies. These institutional factors affect the nature of the business cycle in a way that is ambivalent. On the one hand, they act as 'thwarting systems' whose purpose is to counteract and to contain the naturally explosive amplitude of economic fluctuations. On the other hand, they themselves can change into and become factors of instability and inefficiency.

In this chapter, it is shown that this ambivalence of institutional factors appears early in Minsky's first works, more precisely in the late 1950s. The argument is developed in two main steps. First, on the basis of Minsky's analysis, I investigate the actual form that fluctuations analysis can take, explicitly including the institutional context that governs interactions between economic agents (section 1). I then look at the reasons why the stabilizing effects of a given institutional structure are not immutable. In order to remain effective, the institutional structure must, on the contrary, change endogenously in response to actions by private agents in the economy (section 2).

1 THWARTING SYSTEMS OR THE NEED TO 'STABILIZE AN UNSTABLE ECONOMY'[3]

For Minsky, the various institutional mechanisms that make up contemporary market economies are central features in determining economic fluctuations. Their role is to 'halt' and then correct the dynamic process at the origin of the economy's 'endogenous' behavior, which is assumed to be incoherent. Concretely, this procedure amounts to introducing new initial conditions into the system and therefore modifying the behavior of markets and altering the parameters entering into economic agents' decisions. This means of characterizing the change in economic activity is interesting on more than one count. First it ties back in with and supplements a certain type of model of business cycles developed in the 1950s (section 1.1). Secondly, it provides a relevant theoretical framework within which to analyze the role of stabilizing institutional mechanisms occurring in contemporary financially sophisticated economies (section 1.2).

1.1 Reinterpreting Growth Models with 'Ceilings and Floors'

The business cycle models proposed by Minsky in the late 1950s[4] drew heavily on models of interaction between the multiplier and the accelerator developed some years previously by Hicks[5] and Goodwin.[6] Being aware of the inherent limits of linear macroeconomic models of the type proposed by Samuelson[7] and of the fundamentally nonlinear nature of economic activity, Hicks and Goodwin introduced constraints into business cycle models, to act as bounds to expansion or depression. Now, mathematically, this procedure comes down to introducing what can be termed 'type-1' nonlinearity into the model. Type-1 non linearity is thus defined by the introduction of constraints which the unstable solutions of a linear structure system run up against.

In view of the obvious kinship between these growth models with constraints and Minsky's approach, it seems necessary to recall briefly the main assumptions underlying them and the way they generate economic fluctuations. However, it seems more judicious, if we are to highlight the effects of institutional mechanisms, to present these models in a slightly different form from that initially proposed by their authors and given in the standard textbooks on macroeconomic dynamics.

This particular presentation, which is the one utilized by Minsky himself, consists in highlighting the influence of 'initial conditions' (and their variations) on the movement of time series generated in linear models with constraints. Resorting to this type of reasoning has the advantage of emphasizing that the shape of the paths obtained in these models is the outcome of dynamic processes divided into a series of stages. At each stage, the values taken by an economic variable serve as the initial conditions in determining the next value. A dynamic process is then termed 'unconstrained', in Minsky's terminology,[8] when the initial conditions of the following stage are generated endogenously by the process itself. In contrast with this, any process wherein the initial conditions of the next stage differ (because of influence from features exogenous to the process) from those that the process would have generated naturally are said to be 'constrained'. Type-1 nonlinearity therefore appears in the form of functions defined 'piecemeal', the specificity of which is to undergo variations when new initial conditions are defined.

Having made this preliminary remark, we can examine briefly the general behavior of models of interaction between the multiplier and the accelerator. These are usually characterized by a consumption function of the form $C_t = aY_{t-1}$ [a standing for the marginal rate of consumption and Y_t denoting the net national product in period t] and by an induced investment function of the form: $I_t = b(Y_{t-1} - Y_{t-2})$ [where b represents the accelerator]. When introduced into the equilibrium condition $Y_t = C_t + I_t$, these relations yield a second-order linear difference equation:

$$Y_t = (a + b) Y_{t-1} - bY_{t-2} \qquad (14.1)$$

This latest equation means that when the value of the reaction coefficients a and b and the values of Y_{t-1} and Y_{t-2} (the initial conditions) are known, it is possible to determine recursively any solution Y_n (where n is a previous or subsequent period) to the system. In addition, we know that the solution to (14.1) is of the form:

$$Y_t = A_1 U_1^t + A_2 U_2^t \tag{14.2}$$

where U_1 and U_2 are the roots of the associated characteristic equation $U^2 - (a + b) U + b = 0$ and A_1 and A_2 are constants depending on the value of parameters a and b and on the initial conditions.[9]

Solving equation (14.2) yields different types of dynamics depending on the value of the parameters, namely: (a) monotonic convergence of net national product toward an equilibrium value (if the roots are real and of absolute values less than unity); (b) damped fluctuations: the system is stable and converges towards the long-term equilibrium level of Y_t by values that are alternately less than and greater than this equilibrium value (if the roots are complex and their modulus is less than unity); (c) explosive fluctuations: the amplitude of fluctuation of national output increases around the equilibrium value at each period (if the roots are complex and their modulus is greater than unity); (d) instability in the form of monotonic divergence or regular explosive growth, the national product diverging increasingly from the equilibrium level (if the roots are real and greater than unity in absolute value).

Unlike Samuelson's analysis,[10] which investigates the range of different solutions set out above, Hicks concentrates exclusively on parameter values which when combined give either accelerated growth, or amplified fluctuations [cases (c) and (d) above]. Hicks therefore situates his approach in a configuration such that both roots U_1 and U_2 are greater than unity with $U_1 > U_2 > 1$. He further assumes that there is a maximum growth rate ('ceiling') of the economy which we shall note as g (this gives therefore $Y_t = Y_0 e^{gt}$ when the ceiling is effective) and the dominant root U_1 is very much greater than the growth rate of the ceiling income. Finally, both roots U_1 and U_2 are such that $U_1 > U_2 > g > 1$.

Under these assumptions, the economy would evolve in the following way. Let us suppose that the economy is initially defined in such a way that it generates two consecutive incomes Y_0 and Y_1 ($Y_1 > Y_0$) such that both these incomes are less than their corresponding 'ceilings' and that, in addition, $U_1 > Y_1/Y_0 > U_2$. These initial conditions determine positive coefficients A_1 and A_2 (with, in addition, A_2 being much greater than A_1 because U_1 is assumed to be much greater than g^{11}). Equation (2), characterizing the dynamics of the system, then generates an explosive type evolution over time.

However, after a certain time, let us say the period n, the income generated in accordance with equation (14.2) finishes by levelling out at a higher value than the ceiling corresponding to that period. At that juncture, the constraint becomes effective and the income realized is no longer determined by the previous equation (14.2) (specifying the unconstrained dynamics) but, for two successive periods, by the equation:

$$Y_1 = gY_0 \qquad (14.3)$$

This takes us back to a situation where $Y_1/Y_0 = g < U_2$. The prominent feature is that the coefficient A_1 of the dominant root U_1 will change sign and become negative in the new solution equation (14.2) which will prevail. This change in sign indicates the start of the 'rebound' of the path against the ceiling, i.e. the turnaround point of the cycle. A cumulative depression process results from this. The economy is henceforth subjected to change that is guided essentially by the negative term of increasing absolute value: $A_1(U_1)^t$.

This explosive downward movement of income can only be slowed if there is a lower limit, a 'floor', to counter the process generated by the unconstrained dynamics, as with the ceiling examined above. As in Hicks's model, the floor may consist in setting a maximum value of disinvestment by firms. When this maximum value is reached, the realized value Y_t is different from that obtained with equation (14.2) previously. A new solution equation then determines the change in the economy. This new equation is characterized this time by a negative and comparatively large coefficient A_2 and by a positive and comparatively small coefficient A_1. As in the previous case, there then comes a point where the cycle reverses. A new expansion phase arises, which is initially moderate and then explosive. It continues until the economy 'rebounds' again on the ceiling for the reasons described previously and so on and so forth.

When we compare the general form of Hicks's model with that of the models proposed by Minsky in the late 1950s, the two approaches look very similar. In both cases, the authors have opted to take nonlinearities into account by introducing constraints on booms or slumps, in the form of 'floors' or 'ceilings'. These models are therefore capable, as we have just seen, of generating persistent fluctuations from an unstable solution of the Samuelson model.

Nonetheless, this apparent similarity conceals a marked difference in interpretation between the two economists. This difference depends mainly on the exact sense each gives to the constraints that stabilize the dynamics of the economy.

In Hicks's model, commonsense justifies the existence of these constraints: real investment cannot be negative, hence the existence of a 'floor' (determined by the growth of autonomous investment and the size investment due to depreciation). In addition, output, consumption and investment are limited by the bounded availability of natural resources, labor and productivity gains. Hence the existence of a 'ceiling'.

Things are very different for Minsky. Of course, Minsky does not deny that such constraints can influence the level of economic activity. Nevertheless, he does not think they are primordial in explaining the cyclic dynamics observed in market economies. He argues that floors and ceilings reflect primarily the set of institutional mechanisms set up by public authorities in order to confine the amplitude of economic fluctuations within reasonable bounds. This is why Minsky terms these institutional arrangements 'thwarting systems'.

The original idea developed by Minsky is therefore that the main purpose of these thwarting systems is to modify the initial conditions governing the future evolution of economic time series during phases of explosive expansion or cumulative depression (or to speak in nominal terms, during periods of intense inflation or deflation). As we have emphasized, such changes in 'initial conditions' have the effect of inverting the sign of the dominant root of the equation that solves the oscillator model. Consequently, the movement of the economy ends up slowing down and reverting to the opposite direction. Depression or deflation is thus converted by an 'institutional' type floor, into a moderate and then explosive recovery, which in turn runs up against an 'institutional ceiling'. The time series observed thus appear to be the outcome of incessant 'rebounds' of economic dynamics, hitting alternatively the ceilings and floors generated by the institutional thwarting mechanisms set up in the economy.

Such a model, explicitly integrating the role of institutions on the changes in economic activity is interesting in more than one way. First, unlike Samuelson's oscillator type unconstrained linear models, it accounts for the complexity of changes of capitalist economies over time that Minsky highlighted. This evolution is made up of *'steady growth [when $U_1 > g > U_2$], cycles [when $U_1 > U_2 > 1$], booms, or depressions [when $g > U_1$'*.[12] In other words, this linear model with constraints *'exhibits the features of chaotic models, including the sensitivity of the time series that is generated to initial conditions'*.[13]

Secondly, unlike usual linear models with constraints which spirit away institutional thwarting systems,[14] this model makes it easier to understand the role played by institutional changes and interventions by public authorities on economic dynamics. In Minsky's model, the policy and institutional dependence of the floors and ceilings can be made quite precise. The 'incoherence' of economic paths [in particular the occurrence of explosive, amplified changes leading to either very large values (even infinite) or... negative values] inherent in unconstrained linear models can thus be countered by setting up institutional thwarting mechanisms. Under these circumstances, *'business cycles can result either from the values of the "U's" being complex, from regular interventions that contain the economy between "floors and ceilings" if the "U's" are greater than one, and from introductions of energy from outside if the "U's" are less than one'*.[15]

In Minsky's approach, the concrete stabilizing procedures of economic activity that are able to lay down new initial conditions and to contain the amplitude of time series are essentially the concern of the government, via its budgetary policy, and of the central bank, through its role as lender-of-last-resort.

1.2 'Big Government', Lender-of-last-resort and Stabilizing Economic Activity

Minsky views budget deficit and interventions by the central bank as lender-of-last-resort (the Fed in the US) as extremely effective instruments with which to stabilize economic fluctuations. Even if they do not lead to a situation of full employment, these instruments help limit variability to the fall in income and liquidity during economic recessions and during the onset of a financial crisis.

Let us consider the role of budget deficit first. In Minsky's theory, investment is the essential determinant of economic activity. This investment is largely influenced by aggregate (realized or anticipated)[16] profits. It follows, he emphasizes, that '*a main aim of policy is to constrain the variability of profits*'.[17] Now, recalls Minsky, in a closed economy, these aggregate profits are, in accordance with the approach utilized by Kalecki,[18] equal to the sum of investment and of budget deficit. Consequently, this deficit, by supporting aggregate demand when private investment flags, allows a lower limit (a 'floor' to continue with the vocabulary of linear models with constraints) for profits, wages and current production prices.[19] In other words, '*policy will be stabilizing if a shortfall of private investment quickly leads to a government deficit and a burst of investment quickly leads to a budget surplus*'.[20] This stabilization of actual and expected profits is crucial to ensure the continuity of the economic system. It is utilized in particular to maintain the viability of debt structures and therefore the level of private investment. In fact, '*once rational bankers and business men learn from experience that actual profits do not fall when private investment declines, they will modify their preferred portfolios to take advantage of the stability of profits*'.[21]

Thus the presence of a 'big government', characterized by a budgetary policy that is very sensitive to variations in overall profits is necessary to improve the stability of the economy. Nonetheless, isolated action of this type of policy may prove insufficient during periods of economic turmoil. True, public deficits partly offset the reduction in profit flows resulting from a fall in investment and in this way maintain current production prices and consumer goods prices. However, these deficits do not make it possible to counteract directly, during an economic crisis, the drop in another type of price, and one which is essential in Minsky's investment theory, namely the price of capital assets. This latter price is dependent upon the amount of money in circulation but also on more subjective variables such as liquidity preference, the debt level that is judged acceptable or the expected profits of different agents in the economy.[22]

It is necessary then to turn, as a supplementary step, toward a second type of 'institutional thwarting mechanism', the role of the central bank as lender-of-last-resort.[23]

The main purpose of this type of intervention is to counter the 'debt deflation' phenomena or at least the different forms of financial instability that contemporary market economies have experienced, especially in the last decade. In the case of the US, which Minsky gives precedence to, one obviously thinks of the financial market crash of October 1987, the Federal Savings and Loan Insurance Corporation (FSLIC) debacle and the extreme fragilization of junk bond markets. Through their sheer scale and the difficulties experienced in correcting them, these different examples emphasize the idea that the stability of the current financial system cannot be based exclusively on government budgetary policy.

For Minsky these phenomena also emphasize the necessity for an extended interpretation of the role of lender-of-last-resort. This is why he distinguishes three aspects of this type of intervention in his approach.[24] First, in the event of insufficient funds on the money market (generally synonymous with substantial falls in the value of claims utilized by agents to obtain liquidities), the central bank must intervene by increasing the amount of money in circulation. Secondly, during the financial restructuring period that follows a crisis, the central bank must take care to favor recourse to long-term rather than short-term borrowing by acting accordingly on interest rates. Finally, the central bank is responsible for guiding the development of the financial system, both through regulations and through banking system controls so that the impact of 'speculative' banking operations (notably excessive recourse to liability management) can be restricted.

There is no denying that, in the last twenty years, the 'endogenous' aspect of central bank policy has been considerably reinforced, in accordance with the approach advocated by Minsky and contrary to the claims of the monetarist school.[25] Its function as lender-of-last-resort has extended constantly to new institutions and new instruments.[26] By the end of the 1960s, the Fed had to intervene to protect the municipal bond market. In 1970 it had to guarantee the commercial paper market. In the 1980s it had to intervene during the foreign debt crisis, during the Continental Illinois bankruptcy and during the financial market crash. In each of these situations, the Fed (which is supposed to follow a 'monetarist' policy) provided liquidity and was compelled to validate to some extent many risky financial practices.

The analysis of institutional constraints of the system thus marks the clear opposition between Minsky's approach and the 'Smithian' conception of economic behavior characterizing current business cycle theories of neo-classical inspiration. The idea highlighted by this author is that the institutional structure of contemporary economies contains a number of regulatory mechanisms, which are exogenous to the market, whose actions prevent the free exercise of the internal dynamics of the economic system. In this context, each specific institutional structure will have the effect of producing realized values (asset values, income flows) that are different from those that would have been determined by unconstrained internal dynamics. The central bank in particular intervenes almost daily on the money and financial markets in its activity as lender-of-last-resort. The main implication of these interventions is to prevent the present results obtained on these markets from becoming the initial conditions that will govern future dynamic processes. Thus when the central bank intervenes in the money market to shore up a failing financial institution or to stabilize the foreign exchange market, the values of the interest rate, of asset prices or of exchange rates will differ from the values determined by the working of the market alone.

2   THE AMBIVALENCE OF INSTITUTIONAL THWARTING SYSTEMS

The line of argument developed in the previous section implies that in the long run, the satisfactory working of the economy is dependent on the 'accuracy' of the regulating structure set up by the public and monetary authorities. Now, the effects of an intervention structure are not immutable: its capacity to stabilize the amplitude of economic fluctuations and to compel market agents to undertake moderately risky actions varies greatly over time. This is so because *'profit-seeking agents learn how a regulatory structure operates and because regulation means that some perceived opportunities are not open to exploitation, there are incentives for agents to change their behaviour to evade or avoid the constraints'*.[27]

This means that some institutional interventions and mechanisms, that were initially stabilizing, may change into factors of instability and inefficiency. One need only recall the Savings and Loan debacle and the powerlessness of the FSLIC when confronted with problems of financial instability in the 1980s to be persuaded of this: a regulation and intervention structure which was at first effective can begin to backfire if the political and institutional decision-makers do not take adequate account of the behavior of market agents in response to the institutional changes they are up against.

This basic aspect of the effects of interaction between market dynamics and institutional dynamics appears to be a key element in Minsky's cycle theory. This issue was investigated in depth by the author's very first publication titled 'Central Banking and Money Market Changes'.[28]

In that paper Minsky develops an approach based on a money supply function reflecting, on the one hand, complex interactions between the central bank and private banks on the money market and on the other hand the institutional dynamics derived from such interaction. In order to examine the role of commercial bank behavior on the money market, the author reasons firstly on the assumption that the central bank conducts a restrictive monetary policy. He argues that if economic expansion generates fears of inflation, the monetary authorities may be led to apply this type of policy, which is liable to entail interest rate rises which reflect, during such periods of upturn in activity, '*a vigorous demand for financing relative to the available supply*'.[29] Minsky then envisages two cases: the first consists in reasoning on a stable institutional environment. In this case Minsky acknowledges that '*a tight money policy will be effective and the interest rate will rise to whatever extent is necessary in order to restrict the demand for financing to the essentially inelastic supply. [...] This can be represented as a positive sloped curve between velocity and the interest rate*'.[30]

This assumption of institutional stability is, however, not the one that the author favors, having regard to the major changes occurring on the money market in the early 1950s, characterized in particular by the substantial development and boom in the federal funds market and 'repurchase agreements'. Minsky contends that these changes reflect 'institutional instability' which is driven mainly by the maximizing and innovating behavior adopted by commercial banks.

Restating and supplementing the analysis of Schumpeter[31] (1951) on the question, Minsky emphasizes that the search for market power is a fundamental determinant in innovation: banks are viewed as enterprising firms that innovate to improve their profitability. The idea behind this is that as financial institutions innovate, the financial system changes, imagining new ways of financing the maximizing behavior of other institutions. Consequently, the innovators who develop new financial instruments, new financial usages and new financial institutions are rewarded in the form of monopoly rents which vanish only with the propagation of the innovations. More specifically, the mechanism studied by Minsky in 1957 works as follows. Interest rate rises act as a signal for the private operators in the money market who interpret these increases as new opportunities for profit. In particular, in the case of commercial banks, the interest rate rise induces an increased opportunity cost of idle balances for those establishments with excess reserves on hand. It is therefore in their interest to lend such reserves on the federal funds market. Likewise, banks with deficit reserves can take advantage of the gap between interest rates on federal funds and the discount rate; the former, observes Minsky, being never greater than the latter.[32] For identical reasons, non-bank financial institutions such as government bond houses are encouraged to borrow through repurchase agreements from nonfinancial corporations. This operation is made easier in periods of high interest rates, the non-financial corporations turning away from non remunerated demand deposits and therefore seeks to place their funds in more profitable liquid assets.[33]

To sum up, the rise in interest rates creates a favorable environment for the emergence and development of institutional innovations. Now, these innovations have an important implication: they increase the velocity of money and, in itself, the quantity of money on offer to potential borrowers.

There are two essential reasons behind this fundamental relationship that emerges between increased velocity and increased quantity of money. First, it is clear that the increased recourse by banks to the federal funds market produces an increase in the volume of demand deposits for a given amount of central bank money: '*a given volume of reserves now supports more deposits*'.[34] Secondly, the innovation process described implies henceforth that for a given volume of demand deposits, banks increase the amount of loans granted to firms.[35] Commercial bank assets undergo two important changes: (1) a fall in the proportion invested in short-term government bonds, such as Treasury Bills; this is a consequence of the rising share being held by nonfinancial corporations following the increase in rates; and (2) reduction in loans granted to government bond houses which are increasingly financed, as we have seen, from these nonfinancial corporations through repurchase agreements. It can be seen then why Minsky rightly assimilates these different changes in bank balances generated by the innovation process to an increase in bank reserves[36] and why the velocity and the quantity of money vary jointly during the expansion phase of economic activity.

These different changes on the money market therefore engender institutional instability which is reflected concretely by a shift to the right in the relationship linking interest rates and the velocity of money. This leads eventually to an upward stepped money supply curve similar to that in Figure 14.1.

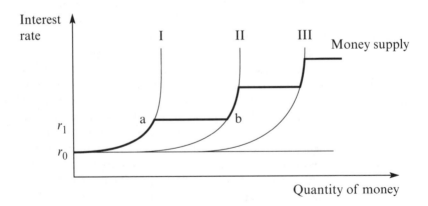

Figure 14.1   Institutional dynamics and interest rates

The increasing parts of the curve represent the effect on the interest rate of a restrictive monetary policy in a stable institutional environment. However, this movement does not last indefinitely: interest rate rises (from r_0 to r_1) generate profit opportunities, innovations on the money market and therefore institutional instability reflected by the shift of curve I to II. This gives rise to a horizontal plateau (a – b) characterizing the period during which institutional innovation propagates.

During this period, the effects of the restrictive monetary policy on the interest rate are completely offset while the velocity and the supply of money seem to be infinitely elastic. As Minsky emphasizes, in such a context, the effectiveness of monetary policy for controlling monetary aggregates is very low and, to react to inflationary fears, the central bank has no other solution than to act directly on banking system liquidity. It therefore tries to reduce reserves sufficiently to offset the increase in the velocity. This reaction by the central bank to the maximizing and innovating behavior of commercial banks has the effect of directing interest rates up again, and consequently, recreating eventually the entire process described above, hence the succession over time of increasing portions and horizontal plateaux as shown in Figure 14.1.

In this way, the behavior of commercial banks in response to profit possibilities and to the policy conducted by the central bank does not allow the central bank to set the interest rate at the level it judges desirable. The change in the interest rate is largely dependent upon the series of phases of institutional stability and instability induced by the behavior of commercial banks in response to stabilization policies conducted by the monetary authorities.

This interest rate also appears to be 'pro-cyclic': on the assumption used here, the interest rate rises simply reflect the dynamic process that is set up between the innovations of commercial banks and the reactions in the form of restrictive monetary policy of the central bank during the expansion phase of economic activity. The rise in interest rates on the money market and the institutional innovations of the commercial banks finish up by fragilizing the banks' balance sheets. This fragilization leads to increased preference for liquidity on the part of banks and revaluation of what are deemed acceptable debt ratios for borrowers. Accordingly, banks are led to restrict their lending policy on the credit market. This is reflected in the fall of the supply of finance and in the increase of interest rates on the market for loans. Greater financial constraints are then liable to have dramatic consequences in terms of economic and financial instability if they arise in an economy dominated by agents with an already fragile financial structure.[37]

These problems which are inherent to intervention by the monetary authorities, much as the difficulties encountered by organizations such as the FSLIC in the US, are not, however, an argument in favor of '*laissez-faire*' or for rejecting institutional thwarting systems. On the contrary, they suggest the conclusion that '*intervention cannot be frozen in time but must adapt as institutional and usage evolution takes place; successful capitalism requires both a structure of regulation and a sophisticated awareness of the way profit seeking drives the evolution of structures and behaviour*'.[38] In other words, while '*thwarting systems are analogous to homeostatic mechanisms which may prevent a system from exploding*'[39] they are not mechanical for all that.

In this context, any incapacity of the public authorities to interpret correctly the change in their economic environment and more particularly to take account of the consequences of their interventions on the behavior of private agents can have harmful consequences on macroeconomic dynamics. Three types of difficulties are liable to arise.

A first problem arises when policy-makers have to rely on the data drawn from time series generated, precisely, by a potentially explosive system that is constrained by interventions and institutional mechanisms. These data may give the misleading impression that they result from a 'naturally' stable dynamic process and cannot suitably support policy-making. In a setting of this sort, economists and policy-makers may mistakenly conclude that a system is endogenously stable and that institutional thwarting mechanisms are useless. In addition, once the problems of macroeconomic instability have seemingly been eliminated, the public authorities may become prone to take measures in order, for example, to improve the microeconomic efficacy of the system. In finance, scrutiny of contemporary market economies shows that such a policy usually takes the form of a process of deregulation and of slackening of the constraints (notably in balance sheet management) weighing on the operators of the money and financial markets. The periods of great financial instability experienced by Western countries and by Japan in the early 1990s emphasize the adverse effects induced by this quest for microeconomic effectiveness to the detriment of the stability of the system as a whole. Events have provided a harsh reminder that, in accordance with Minsky's approach, inflexible and short-sighted action by the public authorities leads to a weakening of the stabilizing mechanisms set up in the past and to the creation of an environment conducive to the triggering of a financial crisis.

Secondly, Minsky emphasizes that the large injections of liquidity associated with interventions by the government and monetary authorities are inflationary, as they inject purchasing power into the economy more quickly than they encourage the creation of new production.[40] The combination of fragility of the system and anti-deflationary intervention therefore introduces an inflationary bias into the economy. The problem is that it is very difficult to control inflation in 'financially sophisticated' economies. Cost inflation acts on the price level of current output. Now, as Kregel[41] shows, monetary policy appears to be an overweildy instrument for combating inflation and may aggravate recession and lead to increased unemployment. This policy appears *a priori* more effective for controlling 'speculative inflation' of the prices of capital assets by acting directly on variables such as interest rates and financial system liquidity which are directly involved in determining this type of price. Nevertheless, the effect of a restrictive monetary policy on the prices of assets remains difficult to predict accurately: these prices also depend to a large extent on potentially volatile expected profits in an uncertain environment. Consequently, any attempt by the monetary authorities to hold down inflation (e.g. interest rate rises) on the financial markets may well force expectations to be revised downward and trigger behavior leading to marked instability of the system.

Thirdly, it is clear that even if actions taken by public authorities can offset financial instability in the short run, they do not necessarily drive the economy toward a stable situation of full employment. Their interventions also tend to validate fragile financial structures that have come into existence and, as an effect, to sustain or even amplify the problems associated with such structures. This is so because rational agents, observing a rise in the level of financial fragility at the macroeconomic level, will be prone to adopt financial behavior that will become increasingly risky, and engage in more debt. Such behavior is explained essentially by the fact that potential costs associated with risky financial practices of private agents are, to a very large extent, 'socialized': it is the task of the public authorities (the government, the central bank) rather than of the private agents themselves to absorb the costs inherent in the increase of the budget deficit or intervention as lender-of-last-resort.

Finally, the inclusion of the role of institutional mechanisms implies that Minsky's theory does not simply describe the cycle as a mechanical phenomenon of succession of phases of the type: increasing financial fragility → financial crisis → gradual return to a more safety and soundness of the financial system. This is so because, as a rule, financial crises thwarted by institutional mechanisms do not develop all their effects (debt-deflation, widespread bankruptcies, disappearance of agents with more fragile financial structures, etc.). As a consequence, the natural tendency towards greater financial fragility is temporarily mitigated but is in no way reversed. Fragilization on the contrary takes the form of a sustained trend, permanently transforming the fundamentals of the economy and behavior of agents within the system. Such a tendency , in an economy that is becoming increasingly fragile in the long run, makes it necessary then for there to be greater frequency and extent of actions taken by the public authorities aimed at offsetting the emergence of instability until the time comes when the crisis can no longer be contained, as is noted by Minsky.

Thus in 'financially sophisticated' economies on which Minsky concentrates, the natural tendency of the system to generate periods of great instability may be controlled in part by thwarting systems. Nevertheless, such systems cannot lead to a stable equilibrium with full employment. Downward instability (debt-deflation) tends to transform under the effect of institutional thwarting processes set up by the public authorities into upward instability (characterized by a sustained trend toward excessive borrowing, increased interest rates and persistent inflationary pressures).

CONCLUSION

For more than two centuries, there have been two opposing conceptions of the evolution of economic activity. In his memorial of Wesley Mitchell, Schumpeter distinguishes between those economists who hold that '[...] *the economic process is essentially non-oscillatory and that the explanation of cyclical as well as well as other fluctuations must be sought in particular circumstances (monetary or other) which disturb that even flow*' and those holding that the '*economic process itself is essentially wave like – that cycles are the form of capitalist evolution*'.[42]

The analysis in this work, while it does not fundamentally challenge this distinction, shows that it must nevertheless be substantially completed if the institutional factors that constitute contemporary market economies are to be integrated explicitly in business cycle analysis. The taking into consideration of the institutional dimension of economic dynamics emphasizes that there is room within contemporary analyses of economic fluctuations for a new family of business cycle theories. It would fit somewhere in between the purely exogenous conceptions of New Classical Economics and those purely endogenous ones underpinning recent nonlinear models. It implies that the economic process is not 'essentially non-oscillatory' just as it is not 'essentially wave-like'. This different way of analyzing fluctuations is stimulating for many reasons.

First, it allows one to explain the complexity of the evolution of contemporary economies. Such modeling can incorporate both steady growth and regular business cycles as possible transient characterizations of economic time series, but, in addition, it does not exclude the emergence of the potentially 'incoherent' (or chaotic) dynamics created by the interaction of economic agents. Accordingly, the effective character of the transformation of potential incoherence into realized incoherence is dependent, mainly, on the various institutional thwarting systems characterizing the economic system under consideration.[43]

This kind of approach also has the merit of renewing the treatment of the relations between institutions and economic activity, which is something that we do not find in traditional macroeconomic models. In New Classical Economics, it is postulated that governmental institutions can only disturb the operation of otherwise clearing markets. On their side, Keynesians of the IS–LM synthesis consider economic policy as entirely exogenous. The analysis referred to in this chapter shows on the contrary that the public authorities (the government, the central bank) react in an endogenous way to the behavior of private agents. They thus create a true 'institutional dynamics' which interweaves with the real and financial dynamics of the economy and changes the 'unconstrained' results of the latter two.

The essential consequence of this permanent interaction between institutions and markets is that the economic system never reproduces itself identically.[44] In this context, the emplacement of adequate institutional thwarting mechanisms becomes extremely complex and demands increased vigilance on the part of the public authorities. Vigilance is necessary as the stabilization processes put in place at a certain time may eventually prove to be highly destabilizing. The 'institutional' changes imposed by the public authorities on the initial conditions of dynamic processes generate constrained time series or, more precisely, 'truncated' business cycles. The same is notably true when stabilizing mechanisms that have been instituted have the effect of guarding, for a comparatively long period, against a financial crisis or a deep depression. In this case, stability becomes destabilizing: private agents tend to become less risk averse and to adapt their maximizing behavior to the new institutional structure that gradually comes to prevail, thereby gradually undermining the stabilizing capacity of this structure, which causes the effects of the crisis to be amplified when it eventually breaks out. The extent of the problems raised by the bailing out of the US Savings and Loans Associations and more recently the difficulties faced by the central banks and the International Monetary Fund in containing the crisis in the Asian markets are painful evidence of this idea. They also strongly underline the need for contemporary business cycle theorists to integrate the institutional dimension of economic fluctuations into their analyses, in accordance with the view developed by Hyman Minsky.

NOTES

1. See Minsky (1975, 1982, 1986).
2. For instance, we have Franke and Semmler (1989), Skott (1995) or Delli Gatti and Gallegati (1993).
3. To cite the title of one of the main works of Minsky (1986).
4. Minsky (1957a, 1959).
5. Hicks (1950).
6. Goodwin (1951).
7. In the linear model of Samuelson (1939), regular, self-sustaining oscillations appear only for very special values of parameters characterizing the multiplier and accelerator. Apart from these values, the model is not very satisfactory for explaining the occurrence of self-sustaining fluctuations and accounting for the evolution of the different economic series, where, as is known, irregular fluctuations with hardly any damping are observed. This mismatch between empirically observed fluctuations and theoretical results of linear models emphasizes an absolutely general property of this type of formalization: its inability to account for persistent fluctuations, i.e. fluctuations that are neither damped nor amplified.
8. Ferri and Minsky (1992).

9. If m is the effective growth rate of income, then for any two successive dates chosen as initial conditions, $Y_1 = mY_0$. This therefore gives (since $Y_1 = A_1U_1 + A_2U_2$ and $Y_0 = A_1 + A_2$):

$$A_1 = (m - U_2) + (U_1 - U_2)Y_0$$
$$A_2 = (U_1 - m) / (U_1 - U_2)Y_0$$

Assuming that values a and b are such that $U_1 > U_2 > 1$ (i.e. the case of explosive time series in an unconstrained system), it follows that:

$$U_1 > U_2 > m, \text{ therefore } A_1 < 0 \text{ and } A_2 > 0$$

whereas

$$U_1 > m > U_2, \text{ therefore } A_1 > 0 \text{ and } A_2 > 0.$$

10. Samuelson (1939).
11. Cf. footnote 9. This characteristic implies that during the early periods (t small), the weight of U_2 is predominant in determining the dynamic evolution whereas during subsequent periods, it is the root U_1 that tends to dominate. It ensues that the income growth rate finishes by converging towards U_1 when t goes to infinity.
12. Minsky (1959, p. 134).
13. Ferri and Minsky (1989, p. 138).
14. Such as Hicks's model examined earlier but also Goodwin's (1951) model, based on a non-linear accelerator.
15. Ferri and Minsky (1989, p. 137).
16. Cf. in particular Minsky (1986, Chapters 7 and 8).
17. Fazzari and Minsky (1984, p. 107).
18. Kalecki (1971).
19. For an analysis of the relationship between profits and the fixing of wages and current production prices, cf. Ferri and Minsky (1984) and Minsky (1986, Chapter 7).
20. Fazzari and Minsky (1984, pp. 107–8).
21. Minsky (1992, p. 12).
22. Cf. Minsky (1975, 1986).
23. In the US, the central bank includes not only the Federal Reserve system but also the different insurance-deposit organizations.
24. Minsky (1986).
25. On this point, see the useful paper by Friedman (1992).
26. Cf. Wojnilower (1987).
27. Minsky (1992, p. 17).
28. Minsky (1957b).
29. Ibid. p. 163.
30. Ibid. p. 172.
31. Schumpeter (1951a).
32. Minsky (1957b, p. 164).
33. As Minsky points out, in mid 1956, nonfinancial corporation funds became the major source of financing for government bond houses.
34. Minsky (1957b, p. 171).
35. Ibid. p. 163.
36. Ibid. p. 170.
37. For a more extensive development of this point, see Nasica (1997).
38. Minsky (1992, pp. 17–18).
39. Ferri and Minsky (1992, p. 84).
40. Cf. Friedman (1992). This reflects a problem that Minsky often pointed out: the necessity for the Federal Reserve to act as lender-of-last-resort may often be incompatible with its other objectives, in particular with keeping the inflation rate down.

41. Kregel (1992).
42. Schumpeter (1951b, p.252).
43. The necessity to integrate the 'institutional' dimension and the thwarting systems is not really taken on board in recent non-linear models of the financial instability hypothesis with the notable exception of the model proposed by Keen (1995).
44. Consideration of institutional dynamics is thus akin, from the point of view of its consequences on the decision-making environment, to the 'crucial decisions' of Shackle (1955) and the non-ergodic stochastic processes of Davidson (1982–3).

REFERENCES

Davidson, P. (1982–3) 'Rational expectations: a fallacious foundation for studying crucial decision-making processes', *Journal of Post Keynesian Economics*, Fall, 182–98.

Delli Gatti, D., Gallegati, M. and Gardini, L. (1993) 'Complex dynamics in a simple macroeconomic model with financing constraints', in G. Dymski and R. Pollin (eds), *New Perspectives in Monetary Macroeconomics, Explorations in the Tradition of Hyman P. Minsky*, The University of Michigan Press, Ann Arbor.

Fazzari, S. and Minsky, H.P. (1984) 'Domestic monetary policy: if not monetarism, what?', *Journal of Economic Issues*, 18, 101–16.

Ferri, P. and Minsky, H.P. (1984) 'Prices, employment and profits', *Journal of Post Keynesian Economics*, Summer, 489–99.

Ferri, P. and Minsky, H.P. (1989) 'The breakdown of the IS-LM synthesis : implications for Post-Keynesian economic theory', *Review of Political Economy*, July, 123–41.

Ferri, P. and Minsky, H.P. (1992) 'Market processes and thwarting systems', *Structural Changes and Economic Dynamics*, **3**, (1), p.79–91.

Franke, R. and Semmler, W. (1989) 'Debt financing of firms, stability and cycles in dynamical macroeconomic growth model', in W. Semmler (ed.), *Financial Dynamics and Business Cycles: New Perspectives*, M.E. Sharpe, Armonk, New York, pp.38–64.

Friedman, B. (1992) 'Risks in our high-debt economy: depression or inflation?' in Fazzari and D. Papadimitriou (eds), *Financial Conditions and Economic Performance: Essays in Honour of Hyman P. Minsky*, pp.63–70.

Goodwin R. (1951) 'The non linear acceleration and the persistence of business cycles', *Econometrica*, **19**, (1), January, 1–17.

Hicks, J.R. (1950) *A Contribution to the Theory of the Trade Cycle*, Clarendon Press, Oxford.

Kalecki, M. (1971) *Selected Essays on the Dynamics of the Capitalist Economy, 1933–1970*, Cambridge University Press, Cambridge.

Keen, S. (1995) 'Finance and economic breakdown: modeling Minsky's financial instability hypothesis', *Journal of Post Keynesian Economics*, Summer, **17** (4), 607–35.

Kregel, J.A. (1992) 'Minsky's "two price" theory of financial instability and monetary policy: discounting versus open market intervention', in Fazzari and Papadimitriou (1992, pp.85–103).

Minsky, H.P. (1957a) 'Monetary systems and accelerator models', *American Economic Review*, (47), 859–63.

Minsky, H.P. (1957b) 'Central banking and money market changes', *Quarterly Journal of Economics*, May, 171–87.

Minsky, H.P. (1959) 'A linear model of cyclical growth', *Review of Economics and Statistics*, **41**, 137–45.

Minsky, H.P. (1975) *John Maynard Keynes*, Columbia University Press, New York.

Minsky, H.P. (1982) *Can 'It' Happen Again?*, M.E. Sharpe, Armonk, New York.

Minsky, H.P. (1986) *Stabilizing an Unstable Economy*, Yale University Press, New Haven.

Minsky, H.P. (1992) 'Profits, deficits and economic instability: a policy discussion', in D. Papadimitriou (ed.), *Profits, Deficits and Instability*, Macmillan, London, pp. 11–22.

Nasica, E. (1997) 'Comportements bancaires et fluctuations économiques : l'apport fondamental d'Hyman P. Minsky à la théorie des cycles endogènes et financiers', *Revue d'Economie Politique*, **107** (6), November–December, 854–73.

Samuelson, P.A. (1939) 'Interactions between the multiplier analysis and the principle of acceleration', *Review of Economics and Statistics*, May, 75–78.

Schumpeter, J.A. (1951a) 'The creative response in economic history', in R. Clemence (ed.), *Essays on Economic Topics of J.A. Schumpeter*, Kennikat Press, pp. 216–26

Schumpeter, J.A. (1951b) *Ten Great Economists: From Marx to Keynes*, Galaxy Press, New York.

Shackle, G.L.S. (1955) *Uncertainty in Economics*, Cambridge University Press, Cambridge.

Skott, P. (1995) 'Financial innovation, deregulation, and Minsky cycles', in G. Epstein and H. Gintis (eds), *Macroeconomic Policy after the Conservative Era*, Cambridge University Press, Cambridge, pp. 255–73.

Wojnilower, A. (1987) 'Financial changes in the United States', in M. de Cecco (ed.), *Changing Money*, Basil Blackwell.

Index